Economic Growth and Regional Disparities in India

Dr Prabhjot Kaur

KALPAZ

First Published, 2017

Published by

Kalpaz Publications
C-30, Satyawati Nagar,
Delhi – 110052
E-mail: kalpaz@hotmail.com
Ph.: 9212142040

Printed at: G. Print Process, Delhi

Cataloging in Publication Data—DK
Courtesy: D.K. Agencies (P) Ltd. <docinfo@dkagencies.com>

Prabhjot Kaur *(Assistant professor)*, **author.**
Economic growth and regional disparities in India / Dr Prabhjot Kaur.
pages cm
Includes bibliographical references.
ISBN 9789386397119

1. Economic development—India—Regional disparities. 2. Convergence (Economics)—India. 3. Economic development—India—Mathematical models. I. Title.

HC435.3.P73 2017 DDC 338.954 23

Contents

Dedicated

To

My Parents

poverty index. The author has utilised the secondary data on different macro-economic aggregates and social sector variables over time and across Indian states and carried out tests of convergence using sophisticated econometric techniques. She has also worked out the human poverty index and explained its determinants across the states of India in the present book.

The study constitutes an original and innovative contribution to applied development economics in India. The work presented in the book is quite meritorious and impressive. The author demonstrates an adequate understanding of the relevant literature in the field. The study is built on an appropriate base of theory, concepts, tools and techniques. The book also identifies the factors underlying divergence in economic and social activity in India and provides policy suggestions for bringing about more balanced and inclusive development in India.

On the whole, this is a competently worked out study which highlights that signs of progress in economic and social indicates are present in few sates while other sates lag behind, implying thereby unevenness and unequal spread of the benefits of economic growth among the states of India. This book will, no doubt, benefit the researchers, policymakers and students of economics in developing a better understanding of the drivers of sustainable and inclusive economic growth.

Dr Sharanjit Singh Dhillon
Professor
Punjab School of Economics
& Former Registrar
Guru Nanak Dev University,
Amritsar, Punjab.

Preface

India is a country with a population over 1.21 billion and comprising of 29 states and 7 Union Territories. Balanced regional growth is one of the major objectives of each five year plan. Due to the continuous efforts made by the governments through various Five Year Plans, India has achieved success in many areas of social and economic development but still the economy suffers from large scale disparities. All states have not grown at same rate as some states like Kerala, Maharashtra, Karnataka and Gujarat etc. are growing rapidly than others like Bihar, Uttar Pradesh, Assam, Madhya Pradesh and Odisha. The World Bank in its report entitled, "India-Inclusive Growth and Service Delivery: Building of India's Success" has notified huge disparities across states, there are significant differences in the levels of economic development across Indian states. There are also differences in the levels of education, literacy, per capita incomes and health standards, which causes disparities in the standard of living and regional inequalities are still persisting across states.

This book highlights the regional disparities in India by testing the convergence hypothesis in respect of per capita net state domestic product and net state domestic product originating from agricultural, industrial and services sector, human development index as well as in term of its three components for the period since 1980's and for that the book is divided into eight chapters. Chapter 1 provides an introduction. Chapter 2 reviews the literature related to economic development, growth and convergence hypothesis while data base and methodology used in the study have been discussed in chapter 3. Convergence hypothesis in respect of per capita NSDP and NSDP originating from agricultural, industrial and services sector has been examined in chapter 4. The issue of convergence hypothesis in case of Human Development Index as well as in term of its three components has been examined in chapter 5. Composite Development Index based on socio-economic and demographic indicators has been constructed in chapter 6 with an objective to examine the convergence hypothesis for it. Human Poverty Index calculated to compare the positions of major states of India with respect to human development index, human poverty index and per capita NSDP forms the subject matter of chapter 7. Chapter 8 contains summary, conclusions along with policy implications derived from the study.

The result of the study reveals that poor states are getting relatively poorer and rich getting richer in terms of per capita income and the gap between the rich and the poor is widening further. Poor states that have failed to catch up with rich ones in terms of per capita income have managed to catch up in terms of human development index. The convergence observed in case of life expectancy and adult literacy rate helps in bringing convergence in terms of human development index also, despite considerable divergence in per capita NSDP. The book also identifies the factors underlying divergence in economic and social activity in India and provides policy suggestions for bringing about more balanced and inclusive development in India.

Acknowledgement

I take this opportunity to pay a small tribute to all the persons who have been instrumental in the completion of my book.

Completion of this book was made possible with the support of several people. Foremost, I express my sincere debt of gratitude to Dr Sharanjit Singh Dhillon, Professor of Economics, Guru Nanak Dev University, Amritsar for his ever inspiring guidance, constant encouragement and constructive criticism to complete my work. His untiring efforts, unfailing interest, keen observation and constant motivation made this research work a success. Despite of his busy schedule, he has always made himself available to clarify my doubts, gave his valuable suggestions and made corrections. I consider it as a great opportunity to work under his guidance and to learn from his research expertise.

I am thankful to Dr Sanjeev Sharma, Principal, DAV College, Bathinda for providing conducive environment to carry out my research work.

I express my deep sense of gratitude to Dr Amarjit Singh Sethi, Professor, Punjab School of Economics, GNDU, Amritsar who spared his valuable time to sort out my problems whenever I visited him.

I am thankful to Mukhtar Singh and Bakhtawar Singh, Library Staff, Punjab School of Economics who assisted me in searching the required material from department library. I am also thankful to the staff of Bhai Gurdas Library, Guru Nanak Dev University, Amritsar.

I bow my head to my respected mother-in-law Smt. Surjit Kaur for encouraging me to continue with my studies. It is because of her blessings and moral support that I am able to complete this book. I will be failing in my duty, if I do not acknowledge the ever present support, guidance and motivation of my parents. This book would not have been completed without the consistent support and encouragement of my father S. Gurdial Singh and my mother Smt Gurmeet Kaur. I am very much grateful to my beloved husband Dr Kuldeep Singh Dhillon who supported me in every possible way to see the completion of this book. He, by ignoring his own research work, gave priority to my work and was always with me whenever I looked up to his help during the course of my research work. He, with his valuable suggestions, made this work more presentable. Thanks and love to my little son Angadveer, whom I have not given proper time because of completion of my book. I am also very thankful to my dearest sister Amanjot Kaur and my brother Paramjit Singh for their concern and good wishes.

It was my pleasure to share my research experiences with my friends Gurinder Kaur, Gursharan Kaur and Naiya Mahajan. A special thanks to them for being so patient and always willing to lend their service whenever I approached them.

Lastly, I hope that those will forgive my forgetfulness in case I have failed to acknowledge their contribution in this task.

Dr Prabhjot Kaur

Assistant Professor in Economics,
D.A.V. College,
Bathinda, Punjab.

List of Tables

List of Figure

Chapter 1

Introduction

Economic development has been and is a major goal of poor and rich countries alike. The phenomenon that one prefers to denote as "economic development" is very much a matter of what one values as policy goals (Todaro, 1977). 'Development pattern' may be explained as "a systematic variation in any significant aspect of the economic or social structure associated with a rising level of income or other index of development" (Chenery and Syrquin, 1975). Meier (1973) was of the opinion that economic development is "a process whereby the real per capita income of a country increases over a long period of time". Development is not only related to income, despite the fact that "income has a great deal to do with it". In particular, "development is also the eradication of poverty, elimination of unemployment, disease and malnutrition; it is an increase in life expectancy; it is an access to safe drinking water, sanitation, and health services; it is the reduction of infant mortality; it is an increased access to knowledge and schooling, and literacy in particular and elimination of inequalities" (Ray, 2001).

The term development also implies change, as it is associated with social and economic transformation within countries or regions. According to Goulet (1971), the three basic components or core values of development are life-sustenance, self-esteem and freedom. "Life sustenance is concerned with the provision of basic needs. No country may be regarded as fully developed if it cannot provide all its people with such basic needs as housing, clothing, food and minimal education. Self-esteem is concerned with the feeling of self-respect and independence. No country can be regarded as fully developed if it is exploited by others and does not have the power and influence to conduct relations on equal terms. Freedom refers to freedom from the three evils of 'want, ignorance and squalor' so that people are more able to determine their own destiny. No person is free if they cannot choose; if they are imprisoned by living on the margin of subsistence with no education and no skills" (Thirlwall, 2006).

According to Todaro and Smith (2007), "Development must therefore be conceived of as a multi-dimensional process involving major changes in social structures, popular attitudes, and national institutions, as well as the acceleration of economic growth, the reduction of inequality, and the eradication of poverty". Development should have the following three objectives:

1. "To increase the availability and widen the distribution of basic life-sustaining goods such as food, shelter, health and protection.
2. To raise levels of living, including, in addition to higher incomes, the provision of more jobs, better education, and greater attention to cultural and human values, all of which will serve not only to enhance material well-being but also generate greater individual and national self-esteem.
3. To expand the range of economic and social choices available to individuals and nations by freeing them from servitude and dependence not only in relation to other people and nation-states but also to the forces of ignorance and human misery".

It is relatively common to distinguish the term 'economic development' from 'economic growth'. Development is no longer considered identical with growth though they are used interchangeably in some cases. 'Economic Growth' is defined as "the steady process by which the productive capacity of the economy is increased over time to bring about rising levels of national output and income" (Todaro and Smith, 2007). 'Economic growth' is concerned basically with "measuring growth in economic variables and identifying their inter-relationships such as between the national income growth rate and the speed of capital formation". On the other hand 'Economic development' is "a process involving not only quantitative expansions but also changes in non-quantitative factors such as institutions, organisations, and culture under which economies operate". If we follow this usage, "economic growth is considered a quantitative aspect of economic development". If so, in addition to the analysis of economic growth, the study of economic development must examine the effect of cultural and institutional factors on 'economic growth' as well as the influences of economic growth on those factors (Hayami and Godo, 2005). Thus economic development is a broader aspect which comprises of other changes in the economy along with growth.

Since independence in 1947, Indian economy experienced a "low rate of growth", inspite of favourable pre-conditions in the late 1940s of a well-diversified resource base- both physical and human- and a relatively stable political system (Cashin and Sahay, 1996).

Per capita gross domestic product (PCGDP) is an "indicator of the average standard of living of individual members of the population". An increase in PCGDP indicates economic growth. Before 1990, PCGDP and GDP were used to evaluate the human development or country development and for making comparison among countries or regions. Despite its importance, economic theorist finds flaws and problem with PCGDP since this indicator covers only the financial side of human development. The concept of human development index occupies great importance because it covers both social and economic factors of human development. The HDI is now mostly used to evaluate human development in a country or state and for making comparison between countries or states (Shah and Gosavi, 2010).

Since the early-1990s, there has been a remarkable shift in the "focus of development planning" from mere economic growth to an improvement in human well-being. Sen (1985, 1987), Dasgupta (1993) and 'United Nations Development Programme' (UNDP 1990), view development as "a process of enhancing people's capabilities for improving quality of life. Mere economic growth in production of goods and services and the consequent growth in per capita income may not necessarily lead to an improvement in human well-being, which is broadly conceived to include not only consumption of goods and services, but also the accessibility of people to the basic necessities required for leading a productive and socially meaningful life" (Ghosh, 2006).

The term human development seems to be very simple but has a complicated inferred meaning. Human development may mean differently for different people in different contexts. For a poor person, "development may mean his increased earnings for buying better food, clothing and housing, and for a rich person it could abstract into satisfaction in life" (Indrayan et al., 1999). It is the expansion of people's freedoms to live long and healthy life. The phenomenon of human development is "a people-centred approach to development where the primary concern is enhancement of human well-being" (Meghalaya HDR, 2008). Human development (HD) results are "a function of economic growth, social policy, and poverty reduction measures at the macro-level. These, in turn, are the result of various synergies in the form of feedback loops, operating in terms of both inputs and outputs in the development process"(IHDR, 2011).

"The human development index measures the average achievements in a country in three basic dimensions of human development- longevity, knowledge and a decent standard of living. The human poverty index measures deprivation in basic human development in the same dimensions as the human development index. The variables used are the percentage of people expected to die before age 40, percentage of adults who are illiterate and overall economic provisioning in terms of the percentage of people without access to health services and safe drinking water and the percentage of underweight children under five. If human development is about enlarging choices, poverty means that opportunities and choices most basic to human development are denied to lead a long, healthy, creative life and to enjoy a decent standard of living, freedom, dignity, self respect and the respect of others" (UNDP, 1997).

"Poverty is a multi-dimensional concept and is conventionally defined in terms of income poverty, i.e., number of people below the poverty line. The concept of poverty line in terms of income is interpreted as referring to a very minimum level of calories for the people to live, so that they do not die out of hunger, but not adequate to lead a human life with dignity" (Tilak, 2005).

India is a country with a population over '1.21 billion' and comprising of '29 states and 7 Union Territories'. "Balanced regional growth" is one of the major objectives of each 'five year plan'. "Neo-classical economic growth model" suggests that economies would converge in the long run in terms of production or income level. But if we turn our eyes to 'Indian economy', we find that the basic assumption of neo-classical growth theory might not necessarily be fulfilled (Gunji and Nikaido, 2004). The World Bank (2006, cited in Gaur, 2010) in its report entitled, "India-Inclusive Growth and Service Delivery: Building of India's Success" has notified huge disparities across states, there are significant differences in the levels of economic development across Indian states. All states have not grown at same rate as some states like 'Kerala, Maharashtra, Karnataka and Gujarat' etc. are growing rapidly than others like 'Bihar, Uttar Pradesh, Assam, Madhya Pradesh and Odisha'. The report further adds that the gap between India's rich and poor states has widened further during the 1990's. There are also differences in the 'levels of education, literacy, per capita incomes and health standards', which causes disparities in the standard of living and regional inequalities are still persisting across states. The World Bank (2008) in its another report has highlighted the rising income disparities in India during 1993-2005, when the Gini Co-efficient rose from 0.3152 in 1993-94 to 0.3676 in 2004-05.

India is a country of extraordinary diversity. Now-a-days, regional disparity in India is a critical issue. Regions differ enormously in terms of demography, geography, language, social norms as well as in natural resources resulting into significant differences in levels of economic development across Indian states (Nayyar, 2008). In spite of continuous efforts of policy makers and planners, regional disparity remained a serious issue (Bhattacharya and Sakthivel, 2004). Since independence, the issue of 'regional economic growth' and persisting disparities has attracted considerable attention among planners, policy-makers and researchers. The Indian government has been concerned with the issue of how to promote economic growth to attain balanced regional development in the country. 'Balanced growth' of all the regions of the country has been regarded important for political stability, national integration and economic viability. Redressing regional imbalances has been one of the primary objectives of each 'five year plan'. "The Eleventh Five -Year Plan (2007-2012)" with 'faster and more inclusive growth' as its major objective noticed that disparities among regions have increased steadily and the growth failed to pick up in poor states such as Odisha, Bihar, Madhya Pradesh and Uttar Pradesh (Ghosh, 2012).

From a dismal growth rate of 3.5 per cent in 1960's and 1970's (the so-called Hindu growth rate), the Indian economy broke the barriers and achieved GDP growth rate of 5.82 per cent during 1980/1981-1990/1991 and accomplished an impressive growth rate of about 7.5 per cent in the post 2000 period. Thus, after crossing the Hindu rate of growth in 1990's, India has made a noteworthy progress due to the continuous efforts made by the Indian government. But the benefits of growth have not trickle down and regional inequalities are still persisting across states. All states have not grown at the same pace with the states like 'Maharashtra, Kerala, Karnataka, Gujarat, Tamil Nadu' etc. growing rapidly whereas the states like 'Odisha, Uttar Pradesh, Bihar, Assam and Madhya Pradesh' have lagged behind. There are huge differences in levels of education, health, literacy, infrastructure, investment expenditure, population growth, and the structure of regions which causes disparities in per capita income and regional inequalities are still persisting across states (Cherodian and Thirlwall, 2013). This may cause widening of the standard of living across the states of India. Therefore, it is important to know whether the initial poorer states are catching up of with the richer ones or not. This catching up, in the domain of development economics is known as the theorem of convergence. 'The convergence theorem (Barro, 1991)' presumes that "when the growth rate of an economy accelerates, initially some regions with better resources would grow faster than others. But after sometime, when the law of diminishing marginal returns set in, first growth rates would converge, due to differential marginal productivity of capital (higher in poorer regions and lower in richer regions), and this in turn would bridge the gaps in the levels of income across regions" (Bhattacharya and Sakthivel, 2004).

Economic convergence may be divided into two categories: micro convergence and macro convergence. "M*icro convergence* refers to a tendency towards the equalisation of income of identical factors across economies. M*acro convergence* focuses on aggregate variables such as per capita income or output per worker". The theory describes how per capita incomes across countries or regions may converge or diverge over the period of time. The notions of micro and macro convergence are related because per capita income is a weighted average of factor prices (Rassekh, 1998).

According to Baumol (1986), the concept of convergence implies "forces accelerating the growth of nations who were latecomers to industrialisation and economic development give rise to a tendency towards convergence of levels of per capita product or, alternatively of per worker product". According to Barro (1991), the convergence hypothesis postulates that "poor countries, those with relatively low initial per capita income, grow faster than rich ones so that over time income levels converge across countries". As stated in Barro and Sala-i-Martin (1992, 1995) and Mankiw et al. (1992,) and many others (cited in Erdal et al., 2006), "several economic forces including diminishing returns to capital, spatial labour mobility, spatial capital mobility and diffusion of technologies and innovations across regions give rise to convergence". There are three possible and related form of convergence. They are called *'unconditional* β *-convergence,* σ *-convergence and conditional* β *-convergence'.*

"Unconditional β -convergence states that poor countries will tend to grow faster than the rich countries due to the diminishing marginal returns to capital in the rich countries, as the level of capital per labour is high in these countries. Moreover, the further down a country is below its balanced growth path and the higher lags in access to new technology, the higher would be the expected growth when the country gains access to such technology" (Romer, 1986). In the empirical literature, the testing of convergence is done by "running a cross-section regression of the time-averaged per capita income growth rate on the initial level of per capita income. A negative sign for the respective co-efficient reflects the existence of convergence" (Noorbakhsh, 2006).

The illustration of the unconditional convergence can be given with the help of diagram (Fig. 1). The line AB plots the time path of (log) per capita income at the steady state. The path CD represents a country that starts below the steady state level per efficiency unit. According to Solow model, this country will initially display a rate of growth that exceeds the steady-state level and its time path of (log) per capita income will move asymptotically toward the AB line. Overtime, its growth rate will decelerate to the steady state level. Likewise, a country that starts off above the steady state, say at E, will experience a lower rate of growth, because its time path EF of (log) income flattens out to converge to the line AB from above.

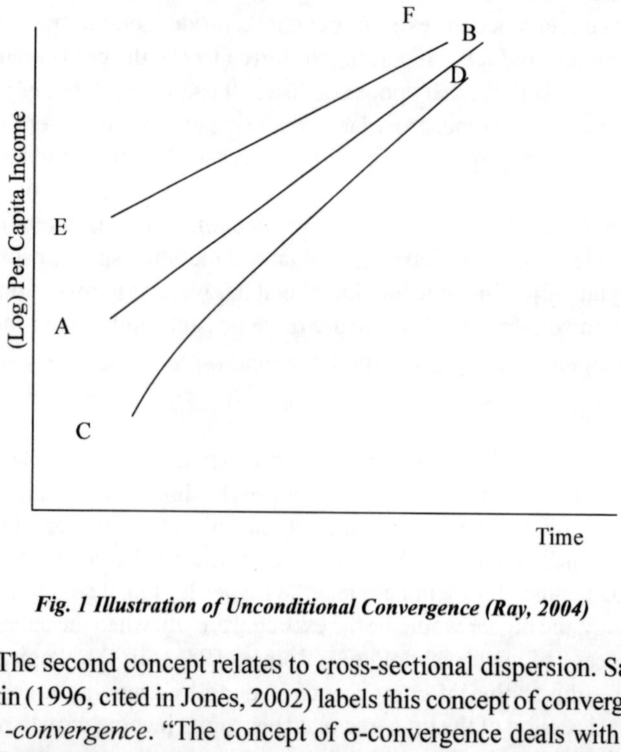

Fig. 1 Illustration of Unconditional Convergence (Ray, 2004)

The second concept relates to cross-sectional dispersion. Sala-i-Martin (1996, cited in Jones, 2002) labels this concept of convergence as *σ -convergence*. "The concept of σ-convergence deals with how the distribution of income or product across economies evolve over time, that is if $\sigma_{t+T} < \sigma_t$, where σ_t is the standard deviation of log $(Y_{i,t})$ across economies at time t". Friedman (1992, cited in Jones, 2002) suggested that "σ-convergence can be more appropriately measured by simply tracking the inter-temporal change in the co-efficient of variation of the given cross-country income distribution, that is, a tendency for the inter-country or inter-regional dispersion in per capita income levels to decline over time".

Quah (1995) and Sala-i-Martin (1996, cited in Jones, 2002) shows that "the existence of β-convergence is a necessary condition for the existence of σ-convergence. For the dispersion of per capita GDP to decline between two countries, the initially poorer countries should grow faster than the initially richer ones, so that the existence of β-convergence generates σ-convergence". According to Shiller (2009), there are significant differences between β-convergence and σ -convergence. "β-convergence is measured between two time periods, while σ-convergence is measured over time. The β-co-efficient is able to predict not only the speed of convergence but also whether the cross-sectional dispersion will fall or rise over time. β-convergence is necessary but not a sufficient condition for σ-convergence. The cross-sectional dispersion can be affected by external shocks, which would cause the σ-co-efficient to increase in spite of a positive β-co-efficient".

Figure 2 displays "the behaviour of the log of GDP per capita (log GDP) for two economies over time. Suppose we observe the data at two discrete intervals, t and t + T. Economy A is richer than economy B. There is an initial distance or dispersion between the two levels of income. In panel A, the growth rate of an economy A is smaller (actually negative) than the growth rate of an economy B between time t and t + T and, therefore, we say that there is β-convergence. Moreover, because the dispersion of log (GDP) at t + T is smaller than at time t, we also say that there is σ-convergence. It is impossible for the two economies to be closer together at t + T without having the initially poor economy growing faster (in this case economy B). In other words, a necessary condition for the existence of σ-convergence is the existence of β-convergence.

When an initially poor economy grows faster than a rich one, then the levels of GDP per capita of the two economies will become more similar over time. In other words the existence of β-convergence will tend to generate σ-convergence. Panel A in Fig. 2 is an example where β-convergence exists and is associated with σ-convergence. Panel B shows that the lack of β-convergence (the initially rich economy grows faster) is associated with the lack of σ-convergence (the distance between the two economies increases over time). In panel C, the initially poor economy (B) grows faster than the initially rich economy (A), so there is β-convergence. However, the growth rate of B is so much larger than the growth rate of A at time t + T, B is richer than A. So, at time t + T, the distance between A and B is the same as it was at time t (except that now the rich economy is B). Hence, the dispersion between these two economies has not fallen, so there is no σ-convergence". (Sala-i-Martin, 1996).

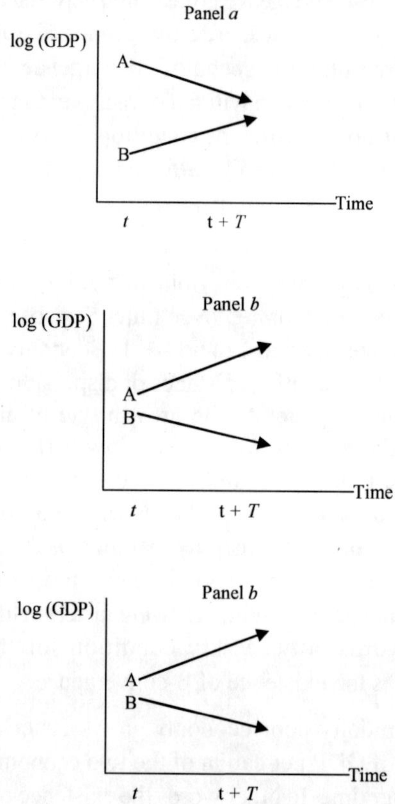

Fig. 2 The relation between s and b-convergence (Sala-i-Martin, 1996).

Economic theory describes why poor countries may "catch-up" with rich ones over the period of time. Romer (1986, cited in Chowdhury, 2004) gave three significant causes for the convergence process. "First, the prediction of the neo-classical growth models that countries will converge to their balanced growth paths, one would expect the poorer countries to catch up with the richer ones. Second, the Solow model implies that the return on capital is lower in richer countries, as the level of capital per labour is high in these countries. Thus capital flow from rich to poor countries will eventually lead to convergence. Lastly, if there are lags in the diffusion of knowledge, income differences can arise since some countries are yet to employ the appropriate technique of production. These differences can disappear once poorer countries gain access to the cutting edge technology". The central idea regarding the convergence hypothesis is based up on 'neo-classical growth models'. 'In neo-classical growth models', such as 'Solow (1956), Cass (1965) and Koopmans (1965)', "a country per capita growth rate tends to be inversely related to its starting level of income per person. In particular, if countries are similar with respect to structural parameters for preferences and technology, then poor countries tend to grow faster than rich countries. Thus, there is a force that promotes convergence in levels of per capita income across countries" (Barro, 1991). The convergence hypothesis in neo-classical growth models is based up on the assumption of "diminishing marginal returns to physical capital". "Countries with low initial income per capita have low ratios of capital to labour, hence a higher marginal product of capital and thereby tend to grow at high rates. This tendency for low-income countries to grow at high rates is reinforced in extensions of the neo-classical models that allow for international mobility of capital and technology. International capital would flow to areas with relatively high rates of return, which is to areas where capital is relatively scarce. Therefore capital-labour ratios will move over time to equality and with them factor prices. This is the classical prescription of the neo-classical growth model with decreasing returns. This would imply that capital would flow from rich to poor countries and income in poor countries would grow faster than incomes in rich countries and that the two would eventually converge" (Jones, 2002). Following neo-classical growth framework, a numerous studies have attempted to examine the differences in growth rates and convergence.

According to the 'neo-classical growth model', "countries with a low capital-labour ratio are expected to have a high marginal productivity of capital. This will prompt a faster accumulation of capital and a higher rate of economic growth. As an economy moves towards its steady state income, marginal product tends to zero. Hence, the growth rate of an economy is positively related to the distance from its steady state value" (Sala-i-Martin, 1996). "If countries differ only with regard to the initial level of income, and if poorer countries are growing faster than richer ones in the long run, they will all converge to the same steady state income. This is known as absolute beta convergence. But if countries are different with regard to technology, population growth rates and so on, then countries will converge to different steady states" (Dobsan and Ramlogan, 2002). This concept is known as "conditional convergence" because convergence is

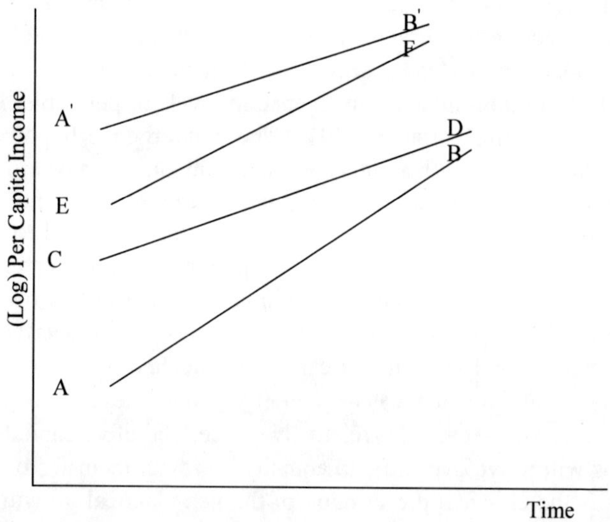

Fig. 3 Illustration of Conditional Convergence (Ray, 2004)

conditional on the different structural characteristics or "fundamentals" of each economy, such as its rate of 'population growth, technologies, societal preferences, and government policy'. "Different structural characteristics imply that different countries will have different steady-state relative per capita incomes". In order to test for conditional convergence, therefore, it is necessary to hold constant the steady state of each economy by introducing into the basic "growth regression" additional variables that proxy for the steady state. If β is negative after including other explanatory variables, then there will be conditional β-convergence. "The conditional convergence and absolute convergence hypotheses only coincide if all countries have the same steady state income" (Sala-i-Martin, 1996).

Now there is no single line that depicts the steady-state time path of (log) per capita income of all countries. Instead, different countries have their own steady-state paths. The line AB and A¢B¢ represents the steady state paths of two different countries. These lines are parallel to one another on the assumption that same rate of technical progress (and therefore, the same rates of steady-state growth) is maintained across all countries.

Now, imagine that a country with steady state path AB starts at a point C above the steady state path. The Solow model suggests that over time, this country will exhibit a slower rate of growth than the steady-state path, as it is converging with the steady-state path AB. This path is given by the curve CD. Likewise a country that starts at point E, below its steady-state path AB¢ will exhibit a higher growth rate than that of the steady state, with the resulting path EF converging upward to its steady-state path.

"The steady states levels of incomes of the economic units are held constant for testing the hypothesis of conditional convergence across different economic units. Different variables were used by the researchers in their studies as determinants of the steady state level of income" (Jan and Chaudhary, 2011). Sala-i-Martin (1997) preferred the "initial level of income, life expectancy and primary school enrollment rate"; Nayyar (2008) uses the initial income level, loans extended by All-India Financial Institutions (AIFIS) (as a proxy for private investment), government capital expenditure (as a proxy for public investment), literacy rate and the infant mortality rate in a conditional framework; Cherodian and Thirlwall (2013), points out the importance of the share of agriculture in state GDP, population growth, male literacy, credit growth, and state expenditure as share of GDP for testing conditional convergence hypothesis.

Due to the continuous efforts made by the governments through various Five Year Plans, India has achieved success in many areas of social and economic development but still the economy suffers from large scale disparities. Various factors such as per capita income, literacy rate, health standards and different level of infrastructure development contribute to the present inequalities among Indian states. There is a substantial literature covering different time periods which examined the issue of convergence or divergence across states and results are, more or less sensitive to the sample, period and estimation techniques. Inspite of many efforts and much progress made in recent past, there is still a wide scope for testing the convergence hypothesis in respect of economic development by taking into consideration various socio-economic and human development indicators which have non-income components also. This provides a strong motivation for studying the variability of inter-state development and to find out the various reasons responsible for existing variations among Indian states. The overall objective of this study is to examine the convergence hypothesis across Indian states over the period 1981 to 2011. Specifically, the objectives are:

1. To examine the hypothesis of convergence in respect of *per capita net state domestic product* and *net state domestic product* originating from agricultural, industrial and services sector of Indian states for the period since 1980's.
2. To examine the issue of convergence hypothesis in case of Human Development Index as well as in term of its three components and to measure the speed of convergence and the 'half-life convergence-the time it takes for 50 per cent of the initial gap to be eliminated'.
3. To construct Composite Development Index based on socio-economic and demographic indicators with an objective to examine the convergence hypothesis for it.
4. To examine the deprivations in three basic elements of human life *(health, knowledge and a decent living standard)* and work out the level of human poverty in the light of the experience of Indian states and to compare the positions of major states of India with respect to human development

index, human poverty index and *per capita net state domestic product.*

5. Identify reasons for the convergence or lack of it among the Indian states.

Plan of the Study

To achieve the above objectives, the study has been divided into eight chapters including the present one. The second chapter reviews the literature related to economic development, growth and convergence hypothesis while data base and methodology used in the study have been discussed in chapter third. Convergence hypothesis in respect of per capita NSDP and NSDP originating from agricultural, industrial and services sector has been examined in chapter fourth. The issue of convergence hypothesis in case of Human Development Index as well as in term of its three components has been examined in chapter fifth. Composite Development Index based on socio-economic and demographic indicators has been constructed in chapter sixth with an objective to examine the convergence hypothesis for it. Human Poverty Index calculated to compare the positions of major states of India with respect to human development index, human poverty index and per capita NSDP forms the subject matter of chapter seventh. Chapter eighth contains summary, conclusions along with policy implications derived from the study.

Chapter 2

Review of Literature

This chapter reviews studies related to economic development and convergence hypothesis. Various studies addressing the issue of growth and convergence have been carried out in the context of Indian states with different samples over different time periods with varied conclusions. Although attempt has been made to review the research work done in the area of economic development, growth and convergence hypothesis in the context of developed and developing countries, but it may not include all studies. It highlights the type of work done in this direction and will provide great help in identifying the objectives and methodology to be adopted for the present study. The brief review of studies related to the convergence hypothesis is presented below in chronological order:

Barro (1991) by applying *theories of economic growth* and by concentrating on the significance of human capital, present few empirical results on "fertility, growth and investment" across 98 countries during the period 1960-1985. Study found that the simple co-rrelation between per capita growth (1960-1985) and the initial (1960) value of per capita gross domestic product is 0.09, which fails to show convergence. However, the co-rrelation of growth rates and initial levels of per capita income become significantly negative, if variables of initial human capital which is proxied by "school-enrollment rates" are held constant. Given the initial levels of per capita gross domestic product, the growth rate is significantly and positively related to the starting amount of human capital. According to study, poor countries are catching up with rich countries if the former have high per person human capital in relation to their level of PCGDP. Study also found that "per capita growth and the ratio of private investment to GDP are negatively related to the ratio of government consumption expenditure to gross domestic product". Variables of "political instability" which were proxied by "coups, resolutions, and political assassinations" were found to be negatively related to investment and growth. Furthermore, the study found that a proxy for "price distortions which is based on purchasing-power parity numbers" is inversely related to growth. Thus, overall study supported the convergence hypothesis for 98 countries by using neo-classical growth model.

Cashin and Sahay (1996) examined convergence hypothesis across 20 Indian states over the period 1961-1991. Study found an evidence of "absolute β-convergence", indicating that "initially poor states have grown faster than initially rich states". After taking into account "exogenous shocks to the agricultural and manufacturing sectors", study found convergence at the speed of 1.5 per cent per year. Further, study found that "it would take about 45 years to close one-half of the gap between any state's initial level of per capita income and 20 states' common long-term level of per capita income". Furthermore, study observed that over the period 1961-1991, the disparities has widened across Indian states in terms of PCI, excluding the sub-periods 1962-68, 1972-75, 1977-78 and 1980-84. Disparities have narrowed down during the period 1961 and 1971 in terms of PCNDP across Indian states due to the "strong growth rates in initially poor states (Manipur, Kerala and Himachal Pradesh) and slow growth rates in initially rich states (Delhi, West Bengal and Maharashtra). However, study found that during the sub-periods 1971-81 and 1981-91, the initially poor states (Manipur, Bihar and Odisha in 1971; Bihar, Assam and Odisha in 1981*)* and the initially rich states (Delhi, Punjab and Haryana in 1971; Delhi, Punjab and Maharashtra in 1981) had similar rates of economic growth".

Evans and Karras (1996) investigated whether the 48 contiguous U.S. states are converging or not and, if they are converging, whether the convergence is absolute convergence or not. Unit-root methods for Panel data were applied for these states over the period 1970-1986. Study found the evidence that levels of technology are stationary around a common trend and the contiguous U.S. states have eventual access to technical knowledge and they are converging. Study also investigated whether convergence is absolute or not and found strong evidence that technology and capital's share have state fixed effects but the rental rate does not have state fixed effects. Furthermore, these estimated state fixed effects produce economically important state fixed effects in output per worker, accounting on an average for 87 per cent of the cross-economy variance of output per worker over the period 1970-1986 which significantly rejected the absolute convergence. Finally, they investigated how rapidly proportional cross-economy differences in output per worker revert toward their non-zero unconditional means and found evidence of rapid mean reversion. The study ends up with the suggestion that technology and factors must flow freely across the contiguous U.S. Sates.

Sala-i-Martin (1996) tested "σ-convergence, absolute β-convergence and conditional β-convergence" in his study and applied these concepts to "a cross-section of 110 countries, the states within the United States, the Prefectures[1] of Japan, sub-samples of OECD countries and regions within several European countries". Summers-Heston data set (1960-1990) was used for the purpose of the study. Study found that in the cross-country distribution the world has become increasingly unequal and the set of 110 countries are not converging in the form of "absolute β-convergence". The cross-sectional countries reveal "σ-divergence and conditional β-convergence". Regarding OECD countries, study reveals "σ convergence, absolute β-convergence and conditional β-convergence" and the same results were found for "the Prefectures of Japan, the United States, and regions within several European countries". Overall, it was concluded in the study that with the exception of cross-sectional countries, the remaining data exhibits "σ-convergence and absolute β-convergence". The cross-sectional countries display "σ-divergence and conditional β-convergence". The rate of "conditional convergence" was found to be same across data set used in the study which was near to 2 per cent per year.

Park (1997) examined convergence hypothesis during 1960-1990. Data set used in the study is from "Penn World Tables consisted of 16 countries and territories". "International inequality" was computed by the "Theil Index and Gini Co-efficient". Evidence exhibits that international inequality improved during the period 1970-1990. Reduction of the "Gini Co-efficient and the Theil Index" for the cases- 5 per cent, 10 per cent, 20 per cent provided empirical support for the convergence hypothesis which states that the initial level of PCI of poor countries increases over the period of time and "poor countries are catching up with the rich countries". The study ends up with the interpretation that the gap between developed and developing countries has increased during 1960s due to the reason that developed countries experienced considerable amount of economic growth, but the gap decreased during 1970s and 1980s as a developing countries also started to take off economically.

Sarkar (1997) examined "absolute convergence" for a sample of 110 countries during 1960-1993 in terms of PCGDP. The sample consists of "24 countries of the North and 86 countries of the South (42 countries from Africa, 24 countries from Latin America, 18 countries from Asia, and Caribbean LAC, and 2 countries from Oceanea)". Ordinary Least Squares procedure was used for the purpose of analysis. The study found a positive and statistically significant relationship between "the initial level PCGDP and its growth rate" in real terms for the whole world and concludes that the gap between the per capita income levels of poor and rich countries have widened during the period of study. Study also found the relationship for the two subgroups, "the North and the South" and the relationship between different regions of the South. The study concluded that there is no catching up of the standard of living of the rich countries by the poor countries and this is true for the North; for the different regions of the South (Asia, Africa and Latin America) and for the South as a whole. Further, it was found that the force of divergence decreases with the rise in income per capita across the countries and still there is a group of highly rich countries which experienced neither 'divergence' nor any 'convergence' among themselves.

Marques and soukiazis (1998) tested the hypothesis of "sigma" and "beta" convergence for countries and regions in the "European Union" over the period 1975-1995 and for the sub-periods 1975-1984 and 1985-1995. The results across countries revealed "sigma" divergence for the period 1975-1995. Regarding the different sub-periods, the study found convergence for the years 1975-1982 and 1986-1991 and divergence over the periods 1983-1985 and 1991-1995. Study revealed 'beta' convergence for the whole period which was "stronger in the years 1985-1995 and weaker in the period 1975-1984". The analysis of regions at NUTS 2[2] level, gave the evidence for "sigma" convergence for the period 1987-1995 and revealed "beta" convergence for the same period. Furthermore, the study found that the poor regions revealed strong "beta" as well as "sigma" convergence, but no convergence was found in rich regions. The study ends up with the suggestion that "the financial support to the less developed regions (with per capita income below 75 per cent of the average) should not be reduced, rather more funds should be concentrated to these regions in order to facilitate their catching up effort and at the same time, a particular attention should be given to the difficulties involved in the transition process from the intermediate level of poverty to higher levels of per capita income".

Stavros and Costas (1998) tried to test "unconditional and conditional β-convergence for the Greek economy". Three issues were taken into account for the study. "Firstly, whether there is a regional convergence in the Greek economy. Secondly, given the interest in the possibility of a North-South divide in Greece, whether there is convergence between Southern and Northern Greece and finally, whether the Greek economy is converging with the other European economies taking part in the European Integration Project". For investigating "Barro and Sala-i-Martin type" β-convergence, the technique of 'Non-Linear Least Squares' has been used for the periods 1971-1981, 1981-1996, and for the whole period (1971-1996). The estimated results rejected the convergence hypothesis and the variables, "the shares of GDP in the manufacturing and industrial sector for each region" were included in the study on the hope that this would stabilise the "β co-efficient", but their inclusion failed to make improvement in the estimated results. Another "North/South dummy variable" was used for estimating convergence between the "Southern and Northern Greece". Estimated results again did not find convergence.

Akkina (1999) ascertained "the role of infrastructure and power shortages on the rate of growth of per capita income using cross-section data on 25 Indian states for the period 1970 to 1990 and for the sub-periods (1970 to 1980 and 1980-1990)". "Barro and Sala-i-Martin models" were implemented on this data set. Study found that the convergence of PCI across the states is not consistent for all the three time periods. However, conditional convergence hypothesis has been found to be consistent after including additional proxy variables such as per capita electric power consumption, percentage share of income from services and industrial sectors of a state to ascertain the effect of human and physical capital existing in the state.

Three infrastructure related variables namely-'railroad length, road transport length per thousand square Kilometres and percentage of electric power shortages' in each state has been used. The results of the study indicated that the railroad network variable has very little impact on the growth rate of PCI across Indian states for all time periods included in the study. Whereas, the road transport variable effect significantly the growth rate of PCI only for the period 1970-80. Further, study found that "a 10 per cent shortage of power supply during the 1970s have reduced the average growth rate of per capita income approximately by 0.1 per cent whereas, the same 10 per cent shortage in power supplies reduced the average per capita income growth by 0.5 per cent during 1980s".

Das (1999) examines the variability of inter-state development by constructing 'composite development index' using four components (i) "economic production and economic condition or in other words level of economic development (ii) common minimum needs (iii) health and health-related services and (iv) communication". Study found that "the states in India marked with wide disparity in socio-economic development. Some states are better-off in terms of economic development, while states like Kerala and Tamil Nadu have recorded remarkable social progress". Study found that the variables like "education, availability of food, minimum purchasing power and facilities like safe drinking water, healthcare infrastructure etc." plays an important role in the development process. Study reveals that "the role of social development such as literacy in promoting basic capabilities emerges as the pre-requisite to overall development". Study suggested "that economic reforms alone are not sufficient for overall development unless it is accompanied by social and political comments; it emphasises the role of well-functioning public actions in improving the overall living conditions of the people. Faster development requires government action to improve elementary education, especially for the younger generation".

Dasgupta et al. (2000) analyses economic position of Indian states in terms of PCSDP over the period 1960-61 to 1995-96. Study found that the trend of the "co-efficient of variation" increased over the period of time and Indian states exhibit σ-divergence. Further, study found no evidence of "β-convergence" across Indian states. The study also examined the behaviour of the states in terms of the ranking of their PCSDP's over the period 1970-71 to 1995-96 and found that the states which had a low ranks in 1970-71, continued to have a low rank throughout the period. Further, the PCSDP data has been divided in to three major sectors, i.e. those originating in "primary, secondary and tertiary sectors" and found that the share of the manufacturing sector has remained almost stable or increased marginally in almost all states, except Assam and Manipur. The share of the primary sector has fallen sharply for all the states and that for the tertiary sector has risen (except Delhi and Goa). Overall, the study found a clear tendency of divergence for the Indian states in terms of PCSDP, but found convergence in terms of different sectors in the SDP.

Asteriou *et al.* (2002) tested convergence hypothesis across "Greek regions" during the period 1971 to 1996. Using the direct test of convergence hypothesis by following "Bernard and Durlauf (1995)", study found absence of convergence and favoured "the existence of inequality" across the "Northern and Southern parts of the country".

For testing the presence of stochastic trends, study made use of "Augmented Dickey Fuller tests" and found that "none of the 13 regions (Eastern Macedonia and Thrace, Central Macedonia, Western Macedonia, Hipiros, Thessalia, peloponisos, Western Greece, Sterea, Athens and Crete) rejected the null hypothesis of a unit root". Further, co-integration has been tested by using "Johansen technique in three separate grouping of a region: a group of 10 regions (5 Southern and 5 Northern regions), a group which contains only the Southern regions and a group for Northern regions only". For the entire 10 region sample, Johansen statistic rejected 4 vectors at the 5 per cent level, whereas rejected 2 or more trends at the 5 per cent level for the Southern region and for the Northern region, the study rejected "the null that there are 5 distinct trends but cannot rejected the null that there is at least 1 trend".

Study supported "the popular view prevailing in Greece about the existence of dualism across the Southern and Northern regions of Greece". The reasons given in the study for divergence is "the lack of experience that the poor countries have in comparison with the rich ones. The rich countries have the combined ability to educate themselves, as they grow rich and the endogenous ability to accumulate the knowledge up on which these efforts are made".

Sachs et al. (2002) examined whether PCI in the 14 major Indian states have been "converging or diverging over the period 1980 to 1998, during the pre-reform period (1980-90) and post-reform period (1992-98)" by using "σ-convergence and β-convergence". Study found "overall rise in inequality of 2.40 per cent per annum during the period 1980 and 1998". For the post-reform period (1992-98), study found divergence at the "rate of 2.14 per cent per annum compared to 1.24 per cent per annum" during the pre-reform period (1980-90). Further, unconditional β-divergence for the overall period as well as for the two sub-periods has been found. Therefore, by using convergence hypothesis, "India demonstrated overall divergence during 1980-98, as well as during the pre-reform and post-reform periods". Furthermore, study found that "the richer states experienced convergence during the post-reform period, whereas the poorer states did not and divergence was most notable within the poorer group of states. 82 per cent of the cross-state variation in growth is explained by just the urbanisation variable in India".

Dholakia (2003) analysed the "regional disparity in India's economic and human development" among 14 major Indian states over the period 1980-81 to 2000-01. Study does not found any "significant trend in regional disparity" over the last two decades in terms of per capita income. Whereas, the overall HDI for the major states shows a clear and highly significant declining trend in regional disparity during 1981-1991 and 1991-2001. Further, the study found that the regional disparity declined sharply during 1983-94 in terms of "inflation and inequality adjusted per capita consumption expenditures (IIAPCCE)", but remained the same during 1993-2000.

On the other hand, the regional disparity increased significantly during 1993-2000, but remained statistically the same during 1983-94 in terms of 'proportion of population below poverty line (PPBPL)'. However, the study found that in terms of overall literacy rate and death rate, the disparity has been consistently falling over the period of time. Overall the study found that the disparity has increased in 'poverty' but decreased in 'deaths, literacy and drop-outs in primary education'. Further, the study found "a two-way causality between human and economic development".

Bhattacharya and Sakthivel (2004) analyse "the growth rates of aggregate and sectoral domestic product of major states during the pre-reform period (1980-81 to 1989-90) and post-reform period (1990-91 to 1999-2000)". Study found that "the regional disparity has widened during the 1990s. The co-efficient of variation of SDP growth rates among states has jumped from 0.14 in the 1980s to 0.29 in the 1990s. In terms of per capita SDP, the co-efficient of variation has become even worse in the 1990s, as it increases from 0.22 in the 1980s to 0.43 in the 1990s". Study found no evidence of convergence across states. Further, the study found negative relationship between "population growth and income growth" across states in the 1990s. The poorer states like that of Bihar and Uttar Pradesh have not performed well in terms of SDP growth in the 1990s.

Regarding the relationship between growth and inflation, study found negative and significant relationship between "the growth of SDP and inflation rate at the state level" during 1980s, but no "significant relationship" has been found between the two in the 1990s and for the overall period. Furthermore, the study found that "the tertiary sector rather than the secondary sector has become the engine of growth in the last two decades. The tertiary sector has recorded the fastest growth in most states, both before and after the reforms. During the last two decades, the tertiary sector has grown on an average by 8 to 9 per cent per annum in many states like Gujarat, Haryana, Kerala, Maharashtra, Tamil Nadu and West Bengal".

Costantini and Lupi (2005) tested "the stochastic convergence in real per capita GDP for 15 European countries (Austria, Belgium, Denmark, France, Finland, Germany, Greece, Ireland, Italy, Luxembourg, Netherland, Portugal, Spain, Sweden and the United

Kingdom)". Study assumed that "the null hypothesis is that European economies do not converge stochastically" or we can say that "the pair wise differences of national GDPs with the benchmark GDP (Germany) contain a unit root". The alternative hypothesis does not require the differences to be "Zero-mean stationary processes".

By using the "Independent panel unit root tests" (LLC, IPS and MW)[3] for the entire sample 1950 to 2003, study found that "the null hypothesis of no stochastic convergence" cannot be rejected in all the cases, except for the MW test. Study found strong evidence of "stochastic convergence" for the first sub-period (1950-1976). However, the null of "no stochastic convergence" cannot be rejected for the second sub-period (1977-2003).

Furthermore, study made use of "dependent panel unit root tests" (CH, MP, BNG and PS)[4] and found that the CH and MP tests support "stochastic convergence" for the entire period. Strong evidence of "stochastic convergence" among European countries has been found for the first sub-period by using "dependent panel unit root tests", however, "no stochastic convergence" has been found for the second sub-period.

Mathur (2005) tested 'conditional convergence hypothesis' independently for five South Asian, Eight East Asian, and Sixteen European Union countries and total twenty-nine countries for the period 1961-2001. The study also gave justification for "the per capita growth equations using Solovian model (1956) and its factor accumulation assumptions". Conditional convergence hypothesis and the speed of 'conditional convergence' for the three regions were also worked out. "GDP per capita average annual growth (1961-2001)" was chosen as the dependent variable and "the determinants of the steady state level of GDP per capita" in the study were annual average savings rate, growth rate of population and technology, life expectancy in the initial year, average annual trade openness and average annual industry value added as percentage of GDP. Study found "conditional convergence among almost all pairs of regions except East Asian and South Asian nations together". The rate of "conditional convergence" lies between 0.2 per cent in a year to 22 per cent across samples and over the years. Study ends up with the conclusion "that countries which are poor relatively to their own steady state do tend to grow more rapidly but it does not mean that all countries in the world are converging to the same steady state, rather they are only converging to their own steady states (conditional convergence)".

Cunado and Gracia (2006) examined the convergence hypothesis in terms of per capita output for "13 African countries (both toward an African average and the U.S. economy) by means of using time series techniques such as conventional ADF unit root tests and then allowing for structural breaks by means of applying the minimum LM unit root test proposed by Lee and Strazicich (2001)". By using 'ADF unit root test with no regressors', study found no evidence of unconditional convergence for any of "the African countries neither with respect to the African average nor the U.S. economy". But after including intercept in the study, "the unit root hypothesis" has been rejected in favour of "conditional convergence towards the African average for Benin, Kenya, Namibia, Nigeria and Rwanda but cannot be rejected for any of the African countries when convergence is measured with respect to the U.S. economy". Further, after including "intercept and a linear time trend" in the study, "the unit root hypothesis" has been rejected only for Zimbabwe in favour of the "catch-up hypothesis" toward "the African average".

Furthermore, by applying 'LM unit root test', study found "conditional convergence" for Seychelles toward U.S. economy. But when the "catch-up hypothesis" has been analysed, study found "evidence of convergence towards the African average in case of Benin, Cameroon, Cape Verde, Djibouti, Egypt, Ghana, Kenya, Mali, Uganda and Zimbabwe and towards the U.S. economy in case of Cape Verde, Egypt, Mauritius, Seychelles and Tunisia".

Debasri (2006) investigated "the sectoral convergence dynamics of the Indian economy". Sector level data on production (sector level real GDP) per capita for 21 Indian states and territories were employed. The twelve sectors included were "agriculture, forestry, fishing, mining, manufacturing, construction, transport and storage, hotels and trade, banking and real estate, public administration and other services". The study covers the time period of 1980-1998 in which pre-reform sub-sample covers 1980 to 1992 and post-reform sub-period covers 1993 to 1998. The study found that some of the sectors converge while the others do not. "Reform has led to faster rate of convergence for agriculture, manufacturing and transport sectors. However, it has failed to reduce inequality in banking and other service sectors". Regarding overall convergence co-efficient (or aggregate data) simply no evidence of convergence was found because the combination of convergence and divergence averages out. Furthermore, it was found that high income group states have attained faster speed of convergence after reform.

Ghosh (2006) evaluates performance of "15 major Indian states on human development" and its indicators and examine whether the regional disparity in it has increased or decreased over the period 1981 to 2001. The study also examines "the two-way nexus between economic growth and human development". The 'σ-convergence' estimated by using 'co-efficient of variation' across states shows that while the CVs of HDI, literacy rate and life expectancy at birth have consistently declined, whereas the CV of per capita income has consistently increased over time. Further, the estimates of 'cross-sectional growth regressions' found that the co-efficients on initial level of 'HDI, LR and LEB' are negative and statistically significant, reveals that there has been a strong tendency of convergence in these indicators of human development. On the other hand, "the co-efficient on initial level of per capita income" found positive and significant in all the time periods considered indicates that there has been a tendency of "divergence in per capita income across the states".

Estimated rate of convergence in HDI has declined marginally from 1.65 per cent in the 1980's to 1.48 per cent in the 1990's, the rate of convergence in LR has increased considerably from 1.25 per cent to 4.23 per cent and that in LEB from 1.645 per cent to 1.88 per cent. On the other hand, the speed of divergence in "per capita income" has increased from 1.2 per cent to 2.0 per cent during the same period. Furthermore, the classification of the states based on their performance on 'human development and economic growth' reveals that while only four states have been in the virtuous cycle and seven in the vicious cycle. The study ends up with the suggestion that "the sequencing of policy should be such that the HD-induced growth process has to be strengthened for lifting the states from the vicious to virtuous cycle category".

Purfield (2006) by using net state domestic product (NSDP) examines how "growth and economic performance" varied across Indian states during the period 1970 to 2004. Study found that "the gap in real per capita incomes between rich and poor states has widened over time and rich states have also grown over three times faster than the poorer states". Further, the study found that "the rich and faster-growing states have generally been more effective in reducing poverty and poor and slower-growing states had very little success in generating private sector jobs". Furthermore, the study found that "labour and capital flows appear to do little to close the gap in incomes between poor and rich states and poor states also experienced greatest volatility in economic growth".

The study also examined "the link between state-level policies and economic growth and found that state-level policies are a key factor influencing the pattern of economic growth across Indian states. Greater private sector investment, smaller government and better state level institutions were found to be positively associated with growth performance". Study suggested "that states can affect- their relative growth performance by adopting better economic policies and the economic position of a state can be improved by bringing improvements in its investment, fiscal and infrastructure policies".

Jr and Gomes (2007) investigated "per capita income convergence in 19 Latin American countries" by applying "the time series approach" for testing "stochastic convergence and β-convergence based on structural breaks unit root tests". By applying "ADF and the LM break tests", study found that 12 countries namely "Argentina, Bolivia, Chile, Ecuador, Peru, Uruguay, Mexico, Costa Rica, Honduras, Nicaragua, Panama and El Salvador" present evidence of "stochastic convergence". As the study noticed that most of the non-convergent economies are from "South America", so the convergence hypothesis has been further investigated for "South America and Central America separately". Analysing the eleven "South American countries", study found evidence of "stochastic convergence" in favour of seven countries. Further, the study exhibit "stochastic convergence" for all the eight "Central American countries".

From the "15 stochastically convergent countries", twelve countries present support for "β-convergence". As "stochastic and β-convergence" are necessary for "conditional convergence", therefore the study found evidence of "conditional convergence" for 12 countries.

Ismail (2008) in his study investigated "the issues of convergence and economic growth in the ASEAN" by using "a dynamic, heterogeneous panel approach, namely Pool Mean Group Estimation". Study was based on a "panel data set for five ASEAN countries, mainly from Penn World Tables 6.2 database" during the period 1960-2004. "A dummy for ASEAN as a proxy for regional economic integration in ASEAN (formed in 1967), and a dummy for AFTA as a proxy for the ASEAN Free Trade Area (established in 1992)" was included in the analysis. The Panel has been estimated in two stages. The first stage estimated "unconditional convergence hypothesis", whereas the second stage includes "population growth and the share of capital to test for conditional hypothesis". "β and σ convergence" were examined to see whether "intra regional inequality increased or decreased, particularly after the AFTA was launched". Study found neither of "β nor σ convergence" in ASEAN 5[5] for the overall period 1960-2004. However, "a scatter plot of GDP per capita" revealed that there is an evidence of "β and σ convergence" during the "period of AFTA (1993-2004)". "Based on graphical observation, after the expansion of ASEAN membership, the income gap between regions appears to have been decreasing. Study supports the evidence that poor countries in the ASEAN do catch up with the rich ones. The econometric application supported both the 'unconditional' as well as 'conditional convergence' in ASEAN5 namely Indonesia, Malaysia, Singapore, the Philippines and Thailand, for the 1960-2004 period with a speed of convergence of between 1.6 per cent and 16.6 per cent".

Konya and Guisan (2008) examined whether there existed "an empirically discernable and strong tendency in the world for countries to converge in terms of human development over the last three decades". "Human Development" was measured between the period 1975 and 2004 by using the "Human Development Index" trend of UNDP and convergence hypothesis has been examined by using "β and σ convergence". The results of the study indicate that the world had been converging in the sense "that relatively backward countries managed to increase their HDI faster on average than more developed countries, though this convergence process was rather slow". Similar analysis was performed on "the countries that joined all European Union before its 2004 enlargement and on all current members of the EU too". The study detected "β and σ convergence" in both cases and according to the estimates, convergence was much quicker within these groups of countries than convergence in the world. Further, it was found that although the '12 East- and South- European countries which joined the EU in 2004 and 2007' are relatively under developed compared to the other 15 EU members, so their admission slowed down the convergence process a bit, and the last rounds of enlargement did not seem to have any major impact on HDI convergence among EU member states.

Nayyar (2008) tests the convergence hypothesis among 16 major Indian states for the period 1978-79 to 2002-03 by employing both 'cross-section and panel data regression'. For panel data regression, Fixed Effects Method of estimation as well as Generalised Method of Moments (GMM) estimation has been used. Study did not found "absolute β-convergence". This result holds true for both cross-section and panel estimation, thereby implying that there is no tendency for states to converge to identical steady states. Secondly, after controlling for physical capital formation, both public and private, and proxies for human capital, study found an evidence of conditional β-convergence, revealing that initial poorer states do converge faster to their divergent steady state at the rate of 0.067 per cent per year. Thirdly, study found increasing dispersion in per capita real incomes across states over time, which implies the existence of σ-divergence.

Further, the study identified per capita private investment, literacy rate, infant mortality rate and per capita public investment as important determinants of "a state's steady state level of income". The study ends up with the conclusion that "the Indian states are converging to increasing divergent steady-states, which may be attributed to increasing inter-state disparities in levels of private and public investment and an insignificant impact of centre-state government transfers".

Dayanandan and Arbenser (2009) examined Human Development convergence for six regions of the world for the period 1975-2005 using the 'stochastic convergence framework'. "Panel Unit Root tests developed by Levin, Lin and Chu (LLC) (2002) and Im, Pesaran and

Shin (IPS) (1995)" were used. Convergence in human development was examined on the basis of two sets of panels for each region, viz; (i) Difference in HDI between a particular country and the average HDI of that region. (ii) Difference between a particular country and that of leader (with the highest HDI) in that region. The data on HDI for empirical investigation were obtained from UNDP's Human Development Reports. The regions represented were "East Asia and the Pacific, Europe and Central Asia, Latin America and the Caribbean, Middle East and North Africa, South Asia and Sub-Saharan Africa". The results estimated by LLC (at least based on HDI deviations from the average of each region), found evidence of HDI convergence in all regions except for "Europe and Central Asia". On the other hand, the 'IPS panel unit root tests' found no signs of convergence in all regions. The results based on 'LLC and IPS Panel Unit Root' for group-leader model did not found any evidence of convergence. Overall results of the study did not support the HDI convergence hypothesis for all regions under investigation.

Roy and Bhattacharjee (2009) examined the issue of convergence of "Human Development" among the fifteen major Indian states. State-wise decennial data for HDI (1981-91 to 1991-01) were collected from planning commission's (2002), National Human Development Report (2001). Cluster Analysis was carried out to categorise the states in to clusters/groups based on HDI's. 'OLS Regression Model' was used to examine "β convergence" in which the Growth (1991) and Growth (2001) was regressed on log (HDI 81) and log (HDI 91) respectively and σ (sigma) convergence was examined by 'Standard Deviation'. Equality of variances was tested by using "Levene's and Bartlett's test". The study found that "the low HDI states are growing faster than the high HDI states. However at the same time dispersion of their cross-sectional HDI is not decreasing over time indicating σ (sigma) divergence". Study ends up with the observation that "the absence of convergence of Human Development across Indian states is a serious area of concern".

Dawson and Strazicich (2010) uses data on "real per capita incomes from 1900 to 2001" to test for "stochastic convergence in a diverse group of 29 countries" by utilising "LM unit root tests to endogenously determine the number and location of structural breaks" for each country. "The two-break LM unit root test" results reveal that "in 22 of the 29 relative income series, the unit root null has been rejected at the 10 per cent significance level". Further, the results reveal that "two structural breaks in level and /or trend" are significant in "25 countries, whereas only one structural break is significant in the remaining four countries (Australia, Norway, Sri Lanka and Switzerland)". Study used additional tests for these four countries and reveals that "for Norway and Switzerland, countries for which the unit root null was rejected at the 10 per cent level in the two-break test, can now reject the unit root null at the stronger 5 per cent and 1 per cent levels respectively and the breaks for these countries are also significant at the 10 per cent level".

Furthermore, by using the "one-break tests, for Australia and Sri Lanka, unit root null in Australia can now be rejected at the 10 per cent level, however, the break is not significant at the 10 per cent level" but "the unit root null cannot be rejected for Sri Lanka although the break is significant at the 10 per cent level". So, the study uses "a unit root test without a break" for Australia and rejected "the unit root for Australia at the 5 per cent level" by using conventional "Augmented Dickey Fuller test". Overall, findings of the study revealed "stochastic convergence in 23 of the 29 countries".

Gaur (2010) examined inter-state disparities in "total as well as per capita SDP for 20 major Indian states for the period 1980 to 2002 with the help of inequality indices" based on "properties of Lorenz Curve, Atkinson's Social Welfare Function, Herfindahl's concentration indices etc". The whole time period 1980 to 2002 was further divided into two sub-periods 1980-81 to 1990-91 and 1990-91 to 2001-02 and convergence hypothesis has also been examined by using "σ and β-convergence" notion. Empirical results of the study revealed that "disparity among states in terms of total as well as per capita SDP has risen sharply" as the inequality indices like Gini Theil's Index, Relative Mean Deviation (RDM), Kakwan's as well as Atkinson's Indices have increased over the time period considered. Further, the study found "σ-divergence for total as well as per capita SDP for all the three time periods i.e. 1980-81 to 1990-91, 1991-92 to 2001-02 and 1980-81 to 2001-02". Regarding "β-convergence", study found negative but insignificant co-efficients for "total as well as per capita SDP during pre-reform period (1980-1991)", indicating weak convergence during this period. However, "beta" co-efficients were found to be positive and significant for "total as well as per capita SDP during 1991-2002 period", revealing divergence across states after the reforms. So, study found that the gap has been widening among "rich and poor states especially after 1991" in terms of PCI.

Jayanthakumaran (2010) examined the convergence/divergence hypothesis across 27 Indian states over the period 1980 to 2006 by applying stochastic and beta-convergence tests. "An Augmented Dickey Fuller (ADF) unit root test" was first applied to "the log of relative income for each state" and the results reveals that "the null of a unit root" can be rejected in two states namely "Gujarat and Himachal Pradesh at the 1 per cent and 10 per cent level of significance" respectively. Further, "the one-break LM unit root test" was applied and the study reveals that "the null of a unit root can be rejected in all sample states at least at a 5 per cent significance level". So, as compare to "the ADF unit root test, the one-break LM unit root test that allow for a break under the trend-stationary alternative" show evidence in favour of "stochastic convergence for all 27 states".

Furthermore, regarding beta-convergence, the study found no evidence of pre-break income convergence during the study period, but "14 out of 27" states support evidence for "post-break income convergence". Study ends up with the conclusion "that although approximately half of the states were converging to the national average during the post-break period, but the evidence is not sufficient to show the existence of income convergence in India, because many poor states did not catch up with the rich ones". Study suggested that "poorer states need special attention before further liberalisation".

Kalra and Sodsriwiboon (2010) examined convergence and spillovers across 15 major states over the period 1960 to 2004 using non-stationary panel data techniques. Study found that "states' growth rates were positively co-rrelated with average per capita income. Moreover, growth accelerated in the richer states, poorer states grew moderately, whereas high-income states grew at average annual rates of 3 to 4 per cent over 1970 to 2003, while low income states grew only at 1.5 to 2 per cent". Further, it has been found that "the income differences between high and low-income states become more than doubled and by 2003, the average per capita income of the five richest states (Gujarat, Haryana, Maharashtra, Punjab and Tamil Nadu) was 2.5 times as much as that of the poorest states".

Study found "evidence of divergence over the entire sample period (1960-2003), convergence during sub-periods corresponding to structural breaks and club convergence". In the pre-1980s, study found that of the 15 states in the sample, 7 states support evidence for convergence. "High and low income states" revealed convergence for entire period as well as for each sub-period, whereas "medium-income states (Andhra Pradesh, Karnataka, Kerala, West Bengal and Rajasthan) exhibit divergence over the full sample period and convergence for pre-1980 and 1980-1992".

Study ends up with the conclusion that "the dynamic spillover effects among states are small and there is need for better infrastructure and connectivity throughout the country to allow a dissemination of the benefits of growth across the country".

Chikte (2011) examined convergence hypothesis across 15 Indian states over the period 1970 to 2005 in "per capita income and development input" like "population growth, literacy rate, capital expenditure by state government and commercial credit given by banks". The whole period has been divided into "pre-liberalisation period (1970 to 1990) and post-liberalisation period (1991 to 2005)". Study found an evidence of "σ-divergence" in income for the full sample period as well as for the pre and post liberalisation period. "Literacy shows evidence of convergence across states, as the states have become more and more similar as far as the literacy rates are concerned". However, "population, state capital expenditure and commercial bank credit" have also diverged over time across these 15 Indian states.

The study concluded with the suggestions that "the observed economic divergence calls for the acceleration of reforms and better infrastructural facilities in the poorer states and not for limiting the pro-market reform process that started in 1991. Efforts should be made to make his recent economic growth more inclusive. A well-balanced growth across all regions can provide political stability and boost unity in the country. This is important for the onset of second-generation economic reforms in India".

Cunado (2011) examined the real convergence hypothesis in "13 OPEC countries (Algeria, Angola, Ecuador, Indonesia, Iran, Iraq, Kuwait, Libya, Nigeria, Qatar, Saudi Arabia, United Arab Emirates and Venezuela) for the period 1950-2007 towards the U.S. economy" by means of using "time series techniques". In particular, the study analysed the convergence process for the "13 OPEC countries towards the U.S. economy", first based on "ADF unit root tests and then allowing for structural breaks".

ADF unit root test was carried out to each of the series in order to obtain the integration order of each of the series. The results from the "Augmented Dickey Fuller (ADF)" tests to the difference of each of "per capita GDP series with respect to the U.S. economy", unable to reject "the unit root hypothesis" in favour of "unconditional convergence" for any of the "OPEC countries". After including "an intercept and a time trend", the study again unable to reject "the unit root null hypothesis" for any of the countries. But after allowing for one structural break, study found evidence of a "catch-up process" for Indonesia towards the U.S. economy. Further, when the unit root test was applied by allowing two structural breaks, study found an evidence of a "catch-up process" during the last period, the nineties-2007, for Indonesia and Angola towards the U.S. economy.

Jan and Chaudhary (2011) investigated "the existence or non-existence of conditional convergence across four Pakistani provinces" from 1973 to 2000. For estimating "conditional convergence", the "different steady states of the Pakistani provinces" were controlled by "the time and cross-sectional specific effects, the manufacturing output and the structural variable". Study found that the gap between "the initial levels of per capita gross provincial products (GPP) and the respective steady states of provinces" vanishes at the rate of 11 per cent per annum. The study indicated that "the income gap between the provinces will vanish, if there exists homogenous social and political institutions, the geography, climate, natural resource endowments, initial level of technology and the technological progress are identical and all the provinces will have the same level of industrialisation". Further, the study found that "manufacturing output is statistically significant and positively affects the economic growth in the provinces, however, the structural variable is not statistically significant".

The study ends up with the suggestion that "the state must take the initiative of industrialising and bringing favourable structural changes in the poorer provinces by investing directly in the physical infrastructure and human resource development of the poorer provinces".

K. G. and Kumar (2011) used "the time series data on per capita state domestic product (SDP)" of eighteen Indian states over the period 1980-81 to 2008-09 in order to examine convergence of states per capita income. "The entire period has been divided into two parts 1980-81 to 1990-91 and 1991-92 to 2008-09" to test the convergence hypothesis between pre-reform and post-reform period. Study used "panel unit root tests" such as "LLC test (Levin, Lin and Chu 2002), IPS test (suggested by Im, Pesaran and Shin, 2003), MW (Maddala and Wu, 1999) and PP-Fisher Chi-Square test". "The unit root null hypothesis" has not been rejected by all these four tests, for the period 1980-81 to 2008-09. This indicates that "there is no sign of convergence of per capita income in Indian states, whereas it is diverging, since the panel unit root test results indicates that the mean variations of state per capita income is non-stationary process". Further, the study variable was found to be stationary for the "pre-reform period", whereas it is non-stationary for the "post-reform period". This indicates the convergence of "per capita income in the pre-reform period", while in the "post-reform period" it confirms "divergence in per capita income" among the Indian states.

Ghosh (2012) evaluates "the economic performance of 15 major states in India, and examines whether initially disparate states displayed any tendency towards convergence in real per capita income during the period 1960-61 to 2006-07". The study also evaluates "stochastic convergence" and classifies the states into convergent and non-convergent clubs at the "aggregate and sectoral levels". The whole period 1960-61 to 2006-07 has been divided into two periods i.e. "pre-reform period (1960-61 to 1990-91) and post-reform period (1991-92 to 2006-07)". Study found that "though the growth performance of the states has improved in the post-reform period since 1991, but the states have diverged in per capita income. The states with higher initial levels of per capita income grew faster than those with lower initial levels, particularly during the post-reform period".

Further, stochastic convergence has been examined for "per capita income, per capita income originating from agriculture and allied sector, per capita income originating from industry and services sector" by using Phillips-Perron test statistics. The test statistics for relative per capita income found that "while the null hypothesis of a unit root (non-stationarity) can be rejected for five states only (Andhra Pradesh, Karnataka, Kerala, Rajasthan and Tamil Nadu), it cannot be rejected for the remaining 10 states (Assam, Bihar, Gujarat, Haryana, Madhya Pradesh, Maharashtra, Odisha, Punjab, Uttar Pradesh and West Bengal)". This suggests that "the five states are stochastically converging, sharing a common steady-state path with the national average level, whereas the remaining ten states have been diverging following different steady-state paths".

The results for the agriculture and allied sector found that "the null hypothesis of no convergence can be rejected for 10 states (Andhra Pradesh, Assam, Bihar, Gujarat, Karnataka, Madhya Pradesh, Maharashtra, Rajasthan, Tamil Nadu and Uttar Pradesh)". While the null hypothesis of no convergence can be rejected for three states (Karnataka, Kerala and Odisha) for industrial sector, it can be rejected for four states (Andhra Pradesh, Kerala, Rajasthan and Tamil Nadu) for services". Thus, the study found that most of the states have converged in "per capita income originating from the agriculture and allied sector", the opposite has happened in industry and services. Study explained regional divergence in terms of inter-state variations in "physical and social infrastructure, state-level policy reforms, foreign direct investment flows and economic structure". So, the study suggested for "undertaking investments in physical and social infrastructure".

Kalita and Tiwari (2012) attempted to test income convergence across 27 Indian states over the period 1980-1981 to 2007-2008 by utilising "panel linear and non-linear unit root tests". The study used the panel data framework by "Ucar and Omey (2009) for heterogeneous panel unit root test" due to two reasons. First, it is based on heterogeneous panel, as Indian states are heterogeneous in nature and culture. Second, it has advancement in showing the non-linear nature of convergence. Study found that when constant term is included in the regression or constant and trend terms both are included in both the regression tests "(linear and non-linear panel unit root tests)", the null hypothesis has not been rejected, implying that State Gross Domestic Product (SGDP) of Indian states follows random walk i.e. non-stationary.

Hence, the results of the study provide evidence that there is no convergence of SGDP of the Indian states and these states do not follow balanced growth path and there is strong mismatch in the growth path of SGDP. Study suggested for making proper strategies by Indian government in order to have balanced and equitable growth of SGDP.

Kumar and Subramanian (2012) made an attempt to examine the growth performance of PCNSDP across 21 states during the period 2001-2009 and tested the convergence hypothesis for the same. Study found that the growth increased in 2001-2009 as compared to 1993-2001 in almost all the states except "Himachal Pradesh, Rajasthan and West Bengal". The largest improvements were posted by "Uttarakhand, Maharashtra and Chhattisgarh with Gujarat, Odisha and Bihar not far behind". The laggard states like that of "Bihar, Chhattisgarh, Odisha and Uttarakhand" observed the highest improvements between 2001 and 2009 comparative to 1993-2001. Further, the study found that "despite the strong performance of the hitherto laggard states, the states with a higher per capita income in 1993 grew faster over the next 16 years".

Furthermore, when the "average annual growth rate of per capita income" regressed on the logarithm of the "initial per capita income" in 2001, the study again do not find any evidence of convergence, as the co-efficient on the log of "initial per capita income" found to be positive and statistically significant. But when the exercise was repeated over the period 1993-2009, the study again found that the states have been diverging over this period also.

So, overall the study observed "the phenomenon of divergence or rising inequality" across states and concluded that "on average the rich states in 2001 grew faster in 2001-2009 and demographic dividend do not have any positive effect on economic growth".

Raju (2012) studied the growth performance across states and also examined the convergence/divergence hypothesis by employing two measures of unconditional convergence-sigma and beta convergence. Sigma convergence has been estimated by using co-efficient of variation, whereas beta convergence has been estimated by fixed effects panel models. Growth performance was measured as the growth in the "gross state domestic product (GSDP) at 2004-05 prices" and states were divided into non-special and special category states. Special category states are largely the Border States which traditionally have had smaller economies and historically witnessed social and economic instability, while the non-special category states have larger economies and together accounted for nearly 95 per cent of the total population.

Study found declining co-efficient of variation for all states and for non-special category states also, while alternating rising/declining co-efficient of variation has been found for special category states. Further beta convergence has been observed for all states and the group of non-special category, while evidence of beta convergence among the special category states found to be slightly weaker. Regarding, growth performance of states, it has been found that the growth rate of the non-special category states has been higher (7 per cent) during 2001-10 as compared to 1995-2000 (6.09 per cent) except few states such as "Goa, Karnataka, Rajasthan and West Bengal", which observed low growth rates during 2001-10. Likewise, the special category states also witnessed increase (7.7 per cent) as compared to 1995-2001 (5.8 per cent) except "Mizoram, Manipur, Meghalaya and Jammu and Kashmir".

Cherodian and Thirlwall (2013) examined regional disparities in per capita income in India over the first decade of the twenty first century (1999-2000 to 2010-2011) by estimating "cross-section equations for unconditional and conditional β-convergence and sigma (σ) convergence" across "thirty two regions (twenty-eight states and four union territories)". Study did not find "unconditional convergence" in per capita GSDP for all the 32 regions over the period 1999-2000 to 2010-2011. Further, for testing the "conditional convergence", the study used "per capita GSDP, population growth, the growth of bank credit to the private sector (credit), the male literacy rate, the share of agriculture in state GDP (per cent), state expenditure as a per cent of state GDP" and found weak evidence of "conditional convergence". Furthermore, the study found that "population growth and share of agriculture" exerts a significant negative effect on state per capita growth. "The extension of credit to the private sector exerts a significant positive impact, whereas male literacy rate seems to have no significant effect, nor does the share of state expenditure in state GDP. Sigma divergence has increased continuously except among the poorest states".

Goli et al. (2013) examined the convergence hypothesis across the 15 Indian states from 1981 to 2011 in terms of "indicators of economic inequality, poverty ratios, literacy rate and human development index (HDI) along with per capita SNDP". Study found statistically significant "absolute and conditional β-convergence in literacy rates and HDI, but only conditional β-convergence" has been found in case of "per capita SNDP and poverty ratios" over the period 1981 to 2011. Further, for the period (post-2001), study found divergence in "per capita SNDP and poverty ratios" but convergence in "literacy rates and HDI". The increasing trends in CV for per capita SNDP indicated a divergence phase in PCSNDP across states over the period 1981-2010. Regarding the "estimates of trends of CV for the poverty ratios", study found "a divergent trend in reduction of poverty ratios across the states until 2000, but convergence trend during the post-2000 period". The trends of CV for literacy rates and HDI supported the hypothesis of "σ-convergence" during the period 1981 to 2011. Furthermore, by using "the Kernel Density plots for socio-economic indicators", study found "the existence of convergence clubs but not absolute convergence among all the major states".

Most of the studies, reviewed above, covered only one or two aspects of convergence hypothesis and almost no comprehensive attempt has been made to empirically examine the various aspects. The present study has been planned so as to make a comprehensive attempt to examine the convergence hypothesis across Indian states over the period 1981 to 2011.

Notes

1. An area of local government in some countries.
2. Nomenclature of Territorial Units for Statistics.
3. Levin, Lin and Chu, 2002 (LLC); Im, Pesaran and Shin, IPS (2003) and Maddala and Wu (1999).
4. Choi, 2004 (CH); Moon and Perron, 2004 (MP); Bai and Ng, 2004 (BNG) and Pesaran, 2005 (PS).
5. Malaysia, Indonesia, Singapore, Thailand and Philippines.

Chapter 3

Data Base and Methodology

This chapter describes the data base of the present study, along with concepts and various econometric and statistical techniques applied for achieving the objectives of the study. The present study is based on secondary data. First of all, list of all possible indicators related to study was prepared. An attempt was made to collect the data regarding the maximum possible number of indicators for maximum possible number of states. The data used in the study were collected from Central Statistical Organisation, National Human Development Report 2001, Census of India, Statistical Abstract of Punjab (various issues), Data book for the use of Deputy Chairman (Planning Commission 2012), UNDP India 2011, Centre for Monitoring Indian Economy (CMIE) Report (various issues), Economic Survey (various issues), Economic and Political Weekly Research Foundation 2011, National Family Health Survey (NFHS I and II), Manpower Profile, India Human Development Report 2011. The study has been undertaken for the period 1980 to 2011, the earliest and the latest years as per the availability of data. In order to obtain comparable data for per capita NSDP at 2004-05 prices for the period 1980-81 to 2011-12, shifting of base year from 1980-81 to 1993-94, from 1993-94 to 1999-2000 and then from 1999-2000 to 2004-05 constant prices is necessary. So, as per the requirement, state-wise per capita NSDP at 1980-81 constant prices has been converted into 1993-94 constant prices for each state and then from 1993-94 to 1999-2000 and furthermore, the per capita NSDP at 1999-2000 constant prices for each state has been converted into 2004-05 prices for the entire period 1980-81 to 2011-12.

3.1 Variables of the Study

1. Per Capita Net State Domestic Product at 2004-05 Prices.
2. Adult Literacy Rate.
3. Female Literacy Rate.
4. Primary Pupil Teacher Ratio.
5. Upper Primary Pupil Teacher Ratio.
6. Secondary Pupil Teacher Ratio.
7. Primary Gross Enrollment Ratio.
8. Upper Primary Gross Enrollment Ratio.
9. Primary Drop-out Rate.
10. Percentage of Population below Poverty Line.
11. Percentage of Households with Access to Safe Drinking Water.
12. Percentage of Households with Access to Electricity.
13. Infant Mortality Rate per Thousand Live Births.
14. Crude Death Rate per Thousand Population.
15. Urban Population as percentage of Total Population.
16. Per Capita Consumption of Electricity.
17. Percentage Share of Industry in NSDP at 2004-05 Prices.
18. Percentage Share of Services in NSDP at 2004-05 Prices.
19. Proportion of Undernourished Children (Weight for height per cent below -2SD)
20. Illiteracy Rate for population in the age group of 7 years and above.
21. Non-Enrollment Ratio.
22. Proportion of Population not Fully Vaccinated.
23. Proportion of Population without Access to Safe Drinking Water.
24. Proportion of Population without Access to Electricity.
25. Proportion of Population without Access to Toilet Facility.
26. Annual Per Capita Industrial Consumption of Electricity.
27. Net Irrigated Area as a per cent of Net Area Sown.

28. Percentage Share of Agriculture in NSDP at 2004-05 prices.
29. Bank Deposits as a per cent of NSDP.
30. Bank Advances as a per cent of NSDP.
31. Population Growth Rate.
32. Population Per Bank Office (thousands).
33. Percentage of Villages Electrified.
34. Road Density Per Thousand sq. Km of Area.
35. State-wise Human Development Index.

3.2 Methodology

Various types of econometric techniques and models have been applied to achieve the objectives of the study. All the techniques and models as estimated for specific objectives are discussed as below:

3.2.1 σ-convergence

σ-convergence occurs if the standard deviation of the natural log (ln) $y_{i,t}$ tends to decrease over time. i.e. if $\sigma_{t+T} < \sigma_t$ Where σ_t is the standard deviation of natural log (ln) $y_{i,t}$ across i states; t is initial year of the respective individual state and T is the length of the period considered; y represents the variable selected for examining convergence.

In the present study, σ-convergence has been examined by measuring the standard deviations across states of the natural log (ln) of the respective variable under consideration. If the standard deviation across states tends to decline over time then there will be sigma convergence or sigma divergence otherwise.

3.2.2 Unconditional β-convergence

The second measure called 'β-convergence' refers to "an inverse relation between the relative growth rate of per capita variable under consideration and its value at initial level-occurs when poor states tend to grow faster than the rich ones, in opposite case the situation will be of β-divergence" (Barro, 1991).

For testing unconditional β-convergence hypothesis, this study intends to use the following equation:

$$\Delta yi, t, t{+}T = \alpha - [\ln(Yi,t)]\,(1{-}e{-}bT)\,(1/T) + \varepsilon i,t \tag{1}$$

$$\text{Where } \Delta yi,t, t{+}T = \frac{\ln\left(\frac{yi,\,t+T}{yi,t}\right)}{T}$$

$y_{i,t}$ and $y_{i,\,t+T}$ are the initial and the last year respectively of the individual state

'ln' represents natural log

'i' stands for different states

T is the length of time period considered

Y represents the variable selected for examining convergence

β represents the speed of convergence

$\varepsilon i,t$ is the error term

For solving equation (1), the co-efficient - $(1\text{-}e^{-\beta T})$ 1/T is changed by b and equation (1), becomes:

$$\Delta y_{i,t,\,t+T} = \alpha + b \ln Y_{i,t} + \varepsilon i,t \tag{2}$$

$b = -\,(1-e^{-\beta T})\,1/T$

$-bT = (1-e^{-\beta T})$

$-bT-1 = -e^{-\beta T}$

$bT+1 = e^{-\beta T}$

$\ln(bT+1) = -\beta T$

$-\beta T = \ln(bT+1)$

$-\beta = 1/T \ln(bT+1)$

$$\beta = -\,1/T \ln(bT+1) \tag{3}$$

Equation 3 determines the speed of convergence and if the equation (2) has a negative slope, then there will be unconditional β-convergence.

The half life of convergence is calculated by using the following formula

$e^{-\beta T^*} = \frac{1}{2}$

$T^* = \ln 2/\beta$

$T^* = 0.69/\beta$

Where T* refers to half life of convergence

Equation (2) has been estimated by applying Ordinary Least Squares in which the average growth rate of respective variable is regressed on the natural logarithm of its initial value.

Formal approach to detect the convergence or divergence over time has also been used by plotting annualised growth rates (vertical axis) of respective variable under consideration against natural log (ln) of its initial levels (Horizontal axis).

The growth rate has been calculated using:

$$\frac{\log\left(\frac{yi,\ t+T}{yi,t}\right)}{T}$$

where 't' and 't+T' are the initial year and the last year respectively of the individual state i and T is the length of the period considered and y represents the variable under consideration.

3.2.3 Conditional β-Convergence

According to Sala-i-Martin (1996), "To test the hypothesis of conditional convergence one has to, somehow, hold constant the steady state of each economy". I have also tried to hold the steady state constant by using variable that proxy for the steady state in a regression like (eq.2).

$$\Delta y_{i,\ t,\ t+T} = \alpha + b \ln Y_{i,t} + \psi X_{i,t} + \varepsilon i,t \qquad (4)$$

Where $X_{i,t}$ is a vector of variables that hold constant the steady state of economy i, and $b = (1-e^{-\beta T})\ 1/T$. if eq. (4) has a negative slope once $X_{i,t}$ is held constant, then there will be conditional β-convergence.

For testing conditional convergence in our analysis, I have used 11 variables namely (i) annual per capita consumption of electricity (X1); (ii) annual per capita industrial consumption of electricity (X2); (iii) net irrigated area as a per cent of net area sown (X3); (iv) per cent share of agriculture in NSDP(X4) (v) per cent share of industry in NSDP (X5); (vi) per cent share of services in NSDP (X6); (vii) bank deposits as a per cent of NSDP (X7); (viii) bank advances as a per cent of NSDP (X8); (ix) population growth rate (X9); (x) population per bank office (thousand) (X10); (xi) per cent of villages electrified (X11).

3.2.4 Panel Data Regression Models

"Panel data models examine cross-sectional (group) and/or time-series (time) effects. These effects may be fixed or random. A fixed effect model examines if intercepts vary across group or time period, whereas a random effect model explores differences in error variance components across individual or time period" (Park, 2011). Tests like "F-test, Breush and Pagan Langrangian multiplier (LM) test and Hausman specification test" are applied to find out the appropriate model. 'F-test and Breush and Pagan Langrangian multiplier (LM)' test are used to check the consistency of 'fixed effect model and random effect model' respectively. If both the models found consistent based on these results, then 'Hausman specification test (5 per cent significance level)' is applied to choose the appropriate one. If both the models found inconsistent, then pooled OLS model is most appropriate (Park, 2011).

Pooled OLS

"If individual effect u_i (cross-sectional or time specific effect) does not exist (u_i=0), ordinary least squares (OLS), produces efficient and consistent parameter estimates" (Park, 2011). I have used the following equation for OLS:

$$Y_{it} = \alpha + X'_{it}\beta + \varepsilon it \ (u_i = 0) \qquad (5)$$

Where i = 1,2 ....N; t = 1, 2 ....T

'i' refers to the 'cross-sectional dimension'

't' refers to the 'time-series dimension'

But if individual effect u_i is not zero, then these effects are either 'fixed or random effects'.

Fixed Effects and Random Effects Model

For fixed effects the model becomes

$$Y_{it} = (\alpha + u_i) + X'_{it}\,\beta + n_i \quad (6)$$

For random effects the model becomes

$$Y_{it} = \alpha + X'_{it}\,\beta + (u_i + n_{it}) \quad (7)$$

"where u_i is a fixed or random effect specific to individual (group) or time period that is not included in the regression, and errors are independent identically distributed, $v_{it} \sim IID(0, \sigma^2 v)$" (Park, 2011).

"A fixed effect model examines individual differences in intercepts, assuming the same slopes and constant variance across individual (group and entity). Since an individual specific effect is time invariant and considered a part of the intercept, u_i is allowed to be correlated with other regressors" (Park, 2011).

"A random effect model assumes that individual effect (heterogeneity) is not correlated with any regressor and then estimates error variance specific to groups (or times). Hence, u_i is an individual specific random heterogeneity or a component of the composite error term. This is why a random effect model is also called an error component model" (Park, 2011).

F- test for Fixed Effects

"In a regression of $Y_{it} = \alpha + \mu_i + X'_{it}\,\beta + \varepsilon it$, the null hypothesis is that all dummy parameters except for one for the dropped are zero, $H_0 : \mu_1 = ... = \mu_{n-1} = 0$. The alternative hypothesis is that at least one dummy parameter is not zero. This hypothesis is tested by F test, which is based on loss of goodness-of-fit. This test contrasts LSDV (robust model) with the pooled OLS (efficient model) and examines the extent to which the goodness-of-fit measures (SSE or R^2) changed.

$$F(n-1, nT-n-k) = \frac{(e'e_{pooled} - e'e_{LSDV})/(n-1)}{(-e'e_{LSDV})/(nT-n-k)} = \frac{(R^2_{LSDV} - R^2_{pooled})/(n-1)}{(1-R^2_{LSDV})/(nT-n-k)}$$

If the null hypothesis is rejected (at least one group/time specific intercept u_i is not zero), then we may conclude that there is a significant fixed effect or significant increase in goodness-of-fit in the fixed effect model; therefore, the fixed effect model is better than the pooled OLS" (Park, 2011).

Breusch–Pagan LM Test for Random Effects

Breusch and Pagan's (1980) Lagrange multiplier (LM) test examines "if individual (or time) specific variance components are zero, $H0 : \sigma^2_u = 0$. The LM statistic follows the chi-squared distribution with one degree of freedom" (park, 2011).

$$LMu = \frac{nT}{2(T-1)}\left[\frac{T^2\bar{e}'\bar{e}}{e'e} - 1\right]^2 \sim x^{2(1)},$$

"where $\bar{e}$ is the $n \times 1$ vector of the group means of pooled regression residuals, and $e'e$ is the SSE of the pooled OLS regression" (park, 2011).

According to Baltagi (2001), LM test is of the following form:

$$LMu = \frac{nT}{2(T-1)}\left[\frac{\Sigma(\Sigma\, eit)^2}{\Sigma(\Sigma\, e^2{}_{it}} - 1\right]^2 = \frac{nT}{2(T-1)}\left[\frac{\Sigma(T\bar{e}i.)^2}{\Sigma(\Sigma\, e^2{}_{it}} - 1\right]^2 \sim x^{2(1)},$$

"If the null hypothesis is rejected, we can conclude that there is a significant random effect in the panel data, and that the random effect model can deal with heterogeneity in a better way than the pooled OLS" (park, 2011).

Hausman Test for comparing Fixed and Random Effects

"The Hausman Specification Test compares fixed and random effect models under the null hypothesis that individual effects are uncorrelated with any regressor in the model" (Hausman, 1978). "If the null hypothesis of no correlation is rejected, then individual effects u_i are significantly correlated with at least one regressor in the model and thus the random effect model is problematic. Therefore, we need to go for a fixed effect model rather than the random effect model"

(Park, 2011). The Hausman test uses that "the covariance of an efficient estimator with its difference from an inefficient estimator is zero" (Greene, 2008).

$$LM = (b_{LSDV} - b_{random})'\hat{W}^{-1}((b_{LSDV} - b_{random}) \sim x^2(k),$$

where

$$\widehat{W} = Var\left[b_{LSDV} - b_{random}\right] = (b_{LSDV}) - Var(b_{random})$$

is the difference in the "estimated covariance matrices of LSDV (robust model) and GLS (efficient model)" (Park, 2011).

3.2.5 Factor Analysis

According to Harman (1967), "Some of the variables selected for the construction of composite development index are input and output variables. These variables technically associated with particular phenomenon are highly correlated among themselves. This causes the problem of multicollinearity and the consequences of this problem are inaccurate and unreliable results. The statistical technique that can be more usefully applied in such a situation is 'Factor Analysis'. Factor Analysis attempts to estimate the value for the co-efficients of regression where the variables are regressed up on the factors".

Normalisation of Data

The selected variables were first normalised and the best and worst values in an indicator were computed. The indicators used in the study were of two types i.e. either having positive or negativ——e impact on the index. In case of a positive indicator, the highest value will be considered as the best value and the lowest has been treated as the worst value. On the other hand, in case of a negative indicator, the lowest value will be treated as the best value and the highest will be the worst value. After that the following formula has been used to compute normalised values:

$$Zij = 1 - \left[\frac{\left\{BestX_i - ObservedXi_j\right\}}{\left\{BestX_i - WorstXi\right\}}\right]$$

"Normalised values always lie between 0 and 1" (Mehta and Siddiqui, 2008).

After computing the normalised values, the relative weights of selected indicators have been obtained by applying the scientific technique i.e. 'principal component analysis' also called 'Factor Analysis'. The relative weights of selected indicators have been used for constructing Composite Development Index.

According to Harman (1967), "In Factor Analysis, a given set of 'n' variables are grouped into 'P' number of groups called 'Factors' which are less in number than the set of original variables. The variables within a group (Factor) are of same nature or are complementary with respect to the phenomenon under study but between two groups 'Factors' variables are independent. Thus factors F_i and F_j are orthogonal".

The Factor Analysis used in the present study:

$X = LF + U$

Where X is vector of all the original variables.

$X' = [X_1, X_2, X_3 \ldots\ldots\ldots\ldots X_n]$

F is vector of 'Factors' derived

$F' = [F_1, F_2, F_3 \ldots\ldots\ldots\ldots\ldots\ldots F_p]$

U is vector of error terms

$U' = [E_1, E_2, E_3 \ldots\ldots\ldots\ldots\ldots E_n]$

L is matrix of Factor Loadings (Loading Co-efficient Matrix)

$$L = \begin{pmatrix} a_{11} & a_{12} & a_{13} \ldots\ldots\ldots\ldots & a_{1p} \\ a_{21} & a_{22} & a_{23} \ldots\ldots\ldots\ldots & a_{2p} \\ a_{31} & a_{32} & a_{33} \ldots\ldots\ldots\ldots & a_{3p} \\ \ldots\ldots & \ldots\ldots & \ldots\ldots & \ldots\ldots \\ a_{n1} & a_{n2} & an3 \ldots\ldots\ldots\ldots & a_{np} \end{pmatrix}$$

The coefficient (Factor loading) a_{ij} belongs to i^{th} variable and j^{th} Factor and shows the extent to which variable X_i is related to F_j Factor. "A salient loading is one which is sufficiently high to assume that a relationship exists between the variable and the factor. In addition, it usually means that relationship is high enough so that the variable can aid in interpreting the factor and vice-versa" (Gorsuch, 1974).

The sum of the square of factor loadings of X_i original variables under the derived p Factors is called the communalities for X_i variables.

$$(a_{i1})^2 + (a_{i2})^2 + (a_{i3})^2 + \dots\dots\dots\dots\dots\dots (a_{ip})^2 = (C_i)^2$$

Communality in Factor Analysis is something like R^2 in the Regression Analysis and it shows the extent to which the derived factors explain the ith variable.

The method for determining the relative weights for the variables is explained below:

W_i : $F_{ik}\,\lambda_k$

Wi : is weight of ith variable

F_{ik} : is factor loading of ith variable and k^{th} factor which shows the highest correlation between variable (X_i) and factor (F_k)

λ_k : is the variation explained by k^{th} factor

Index has been calculated by using following formula:

$$Ij = \frac{\sum_{i=1}^{n} W_i Z_{ij}}{\sum_{i=1}^{n} W_i}$$

I_j : is the composite development Index of jth state

Z_{ij} : is normalised value of ith variable for j^{th} state

W_i : is the weight of ith variable.

Sw_i : is sum of the weights (Harman, 1967).

3.2.6 Co-efficient of Variation

In order to examine the trend of inequality across states in the selected indicators as well as the indices over the period of time, 'co-efficient of variation (C.V.)' as a measure of convergence/ divergence has been applied:

Co-efficient of Variation (C.V.) = $\frac{\sigma}{\overline{X}} . 100$

Where σ and $\overline{X}$ are the mean and standard deviation respectively of given variable.

3.2.7 Time Series Unit Root Tests

For testing the convergence hypothesis by applying Time Series Approach, I have used the standard 'Augmented Dickey Fuller (ADF) unit root test'.

For each state i, we examine the natural logarithm of the ratio of Per Capita Net State Domestic Product (PCNSDP) relative to the average of all the states.

Y_{it} = ln ($PCNSDP_{it}$/ average $PCNSDP_t$) (8)

Then, I have applied the 'Augmented Dickey Fuller test' to examine the convergence hypothesis. The ADF test for a unit root developed by 'Dickey and Fuller (1979)' has been used to check whether a data is stationary or not. For this, the following type of Augmented Dickey Fuller (ADF) regression has been applied:

$$\Delta Y_t = \mu + \beta_t + \alpha Y_{t-1} + \sum_{i=1}^{K} \delta_i \Delta Y_{t-i} + e_t \quad (9)$$

Where e_t is white noise. The equation is with intercept and time trend.

The Hypothesis is:

H_0: $\alpha = 0$

H_1: $\alpha \neq 0$

If the calculated ADF statistics are insignificant then the null hypothesis (H_0) is accepted and the series are taken as non-stationary. Hence, unit root exists. Alternatively, if the calculated ADF statistics are significant then the alternate hypothesis (H_1) is accepted and the series are taken as stationary. Hence, unit root does not exist.

3.2.8 Panel Data Unit Root Tests

Levin, Lin and Chu Test

"LLC argued that individual unit root tests have limited power against alternative hypotheses with highly persistent deviations from equilibrium. This is particularly severe in small samples. LLC suggest a more powerful panel unit root test than performing individual unit root tests for each cross-section. The null hypothesis is that each individual time series contains a unit root against the alternative that each time series is stationary" (Baltagi, 2005).

The maintained hypothesis is that

$$\Delta y_{it} = \rho y_{i,t-1} + \sum_{L=1}^{pi} \theta_{iL} \Delta y_{it-L} + \alpha_{mi} d_{mt} + \varepsilon_{it} m = 1,2,3 \quad (10)$$

with d_{mt} indicates the vector of deterministic variables and a_{mi} indicates the corresponding vector of co-efficients for model m = 1, 2, 3. The following steps will be used to implement LLC test:

Step I: 'Augmented Dickey–Fuller (ADF) regressions' for each cross-section:

$$\Delta y_{it} = \rho_i y_{i,t-1} + \sum_{L=1}^{pi} \theta_{iL} \Delta y_{i,t-L} + \alpha_{mi} d_{mt} + \varepsilon_{it} m = 1,2,3 \quad (11)$$

Choose a maximum lag order $p_{\max}$ for a given T and in order to determine if a smaller lag order is preferred, use the t-statistic of $\hat{\theta}_{iL}$.

After determining p_i,

In order to get residuals $\hat{e}_{it}$, Run Δy_{it} on $\Delta y_{i,t-L}$ (L=1, . . . , p_i) and d_{mt}

And

In order to get residuals $\hat{v}_{i,t-1}$, Run $y_{i,t-1}$ on $\Delta y_{i,t'L}$ (L=1, . . . , p_i) and d_{mt}

To control for different variances across i, these residuals will be standardised

$$\tilde{e}_{it} = \hat{e}_{it} / \hat{\sigma}_{\varepsilon i} \qquad \text{and} \qquad \tilde{v}_{i,t-1} = \hat{v}_{it} / \hat{\sigma}_{\varepsilon i}$$

Where $\hat{\sigma}_{\grave{a}i}$ is the standard error from each ADF regression, for $i = 1, \ldots, N$.

Step II. In the second step, 'the ratio of long-run to short-run standard deviations' will be estimated.

$$\hat{\sigma}^2_{yi} = \frac{1}{T-1}\sum_{t=2}^{T} \Delta y^2_{it} + 2\sum_{L=1}^{\bar{k}} \omega \bar{k} L \left[\frac{1}{T-1}\sum_{t=2+L}^{T} \Delta y_{it}\Delta y_{i,t-L}\right] \quad (12)$$

where $\overline{K}$ refers to the truncation lag that can be data-dependent. $W_{\overline{K}L} = 1" (L/(\overline{K} + 1))$.

Step III. The panel test statistics will be computed by running the pooled regression

$$\tilde{e}_{it} = \rho\tilde{v}_{i,t-1} + \bar{\varepsilon}_{it}$$

based on $N\overline{T}$ observations where $\overline{T} = T - \overline{P} - 1$. $\overline{T}$ refers to the 'average number of observations per individual in the panel' with $\overline{P} = \Sigma_{i=1}^{N} P_i / N.\overline{P}$ refers to the 'average lag order of individual ADF regressions'. The 't-statistic' for $H_0 : \rho = 0$ is $t_{ñ} = t_\rho = \frac{\overline{P}}{\sigma(P)}$,

where

$$\hat{\rho} = \sum_{i=1}^{N}\sum_{t=2+p_i}^{T} \tilde{v}_{i,t-1}\tilde{e}_{it} \bigg/ \sum_{i=1}^{N}\sum_{t=2+p_i}^{T} \tilde{v}^2_{i,t-1}$$

$$\hat{\sigma}(\hat{\rho}) = \hat{\sigma}_{\tilde{\varepsilon}} \bigg/ \left[\sum_{i=1}^{N}\sum_{t=2+p_i}^{T_i} \tilde{v}^2_{i,t-1}\right]^{1/2}$$

and

$$\hat{\sigma}^2_{\tilde{\varepsilon}} = \frac{1}{N\tilde{T}}\sum_{i=1}^{N}\sum_{t=2+p_i}^{T} (\tilde{e}_{it} - \hat{\rho}\tilde{v}_{i,t-1})^2$$

is the estimated variance of $\tilde{\varepsilon}_{it}$.

Compute the adjusted t-statistic

$$t^*_\rho = \frac{t_\rho - N\tilde{T}\hat{S}_N\hat{\sigma}_{\tilde{\varepsilon}}^{-2}\hat{\sigma}(\hat{\rho})\mu^*_{m\tilde{T}}}{\sigma^*_{m\tilde{T}}} \quad (12.4)$$

where $\mu^*_{m\tilde{T}}$ and $\sigma^*_{m\tilde{T}}$ are the mean and standard deviation adjustments provided by

Im, Pesaran and Shin Test

"The Levin, Lin and Chu test requires $\tilde{n}$ to be homogeneous across i. Im et al. (2003) (IPS) allow for a heterogeneous co-efficient of y_{it-1} and offer an alternative testing procedure which is based on averaging individual unit root test statistics. The null hypothesis is that each series in the panel contains a unit root, i.e., $H_0 : \rho_i = 0$ for all i and the alternative hypothesis allows for some (but not all) of the individual series to have unit roots" (Baltagi, 2005).

$$H_1 : \begin{cases} \rho_i < 0 & \text{for} \quad i = 1, 2, \ldots, N_1 \\ \rho_i = 0 & \text{for} \quad i = N_1 + 1, \ldots, N \end{cases} \tag{14}$$

Formally, it requires the "fraction of the individual time series that are stationary to be non-zero, i.e., $\lim_{N \to \infty} (N_1/N) = \delta$ where $0 < \delta \leq 1$. This condition is necessary for the consistency of the panel unit root test. The IPS t-bar statistic is defined as the average of the individual ADF statistics as

$$\bar{t} = \frac{1}{N} \sum_{i=1}^{N} t_{\rho_i} \tag{15}$$

where $t_{\tilde{n}i}$ refers to the individual t-statistic for testing $H_0 : \rho_i = 0$ for all i in (14).

$$t_{\rho_i} \Rightarrow \frac{\int_0^1 W_{iZ} dW_{iZ}}{\left[\int_0^1 W_{iZ}^2\right]^{1/2}} = t_{iT} \tag{16}$$

as $T \to \infty$, where $\int W(r)$ dr refers to a Weiner integral with the argument r suppressed in (16), IPS assume that t_{iT} have finite mean and variance. Then

$$\frac{\sqrt{N}\left(\frac{1}{N}\sum_{i=1}^{N} t_{iT} - \frac{1}{N}\sum_{i=1}^{N} E\left[t_{iT} \mid \rho_i = 0\right]\right)}{\sqrt{\frac{1}{N}\sum_{i=1}^{N} \operatorname{var}\left[t_{iT} \mid \rho_i = 0\right]}} \Rightarrow N(0, 1) \tag{17}$$

as $N \to \infty$ by the Lindeberg–Levy central limit theorem. Hence

$$t_{\text{IPS}} = \frac{\sqrt{N}\left(\bar{t} - \frac{1}{N}\sum_{i=1}^{N} E\left[t_{iT} \mid \rho_i = 0\right]\right)}{\sqrt{\frac{1}{N}\sum_{i=1}^{N} \operatorname{var}\left[t_{iT} \mid \rho_i = 0\right]}} \Rightarrow N(0, 1) \tag{18}$$

as $T \to \infty$ followed by $N \to \infty$ sequentially" (Baltagi, 2005).

The present study also employed other two Fisher type tests developed by 'Maddala and Wu (1999) and Choi (2001)'. The MW test (Maddala and Wu 1999) test is based on the combined significance levels (p-values) from the 'individual unit root tests'.

$$P = -2\sum_{i=1}^{N} \ln p_i \tag{19}$$

"which combines the *p*-values from unit root tests for each cross-section *i* to test for unit root in panel data. $-2 \ln p_i$ has a χ^2 distribution with 2 degrees of freedom" (Baltagi, 2005).

Residual-Based LM Test

"Hadri (2000) derives a residual based lagrange multiplier (LM) test where the null hypothesis is that there is no unit root in any of the series in the panel against the alternative of a unit root in the panel. It is based on OLS residuals of y_{it} on a constant, or on a constant and a trend" (Baltagi, 2005). The following two models has been considered by Hadri (2000):

$y_{it} = r_{it} + \varepsilon_{it}$ $i = 1,\ldots, N;$ $t = 1,\ldots,T$

and

$$y_{it} = r_{it} + \beta_i t + \varepsilon_{it} \tag{20}$$

Where $r_{it} = r_{i,t-1} + u_{it}$ is a random walk. By making use of back substitution, model (20) becomes.

$$y_{it} = r_{io} + \beta_i t + \sum_{s=1}^{t} u_{is} + \varepsilon_{it} = r_{io} + \beta_i t + v_{it} \tag{21}$$

Where $v_{it} = \sum_{s=1}^{t} u_{is} + \varepsilon_{it}$. The stationary hypothesis is simply $H_0 : \sigma^2_{\mu} = 0$, in which case $v_{it} = e_{it}$. The LM statistic is given by

$$\text{LM}_1 = \frac{1}{N}\left(\sum_{i=1}^{N} \frac{1}{T^2} \sum_{t=1}^{T} S_{it}^2\right) / \hat{\sigma}_{\varepsilon}^2$$

Where $S_{it} = \sum_{s=1}^{t} \hat{\varepsilon}_{is}$ is the partial sum of OLS residuals $\hat{\varepsilon}_{is}$ from (21) and $\hat{\sigma}^2_{\varepsilon}$ is a consistent estimate of $\hat{\sigma}^2_{\varepsilon}$ under the null hypothesis H_0.

$$\hat{\sigma}_{\varepsilon}^{2} = \frac{1}{NT}\sum_{i=1}^{N}\sum_{t=1}^{T}\hat{\varepsilon}_{it}^{2}$$

3.2.9 Human Poverty Index

The 'Human Poverty Index' measures deprivations in three basic dimensions of human development viz. Health, knowledge and economic. These three deprivations were calculated using the following indicators.

Health Deprivation (P_1): Health Deprivation (P_1) has been captured by using infant mortality rate and proportion of undernourished children, which has been proxied by proportion of children having weight for height percentage below -2SD.

P_1 has been calculated as

$$P_1 = \frac{(IMR + Weight\ for\ height\ percent\ age\ below - 2SD)}{2}$$

Knowledge Deprivation (P_2): Knowledge or educational deprivation (P_2) based on illiteracy rate and non-enrollment ratio has been calculated by giving 35 per cent weight to illiteracy rate for population in the age group of 7 years and above and, 65 per cent weight has been given to the proportion of children not enrolled in schools.

P_2 = (illiteracy rate × 0.35) + (non-enrollment ratio × 0.65)

Economic Deprivation (P_3): Economic Deprivation (P_3) has been calculated by using the following indicators:

Proportion of population below poverty line (P_{31})

Proportion of Population not fully vaccinated (P_{32})

Proportion of Population without access to safe drinking water (p_{33})

Proportion of Population without access to electricity (p_{34})

Proportion of Population without access to toilet facility (p_{35})

$$P_3 = 1/5 \sum_{i=1}^{5} P_{3i}$$

In order to construct Human poverty index (HPI) all the three deprivations *viz:* (P_1), (P_2) and (P_3) were given equal weight. Thus, HPI was constructed by using UNDP's formula.

$$HPI_j = \left[\frac{1}{2} \sum_{i=0}^{3} p_i \right]^{1/3}$$

Where HPI is for the jth state and P_i goes from 1 to 3 refers to the above three deprivations. States were ranked according to value of HPI in 2001 and 2011.

Chapter 4

An Examination of Income Convergence Across Indian States

Indian economy has been experiencing a low rate of growth till the decade of seventies, inspite of favourable preconditions in the late 1940s of a well-diversified resource base-both physical and human-and a relatively stable political system (Cashin and Sahay, 1996). From a dismal growth rate of 3.5 per cent in 1960's and 1970's (the so-called Hindu growth rate), the Indian economy achieved an impressive GDP growth rate of 5.82 per cent during 1980/1981-1990/1991 and accomplished a growth rate of 7.5 per cent in the post 2000 period. Although, after crossing the Hindu rate of growth, India achieved a higher rate of growth due to various policies adopted by government but the benefits of growth have not trickle down and regional inequalities are still persisting across states. All states have not grown at the same pace with Maharashtra, Karnataka, Gujarat, Tamil Nadu etc. growing rapidly and the states like Bihar, Uttar Pradesh, Madhya Pradesh, Assam and Odisha have lagged behind. Even the states/ regions, have witnessed inequalities. This has resulted into widening of gap in the standard of living of people in different states and regions.

Many studies like Ghosh et al. (1998); Rao et al. (1999); Dasgupta et al. (2000); Trivedi (2002); Bhattacharya and Sakthivel (2004); Nayyar (2008); Kalra and Sodsriwiboon (2010) and Cherodian and Thirlwall (2013) points towards increasing regional inequalities. Contrary to the results of the above studies, Cashin and Sahay (1996) and Raju (2012) found convergence in per capita income across Indian states. Thus it becomes important to study how the poor states have grown over time and to find out whether these states are catching up with the rich ones or not. In order to find answer to this question, convergence hypothesis has been examined across states in terms of per capita income. This will also explain whether the regional inequalities have persisted or not.

For this purpose, the chapter has been divided into 5 sections. In Section-I, σ-convergence and unconditional β-convergence in terms of per capita NSDP and NSDP originating from agricultural, industrial and services sector across 24 Indian states namely Andhra Pradesh (AP), Assam (AS), Bihar (BH), Gujarat (GJ), Haryana (HR), Himachal Pradesh (HP), Jammu and Kashmir (JK), Karnataka (KT), Kerala (KR), Madhya Pradesh (MP), Maharashtra (MH), Manipur (MN), Odisha (OR), Punjab (PB), Rajasthan (RJ), Tamil Nadu (TN), Tripura (TR), Uttar Pradesh (UP), West Bengal (WB), Arunachal Pradesh (AR), Goa (GOA), Meghalaya (MG), Nagaland (NG) and Sikkim (SKM) has been examined. Section-II deals with the conditional convergence in terms of per capita income across Indian states. Time series unit root stochastic convergence of per capita income has been analysed in Section-III. Panel data unit root analysis of stochastic convergence in terms of per capita NSDP has been presented in Section-IV. Whole discussion has been concluded in Section-V.

Section-I

σ-convergence:

In this section, σ-convergence has been examined by computing the standard deviations of the natural logarithm of per capita NSDP, NSDP originating from agricultural, industrial and services sector across 24 states for each year at constant prices (2004-05 prices) during the period 1980 to 2011. The results of σ-convergence/divergence for per capita NSDP and NSDP originating from agriculture are shown in table 4.1 and the same has been depicted graphically in figures 4.1 and 4.2.

Table 4.1 shows that the inter-state disparities in terms of per capita NSDP and NSDP originating from agricultural sector have consistently increased over time. The standard deviation in the level of per capita NSDP increased from 0.3189 during 1980 to 0.3503 in

Table 4.1: Standard Deviation (s-convergence) for Per Capita NSDP and NSDP originating from Agricultural Sector

Variables	Period	Standard Deviation	Variables	Period	Standard Deviation
Per Capita NSDP	1980	0.3189	NSDP originating from Agricultural Sector	1980	0.3263
	1981	0.3201		1981	0.3158
	1982	0.3320		1982	0.3485
	1983	0.3131		1983	0.3313
	1984	0.3151		1984	0.3197
	1985	0.3194		1985	0.3480
	1986	0.3181		1986	0.3667
	1987	0.3285		1987	0.3549
	1988	0.3307		1988	0.3587
	1989	0.3454		1989	0.3304
	1990	0.3503		1990	0.3569
	1991	0.3565		1991	0.3586
	1992	0.3881		1992	0.3457
	1993	0.3781		1993	0.3446
	1994	0.3765		1994	0.3475
	1995	0.4066		1995	0.3667
	1996	0.3987		1996	0.3722
	1997	0.4004		1997	0.3616
	1998	0.4187		1998	0.3861
	1999	0.4266		1999	0.3796
	2000	0.4154		2000	0.3923
	2001	0.4246		2001	0.3924
	2002	0.4314		2002	0.3965
	2003	0.4377		2003	0.4028
	2004	0.4379		2004	0.4236
	2005	0.4606		2005	0.3894
	2006	0.4623		2006	0.4385
	2007	0.4719		2007	0.4285
	2008	0.4624		2008	0.4620
	2009	0.4898		2009	0.4874
	2010	0.4993		2010	0.5137
	2011	0.5031		2011	0.5018

1990 to 0.4154 in 2000 and then further to 0.5031 during 2011. The same picture has been revealed for NSDP originating from agricultural sector, as the standard deviation of income originating from agriculture also increased from 0.3263 during 1980 to 0.3569 in 1990 to 0.3923 in 2000 and further to 0.5018 during 2011. Thus inter-state disparities in per capita NSDP and NSDP originating from agricultural sector have increased during the period 1980 to 2011. The estimated standard deviations in per capita NSDP and NSDP originating from agricultural sector from states, plotted against time (figures 4.1 and 4.2

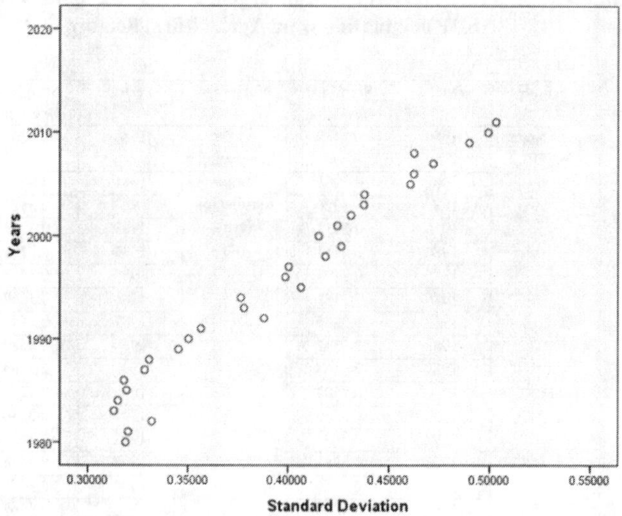

Fig. 4.1 Standard Deviation of the ln of per capita NSDP.

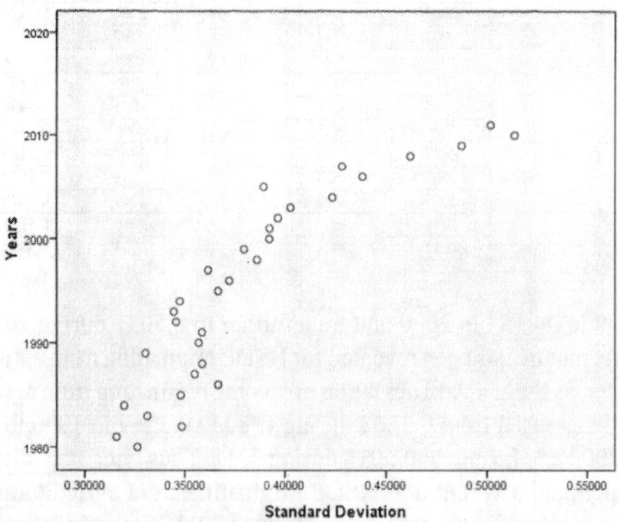

Fig. 4.2 Standard Deviation of the ln of NSDP originating from agricultural sector.

respectively), display an upward trend in both the cases, indicating that the states have diverged in terms of per capita NSDP and NSDP originating from agricultural sector during the period. Thus, there are clear indications of widening of regional disparities in per capita NSDP and NSDP originating from agricultural sector across 24 states during the period under study.

Table 4.2: Standard Deviation (s-convergence) for NSDP originating from Industrial and Services Sector

Variables	Period	Standard Deviation	Variables	Period	Standard Deviation
NSDP originating from Industrial Sector	1980	0.4172	NSDP originating from Services Sector	1980	0.2473
	1981	0.4057		1981	0.2465
	1982	0.4130		1982	0.2385
	1983	0.4026		1983	0.2401
	1984	0.4420		1984	0.2300
	1985	0.4548		1985	0.2330
	1986	0.4440		1986	0.2199
	1987	0.3830		1987	0.2042
	1988	0.4247		1988	0.2074
	1989	0.4120		1989	0.2101
	1990	0.3651		1990	0.1785
	1991	0.3624		1991	0.1751
	1992	0.3626		1992	0.1701
	1993	0.3820		1993	0.1919
	1994	0.3766		1994	0.1965
	1995	0.3482		1995	0.1950
	1996	0.3527		1996	0.1711
	1997	0.2902		1997	0.1459
	1998	0.3492		1998	0.1566
	1999	0.3135		1999	0.1400
	2000	0.3241		2000	0.1286
	2001	0.2977		2001	0.1456
	2002	0.3052		2002	0.1303
	2003	0.3069		2003	0.1516
	2004	0.2957		2004	0.1580
	2005	0.2771		2005	0.1508
	2006	0.2745		2006	0.1503
	2007	0.2600		2007	0.1578
	2008	0.2564		2008	0.1546
	2009	0.2897		2009	0.1531
	2010	0.2881		2010	0.1576
	2011	0.2870		2011	0.1560

The convergence hypothesis for NSDP originating from industrial and services sector has been examined across 24 Indian states over the period 1980 to 2011 and the results are presented in table 4.2.

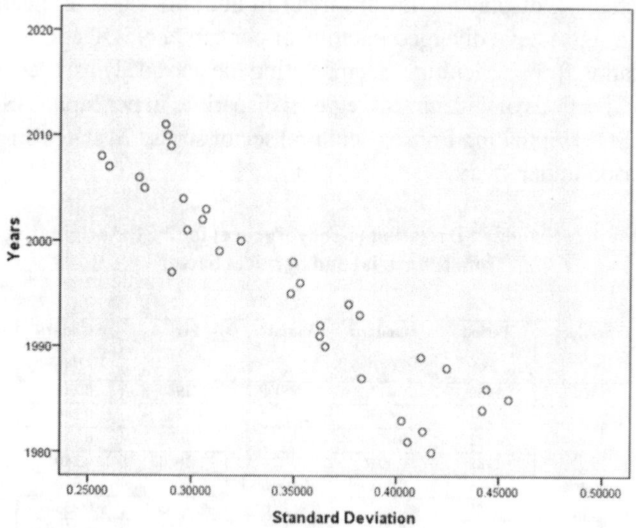

Fig. 4.3 Standard Deviation of the ln of NSDP originating from industrial sector.

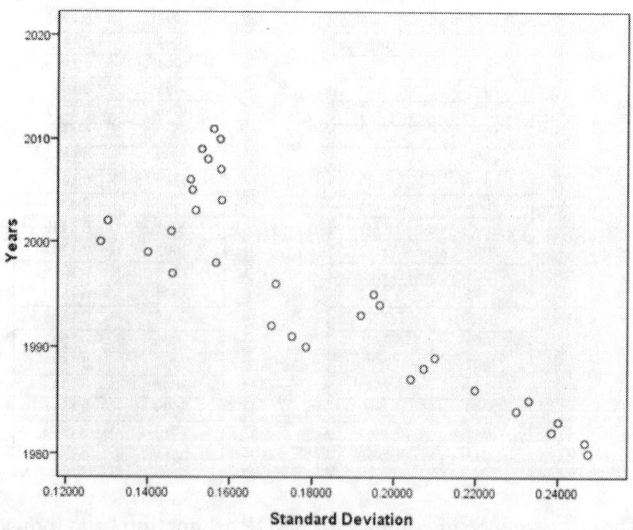

Fig. 4.4 Standard Deviation of the ln of NSDP originating from services sector.

Regional disparities measured in terms of standard deviation of the natural log of NSDP originating from industrial sector fell from 0.4172 in 1980 to 0.3651 in 1990 to 0.3241 in 2000 and then further to 0.2870 during 2011- an evidence of σ-convergence in case of NSDP originating from industrial sector across states over the period 1980-2011 and the same has been supported by figure 4.3. Further, it can be seen from table 4.2 that in case of NSDP originating from services sector the dispersion decreases from 0.2473 in 1980 to 0.1785 in 1990 to 0.1286 in 2000 and then increased to 0.1560 during 2011, however, providing an evidence of σ-convergence across states from 1980 to 2011. The same has been supported by figure 4.4, revealing a downward trend in the standard deviation for NSDP originating from services sector.

Unconditional β-convergence:

"Unconditional β-convergence-a cross section regression of time averaged growth rates on initial levels of per capita income giving inverse relationship-suggests that poor states (regions) tend to grow faster than rich states (regions)" (Barro, 1991). Unconditional β-convergence (or divergence) has been examined for the whole period (1980-2011) as well as for the various sub-periods. In each case, the annual average growth rate of per capita NSDP has been regressed on the natural log of initial level of per capita NSDP and the results of

Table 4.3: Unconditional b-convergence in Per Capita NSDP

Years	Constant	Coefficient	β-convergence	R^2	N
1980-2011	0.0340 (0.06)	0.0621 (0.01)	-0.0346	0.248	24
1980-1985	0.0855 (0.42)	-0.0068 (0.55)	0.0069	0.016	24
1985-1990	0.0047 (0.97)	0.0047 (0.83)	-0.0046	0.223	24
1990-1995	-0.1825 (0.21)	0.0214 (0.16)	-0.0203	0.087	24
1995-2000	0.0733 (0.54)	-0.0039 (0.75)	0.0039	0.041	24
2000-2005	-0.1301 (0.06)	0.0177* (0.06)	-0.0170	0.149	24
2005-2011	0.0104 (0.03)	0.0056 (0.06)	-0.0055	0.039	24

Note: Figures in parentheses are P-values;*denotes significance at 10 per cent level.

this estimated cross-sectional convergence regression has been reported in table 4.3.

Table shows that the Indian states have been diverging but not statistically significantly in terms of per capita NSDP over the period 1980-2011, 1985-1990, 1990-1995 and 2005-2011, however, diverging significantly at 10 per cent level of significance over the period 2000-2005, implying that poor states are not catching up with the rich ones during these periods. But for the periods 1980-1985 and 1995-2000, the coefficient turns out to be negative but not significant, indicating the tendency of weak convergence. Further, the table reveals that the Indian states have been diverging insignificantly at the rate of 3.46 per cent per year for the overall period (1980-2011), however, the speed of divergence has decreased over the period of time from 2.03 per cent during 1990-1995 to 1.70 per cent during 2000-2005 and further to 0.55 per cent per year for the latest period (2005-2011).

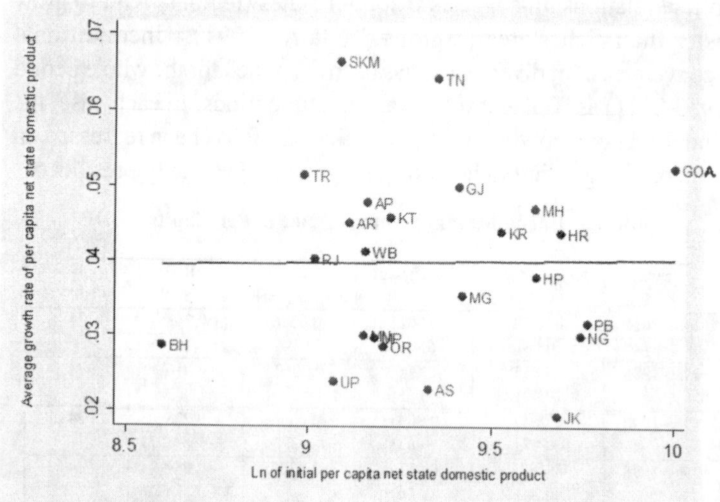

Fig. 4.5 Average growth rate of per capita NSDP (1980-2011) against the ln of initial per capita NSDP (1980).

Figures 4.5 to 4.11 highlight the differential behaviour of states in terms of per capita NSDP for the whole period as well as for the various sub-periods. If there is convergence in the income level across states, the relationship should give downward sloping line but opposite in case for divergence. The positive lines obtained for the states in figure 4.5, 4.7, 4.8, 4.10 and 4.11 reveals the existence of β-divergence during the respective periods. The richer states on average grew faster than the poor states and the inequality among the states is actually increasing during these periods. However, the relation between average growth rate and the natural log of initial level of income is found to be negative but insignificant for the period 1980-1985 and 1995-2000, thus downward sloping lines in figures 4.6 and 4.9, which corroborates the existence of weak β-convergence across states during these two periods.

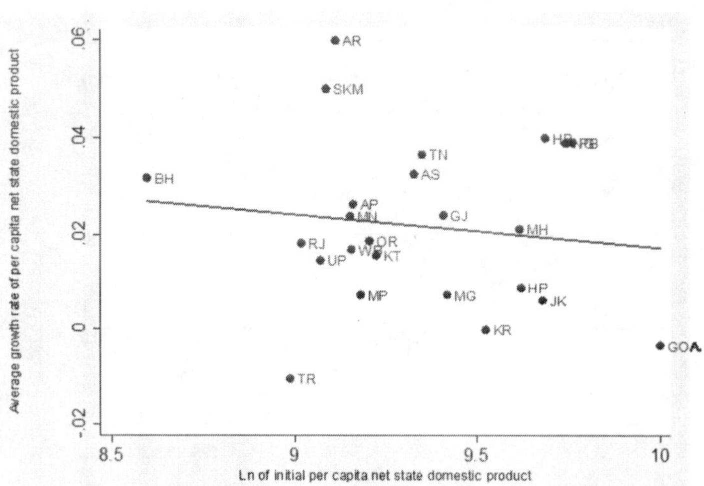

Fig. 4.6 Average growth rate of per capita NSDP (1980-1985) against the ln of initial per capita NSDP (1980).

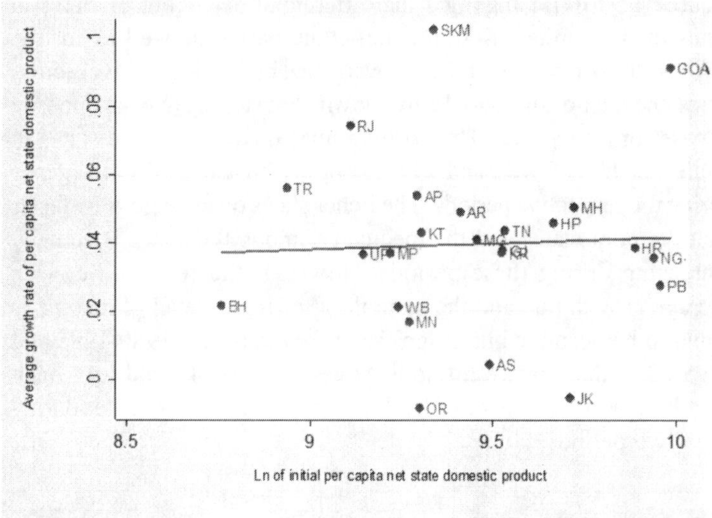

Fig. 4.7 Average growth rate of per capita NSDP (1985-1990) against the ln of initial per capita NSDP (1985).

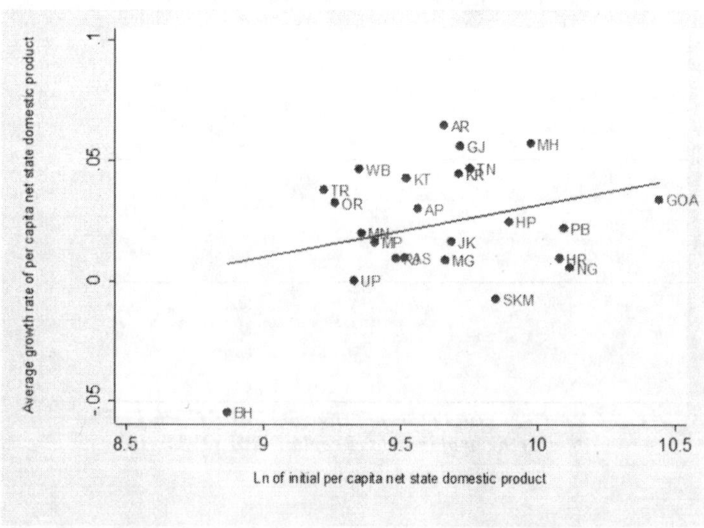

Fig. 4.8 Average growth rate of per capita NSDP (1990-1995) against the ln of initial per capita NSDP (1990).

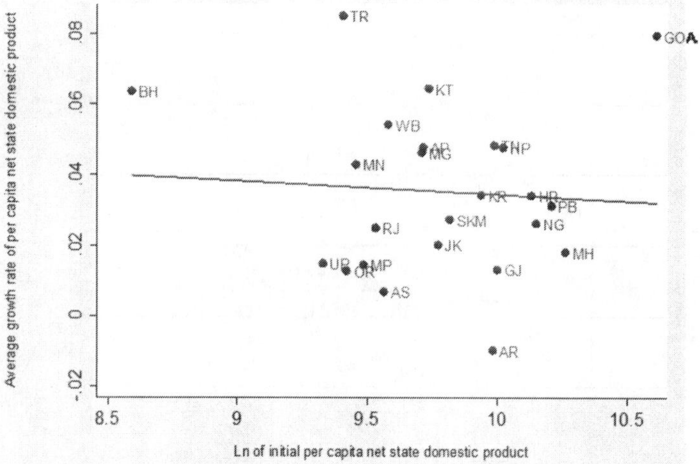

Fig. 4.9 Average growth rate of per capita NSDP (1995-2000) against the ln of initial per capita NSDP (1995).

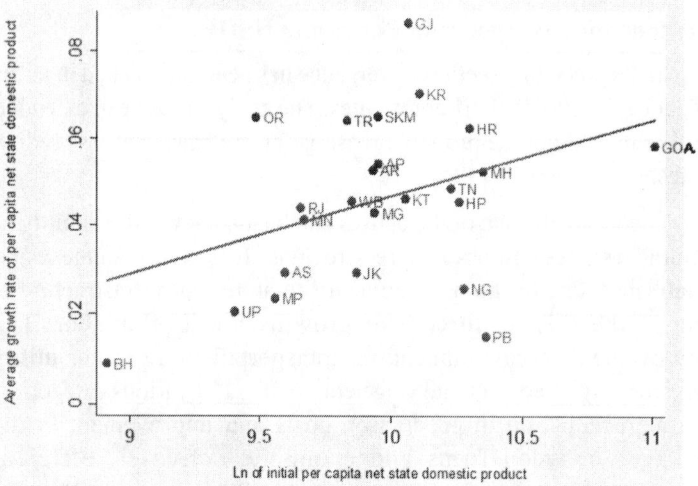

Fig. 4.10 Average growth rate of per capita NSDP (2000-2005) against the ln of initial per capita NSDP (2000).

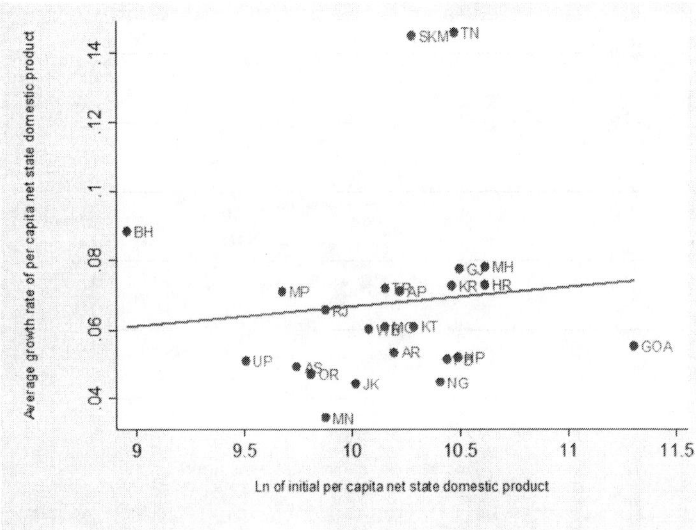

Fig. 4.11 Average growth rate of per capita NSDP (2005-2011) against the ln of initial per capita NSDP (2005).

Reasons for Divergence in Per capita NSDP:

In the preceding section, divergence has been established in terms of per capita NSDP of different states. The analysis has been extended further to find out the probable reasons for divergence across Indian states.

Theoretically, one of the causes can be the uneven availability of natural resources across different regions. It is well document and established fact in the development literature that infrastructure is one of the driving forces for growth and development. The improvement in communication, transportation and other utility services may directly create wage employment of various categories. Through reduction in production costs and improvement in the linkages between firms and economic activities, efficient infrastructure attracts domestic as well as foreign investments and gives rise to economies of scale. The empirical evidence suggests that "investment in public infrastructure generates greater output, improved quality of life and employment and lack of infrastructure constrains growth" (Bougheas et al. 1999; Cutando and Paricio 1994; Esfahani and Ramirez 2003; Looney 1997; World Bank 1994, cited in Nauriyal and Sahoo, 2010).

Table 4.4: Physical Infrastructure Index

States	1981	1991	2001	2011	Average Per capita Net State Domestic Product (1981-2011)
Andhra Pradesh	0.3548 (9)	0.3986 (8)	0.4426 (8)	0.5108 (7)	19774 (14)
Assam	0.1451 (19)	0.2937 (15)	0.1876 (22)	0.2257 (18)	15056 (19)
Bihar	0.2365 (17)	0.2339 (21)	0.2653 (18)	0.1964 (21)	7287 (24)
Gujarat	0.5750 (7)	0.5061 (4)	0.6711 (3)	0.5901 (6)	25444 (8)
Haryana	0.6429 (3)	0.5223 (3)	0.5550 (6)	0.6103 (4)	30179 (3)
Himachal Pradesh	0.2469 (14)	0.3243 (11)	0.4309 (9)	0.6253 (3)	26102 (7)
Jammu & Kashmir	0.3241 (11)	0.3183 (12)	0.3608 (13)	0.3848 (13)	19204 (15)
Karnataka	0.4499 (8)	0.3857 (9)	0.4177 (10)	0.4642 (9)	20856 (11)
Kerala	0.5970 (6)	0.4315 (7)	0.5039 (7)	0.3722 (14)	24332 (9)
Madhya Pradesh	0.2369 (16)	0.3279 (10)	0.3698 (12)	0.3614 (15)	13858 (22)
Maharashtra	0.6268 (5)	0.4628 (6)	0.5610 (5)	0.5032 (8)	30336 (2)
Manipur	0.0796 (22)	0.2501 (19)	0.2208 (21)	0.2183 (19)	14783 (20)
Orissa	0.3350 (10)	0.3122 (13)	0.3262 (14)	0.2593 (17)	14186 (21)
Punjab	0.8423 (1)	0.7051 (1)	0.8357 (1)	0.6975 (2)	28907 (4)
Rajasthan	0.2461 (15)	0.2650 (17)	0.3743 (11)	0.3890 (12)	15312 (18)
Tamil Nadu	0.6336 (4)	0.4864 (5)	0.6158 (4)	0.5981 (5)	27812 (6)
Tripura	0.0744 (24)	0.1409 (22)	0.2460 (20)	0.0955 (23)	16987 (17)
Uttar Pradesh	0.2967 (13)	0.2909 (16)	0.3073 (16)	0.3190 (16)	11939 (23)
West Bengal	0.3145 (12)	0.2490 (20)	0.3088 (15)	0.4253 (10)	17178 (16)
Arunachal Pradesh	0.1011 (20)	0.0576 (24)	0.0874 (24)	0.0954 (24)	20164 (12)
Goa	0.7926 (2)	0.6931 (2)	0.8131 (2)	0.8802 (1)	51883 (1)
Meghalaya	0.0778 (23)	0.0906 (23)	0.1250 (23)	0.1975 (20)	19414 (13)
Nagaland	0.1604 (18)	0.2961 (14)	0.2730 (17)	0.1033 (22)	28066 (5)
Sikkim	0.0977 (21)	0.2620 (18)	0.2537 (19)	0.4062 (11)	23457 (10)

Note: Figures in parentheses are ranks of the states.

In order to examine whether infrastructure has a significant influence on regional disparities in India or not, the physical infrastructure index and social infrastructure index has been constructed at four points of time 1981-82, 1991-92, 2001-02 and

2011-12 by applying Principal Component Analysis. For constructing physical infrastructure index, six variables namely (i) annual per capita consumption of electricity, (ii) annual per capita industrial consumption of electricity, (iii) population per bank office (thousand), (iv) per cent of villages electrified, (v) net irrigated area as a per cent of net area sown and (vi) road density per thousand sq. Km of area have been used. Whereas social infrastructure index is based on literacy rate, infant mortality rate and proportion of population with access to safe drinking water.

Table 4.5: Social Infrastructure Index

States	1981	1991	2001	2011
Andhra Pradesh	0.3299 (17)	0.3319 (16)	0.4470 (16)	0.3970 (16)
Assam	0.1511 (21)	0.3491 (15)	0.3447 (20)	0.2930 (21)
Bihar	0.2178 (19)	0.3037 (19)	0.3899 (18)	0.3549 (18)
Gujarat	0.3572 (15)	0.5200 (10)	0.5563 (11)	0.5581 (12)
Haryana	0.3517 (16)	0.4919 (12)	0.5276 (14)	0.5155 (14)
Himachal Pradesh	0.4394 (11)	0.5370 (8)	0.6576 (4)	0.6508 (7)
Jammu & Kashmir	0.3679 (14)	0.2001 (22)	0.4315 (17)	0.3714 (17)
Karnataka	0.4900 (9)	0.4535 (13)	0.5486 (13)	0.5461 (13)
Kerala	0.8166 (1)	0.8152 (1)	0.6984 (2)	0.7377 (2)
Madhya Pradesh	0.1495 (22)	0.1693 (23)	0.3324 (23)	0.2625 (23)
Maharashtra	0.5620 (5)	0.5785 (4)	0.6661 (3)	0.6982 (4)
Manipur	0.6281 (3)	0.5533 (6)	0.5587 (10)	0.6156 (9)
Orissa	0.1215 (23)	0.1426 (24)	0.2875 (24)	0.3026 (20)
Punjab	0.5327 (6)	0.6146 (3)	0.6517 (5)	0.6380 (8)
Rajasthan	0.2123 (20)	0.2755 (20)	0.3339 (22)	0.2714 (22)
Tamil Nadu	0.4996 (8)	0.5694 (5)	0.6454 (6)	0.7248 (3)
Tripura	0.4627 (10)	0.3983 (14)	0.5547 (12)	0.6654 (6)
Uttar Pradesh	0.1026 (24)	0.2340 (21)	0.3686 (19)	0.3343 (19)
West Bengal	0.5094 (7)	0.5147 (11)	0.6116 (7)	0.6063 (10)
Arunachal Pradesh	0.2693 (18)	0.3124 (18)	0.5138 (15)	0.4247 (15)
Goa	0.6846 (2)	0.6964 (2)	0.7846 (1)	0.8708 (1)
Meghalaya	0.4002 (13)	0.3133 (17)	0.3415 (21)	0.2447 (24)
Nagaland	0.6091 (4)	0.5337 (9)	0.5996 (8)	0.5759 (11)
Sikkim	0.4155 (12)	0.5383 (7)	0.5818 (9)	0.6892 (5)

Note: Figures in parentheses are ranks of the states.

Physical infrastructure index constructed for the 24 Indian states has been presented in table 4.4. Table shows large inter-state disparities in terms of physical infrastructure. Only six states namely Punjab, Goa, Haryana, Tamil Nadu, Maharashtra and Gujarat remained the top six states in terms of physical infrastructure over the period 1981 to 2011. On the other hand states like Meghalaya, Bihar, Manipur, Arunachal Pradesh, and Tripura remained the poor performers in terms of physical infrastructure over the period 1981 to 2011. The states which were initially endowed with better physical infrastructure retained more or less same position till 2011 and the same has happened in case of poor states, as they also remained more or less at the same positions over the period of time.

Table 4.5 shows the relative performance of states in terms of social infrastructure over the period 1981 to 2011. Table shows that the inter-state disparities in social infrastructure remained more or less same, which may be the reason for regional disparities in per capita income across states. Kerala, Goa, Maharashtra and Tamil Nadu were the states with better social infrastructure, whereas the states like Uttar Pradesh, Rajasthan, Madhya Pradesh, Bihar and Odisha remained poor performers in terms of social infrastructure over the period of time. So, the poor performing states remained poor and best remained best over the period 1981 to 2011. Further, it has been observed that the states well endowed in physical as well as social infrastructure also enjoy higher per capita incomes (Table 4.4) over the period 1981-2011, indicating that there could be a significant positive co-rrelation between infrastructure endowment and long run growth performance.

Unconditional β-convergence in case of NSDP originating from agricultural sector has been examined by regressing the average growth rate of agricultural income on the natural log of the initial level of NSDP originating from agricultural sector of respective period and presented in table 4.6. Table shows that when the average growth rate for the period 1980-2011 and 2005-2011 has been regressed on the natural log of initial (1980 and 2005) value respectively, the co-efficients turns out to be positive and significant highlighting that divergence is taking place at the rate of 3 per cent per year across states in terms of NSDP originating from agricultural sector for the whole period as well as for the 2005-2011 period. Further, it is noticeable that speed of divergence remains same for the whole period as well as for the latest period and is maximum during both these periods. The negative but insignificant co-efficients for 1990-1995, 1995-2000 and 2000-2005 reveals that the poor states are catching up with rich ones during these periods but the catch up rate is very weak. The speed of convergence increased from 0.53 per cent per year during 1990-1995 to 1.07 during 1995-2000 and further to 1.53 per cent per year for the period 2000-2005. But convergence is weak for these periods (1990-1995, 1995-2000 and 2000-2005) and also in the last period (2005-2011) there is significant divergence, thus for the whole period it is still divergence.

Table 4.6: Unconditional β-convergence for NSDP originating from Agriculture Sector

Years	Constant	Coefficient	β-convergence	R^2	N
1980-2011	-0.2175 (0.00)	0.0522* (0.00)	-0.0310	0.577	24
1980-1985	-0.0351 (0.41)	0.0056 (0.64)	-0.0055	0.009	24
1985-1990	-0.0246 (0.46)	0.0013 (0.98)	-0.0013	0.009	24
1990-1995	-0.0237 (0.50)	-0.0052 (0.96)	0.0053	0.001	24
1995-2000	-0.0011 (0.98)	-0.0104 (0.63)	0.0107	0.010	24
2000-2005	0.0187 (0.69)	-0.0147 (0.342)	0.0153	0.041	24
2005-2011	-0.139 (0.00)	0.0329** (0.063)	-0.0300	0.148	24

Note: Figures in parentheses are P-values; * &** denotes significance at 1 per cent and 10 per cent levels respectively.

The green revolution has increased inter-state disparities across states, only the states of Punjab, Haryana and Western Uttar Pradesh showed the best results of the green revolution. But results were not impressive in other parts of India. So, Indian states have exhibited divergence in NSDP originating from agricultural sector. Many factors responsible for development of agriculture in states like Punjab, Haryana and Western Uttar Pradesh. After Independence agriculture has developed at a faster pace in the state of Punjab and Haryana due to the initiatives taken at the state level. Land reforms particularly in the form of consolidation of land holdings, introduction of HYV and assured irrigation facilities along with adoptability of Punjabi farmers led to fast growth of agriculture in the state of Punjab. The farmers of Haryana also followed the lead. These two states become the food bowl of India contributing very high percentage of food grains to national buffer stock.

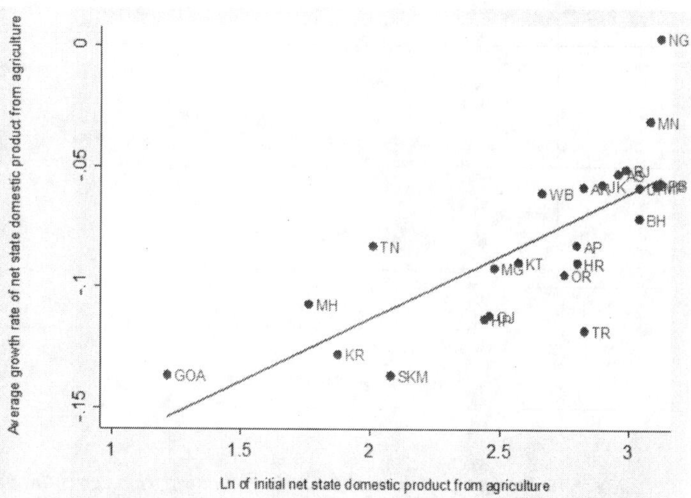

Fig. 4.12 Average growth rate of NSDP originating from agriculture sector (1980-2011) against the ln of initial NSDP originating from agriculture sector (1980).

Figures 4.12 to 4.18 shows the scatter across the set of 24 states in case of NSDP originating from agricultural sector for the whole period as well as for the sub-periods of the study. Figure 4.12, 4.13, 4.14 and 4.18 shows that the relation between the average growth rate of NSDP originating from agricultural sector and the natural log of its initial level is positive, confirming the process of cross-state divergence in terms of NSDP originating from agricultural sector. However, in figures 4.15, 4.16 and 4.17, the relation turns out to be negative. These three figures strengthen our conclusion that poor states are catching up with rich ones and revealing β-convergence in terms of NSDP originating from agricultural sector for the periods 1990-1995, 1995-2000 and 2000-2005 across Indian states.

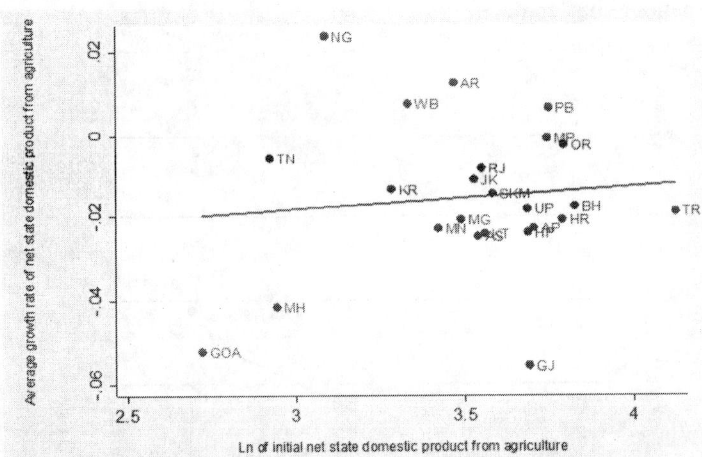

Fig. 4.13 Average growth rate of NSDP originating from agriculture sector (1980-1985) against the ln of initial NSDP originating from agriculture sector (1980).

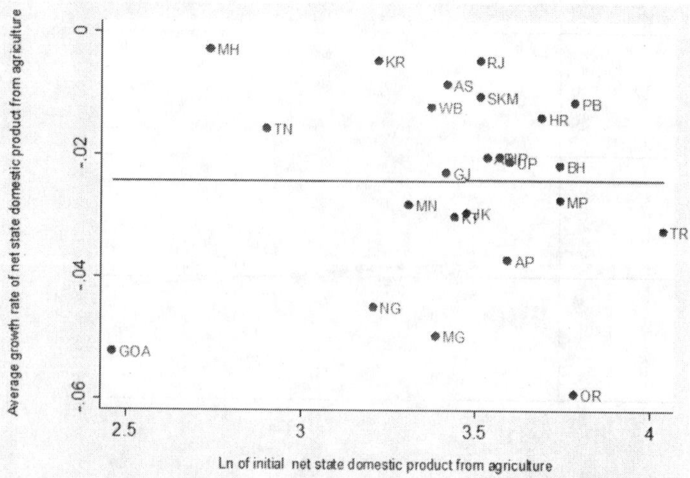

Fig. 4.14 Average growth rate of NSDP originating from agriculture sector (1985-1990) against the ln of initial NSDP originating from agriculture sector (1985).

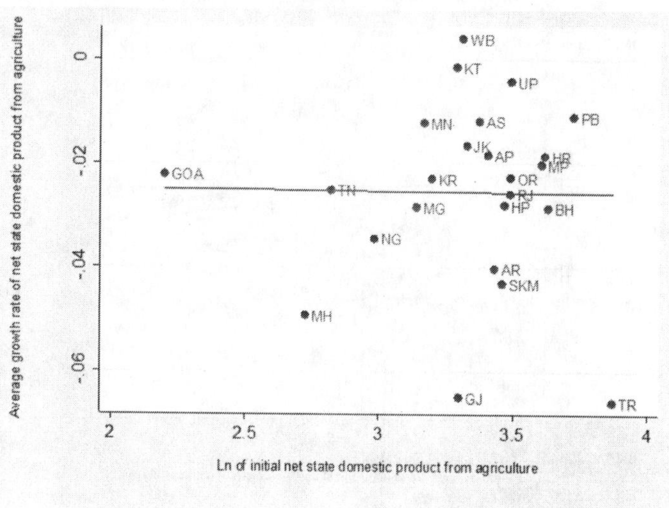

Fig. 4.15 Average growth rate of NSDP originating from agriculture sector (1990-1995) against the ln of initial NSDP originating from agriculture sector (1990).

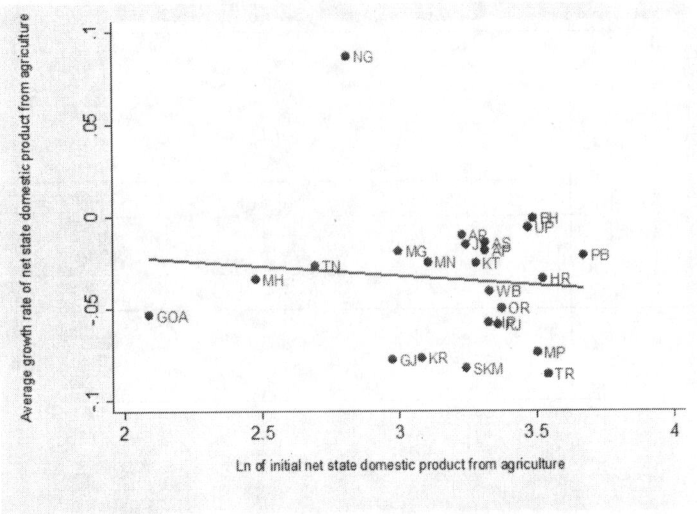

Fig. 4.16 Average growth rate of NSDP originating from agriculture sector (1995-2000) against the ln of initial NSDP originating from agriculture sector (1995).

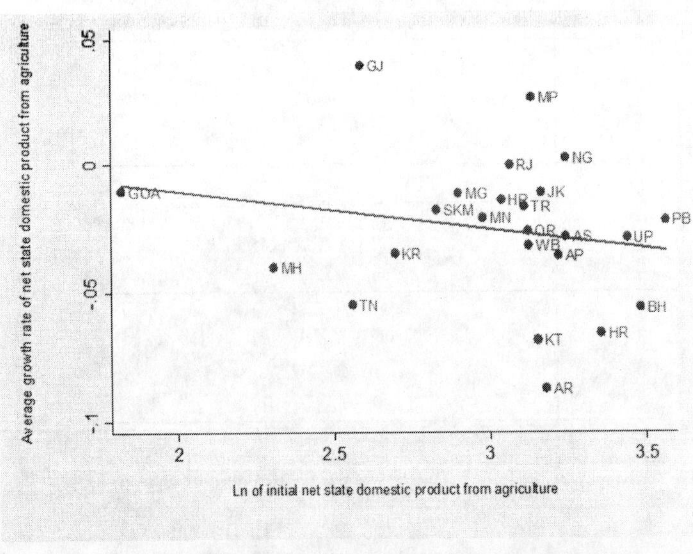

Fig. 4.17 Average growth rate of NSDP originating from agriculture sector (2000-2005) against the ln of initial NSDP originating from agriculture sector (2000).

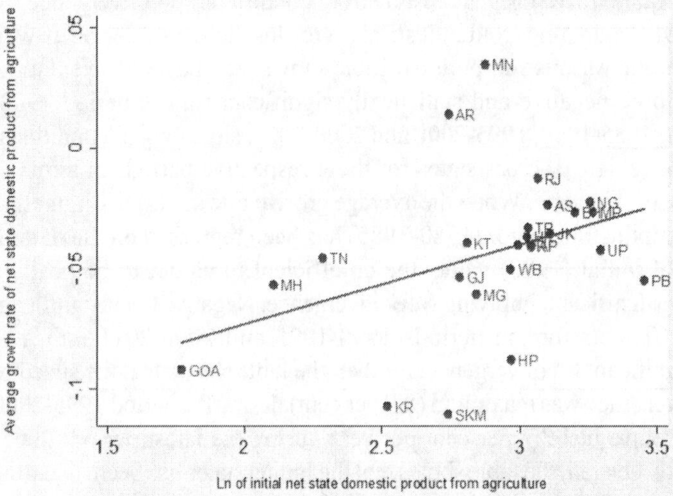

Fig. 4.18 Average growth rate of NSDP originating from agriculture sector (2005-2011) against the ln of initial NSDP originating from agriculture sector (2005).

Table 4.7: Unconditional b-convergence for NSDP originating from Industrial Sector

Years	Constant	Coefficient	β-convergence	R^2	N
1980-2011	-0.0706 (0.00)	-0.0205* (0.00)	0.0326	0.543	24
1980-1985	-0.0015 (0.97)	0.0028 (0.87)	-0.0028	0.001	24
1985-1990	0.1644 (0.00)	-0.0478* (0.00)	0.0546	0.467	24
1990-1995	0.0872 (0.087)	-0.0238 (0.14)	0.0253	0.095	24
1995-2000	0.2238 (0.02)	-0.0719** (0.02)	0.0891	0.221	24
2000-2005	0.1706 (0.003)	-0.0471* (0.008)	0.0537	0.275	24
2005-2011	0.0832 (0.24)	-0.0250 (0.25)	0.0271	0.060	24

Note: Figures in parentheses are P-values; * &** denotes significance at 1 per cent and 5 per cent levels respectively.

Table 4.7 reports the results of unconditional β-convergence for NSDP originating from industrial sector for the whole period as well as for the various sub-periods. Table shows that the co-efficient turns out to be negative and statistically significant for the period 1980-2011, 1985-1990, 1995-2000 and 2000-2005, signalling unconditional β-convergence across states for these respective periods in terms of industrial income. When the average growth rate of NSDP originating from industrial sector (1980-1985) has been regressed on the natural log of initial (1980) value, the co-efficient turns out to be positive but insignificant, implying weak divergence. Negative but insignificant co-efficients for the periods 1990-1995 and 2005-2011 indicates insignificant β-convergence. Further, the table shows that the speed of convergence was maximum (8.9 per cent) during the period 1995-2000 but fell to just 2.7 per cent per year during the latest period (2005-2011). Overall, the table shows that the Indian states has been diverging in terms of NSDP originating from industrial sector during 1980-1985, but after that convergence has been observed at different rates in following sub-periods resulting in overall convergence (1980-2011).

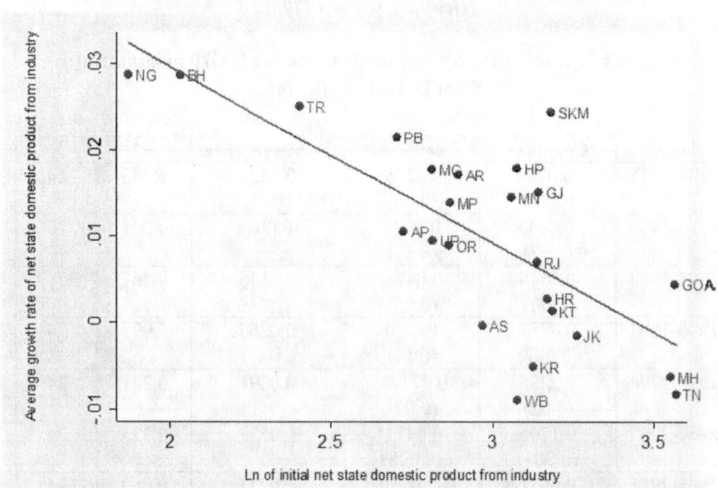

Fig. 4.19 Average growth rate of NSDP originating from Industrial Sector (1980-2011) against the ln of initial NSDP originating from Industrial Sector (1980).

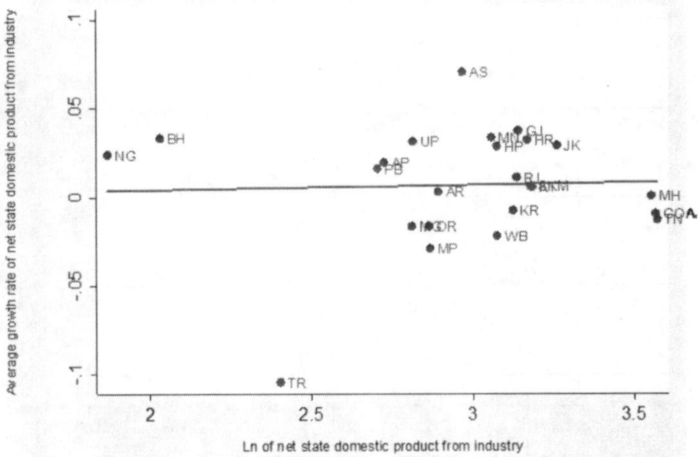

Fig. 4.20 Average growth rate of NSDP originating from Industrial Sector (1980-1985) against the ln of initial NSDP originating from Industrial Sector (1980).

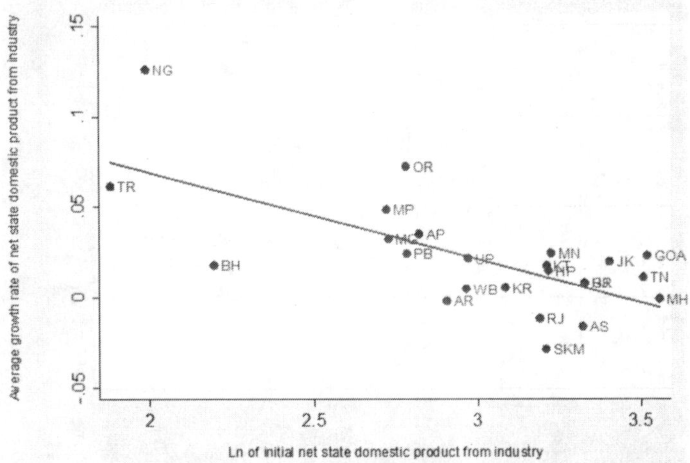

Fig. 4.21 Average growth rate of NSDP originating from Industrial Sector (1985-1990) against the ln of initial NSDP originating from Industrial Sector (1985).

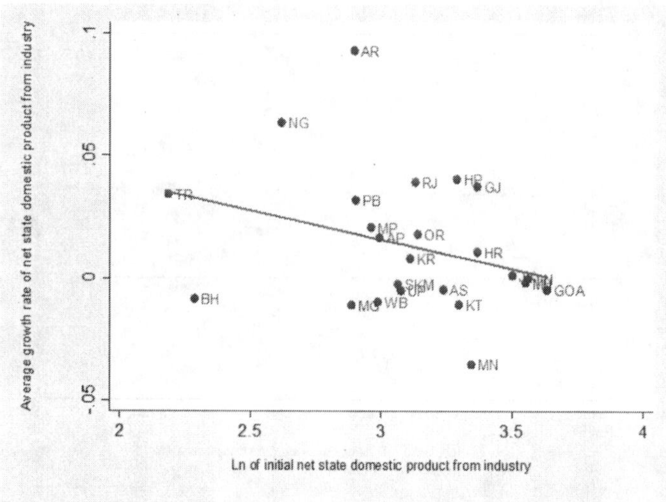

Fig. 4.22 Average growth rate of NSDP originating from Industrial Sector (1990-1995) against the ln of initial NSDP originating from Industrial Sector (1990).

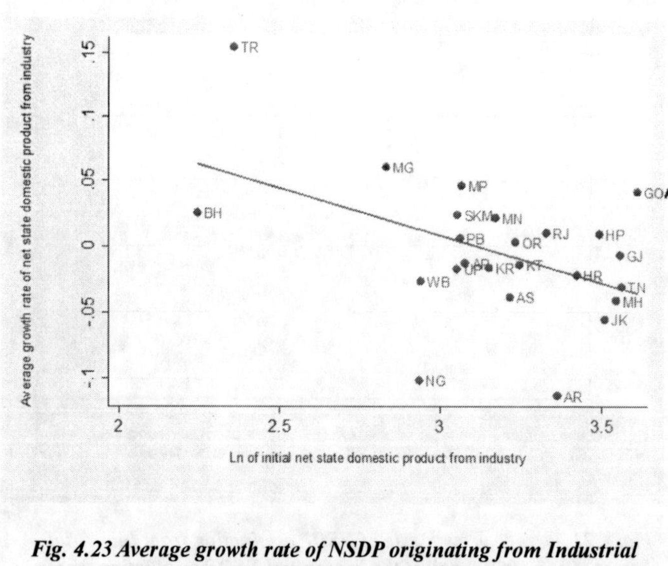

Fig. 4.23 Average growth rate of NSDP originating from Industrial Sector (1995-2000) against the ln of initial NSDP originating from Industrial Sector (1995).

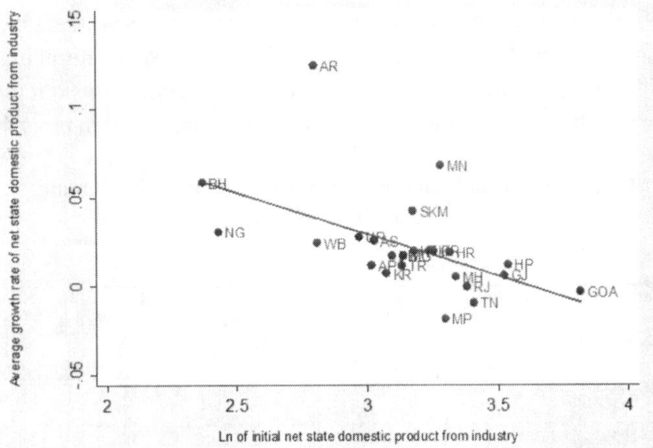

Fig. 4.24 Average growth rate of NSDP originating from Industrial Sector (2000-2005) against the ln of initial NSDP originating from Industrial Sector (2000).

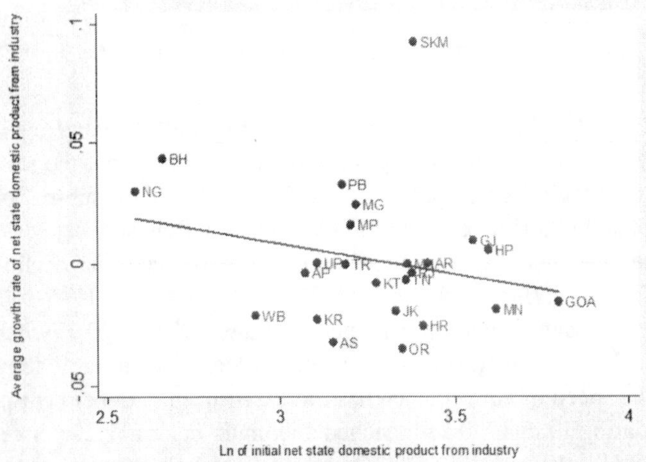

Fig. 4.25 Average growth rate of NSDP originating from Industrial Sector (2005-2011) against the ln of initial NSDP originating from Industrial Sector (2005).

Figures 4.19 to 4.25 bring out the behaviour of 24 states in terms of NSDP originating from industrial sector. For these states, the relation (except figure 4.20 for 1980-1985) between the average growth rate and natural log of initial industrial income turns out to be negative. Thus, supporting regression analysis presented in table 4.7.

Table 4.8: Unconditional b-convergence for NSDP originating from Services Sector

Years	Constant	Coefficient	β-convergence	R^2	N
1980-2011	0.1007 (0.00)	-0.0245* (0.00)	0.0459	0.629	24
1980-1985	0.0893 (0.06)	-0.0217 (0.10)	0.0230	0.112	24
1985-1990	0.1934 (0.00)	-0.0498* (0.00)	0.0573	0.730	24
1990-1995	0.0161 (0.82)	-0.0013 (0.94)	0.0013	0.002	24
1995-2000	0.3689 (0.00)	-0.0918* (0.00)	0.1229	0.597	24
2000-2005	-0.0337 (0.70)	0.0097 (0.66)	-0.0095	0.008	24
2005-2011	0.1272 (0.15)	-0.0289 (0.20)	0.0317	0.072	24

Note: Figures in parentheses are P-values; * denotes significance at 1 per cent level.

Table 4.8 shows the results of unconditional β-convergence for NSDP originating from services sector. Table shows that the states were converging for the period 1980-2011 and for all the sub-periods except 2000-2005 in terms of NSDP originating from services sector. Further, the table shows that the gap between the states has declined significantly during the period 1980-2011, 1985-1990 and 1995-2000, however, insignificantly for the periods 1980-1985, 1990-1995 and 2005-2011 showing weak convergence. Furthermore, the table shows that the speed of convergence has increased from 5.73 per cent per year during 1985-1990 and reached maximum rate of 12.29 per cent per year for the year 1995-2000 but fell to just 3.17 per cent per year during 2005-2011.

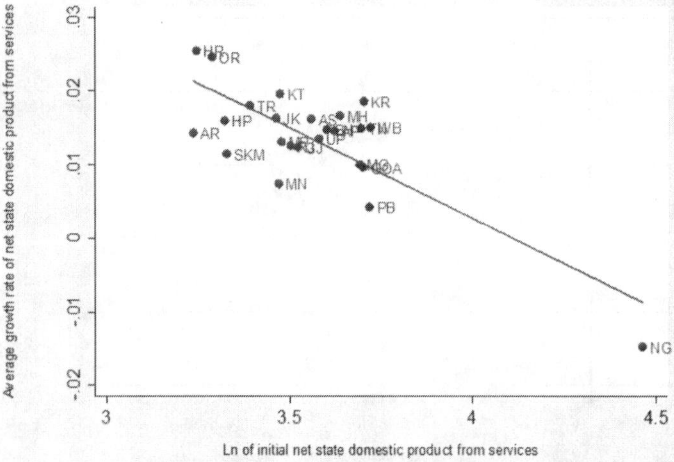

Fig. 4.26 Average growth rate of NSDP originating from services sector (1980-2011) against the ln of initial NSDP originating from services sector (1980).

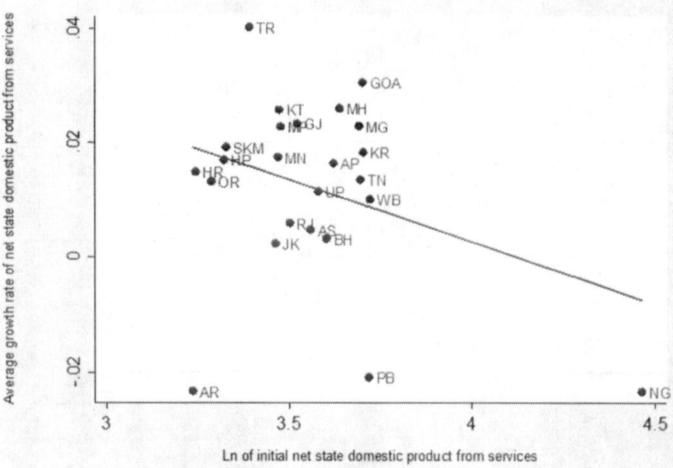

Fig. 4.27 Average growth rate of NSDP originating from services sector (1980-1985) against the ln of initial NSDP originating from services sector (1980).

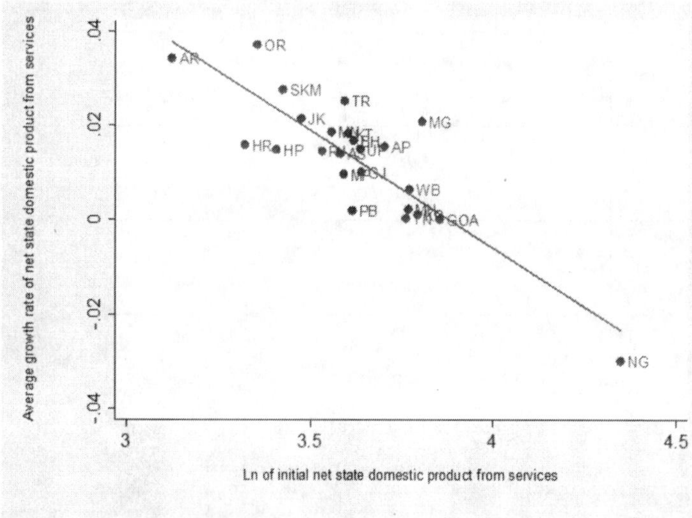

Fig. 4.28 Average growth rate of NSDP originating from services sector (1985-1990) against the ln of initial NSDP originating from services sector (1985).

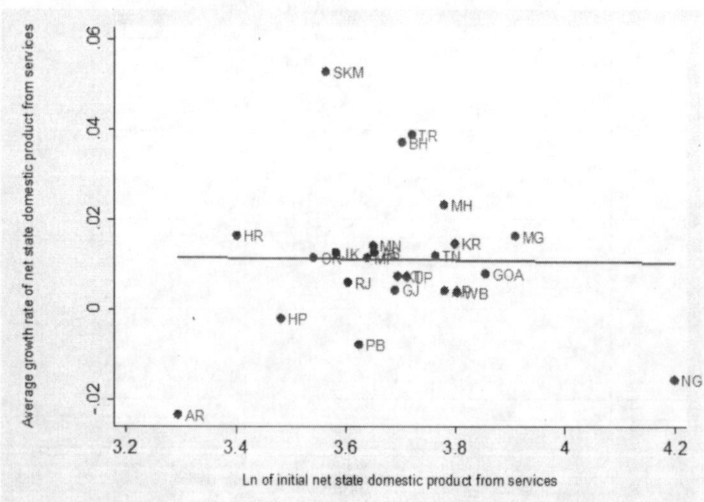

Fig. 4.29 Average growth rate of NSDP originating from services sector (1990-1995) against the ln of initial NSDP originating from services sector (1990).

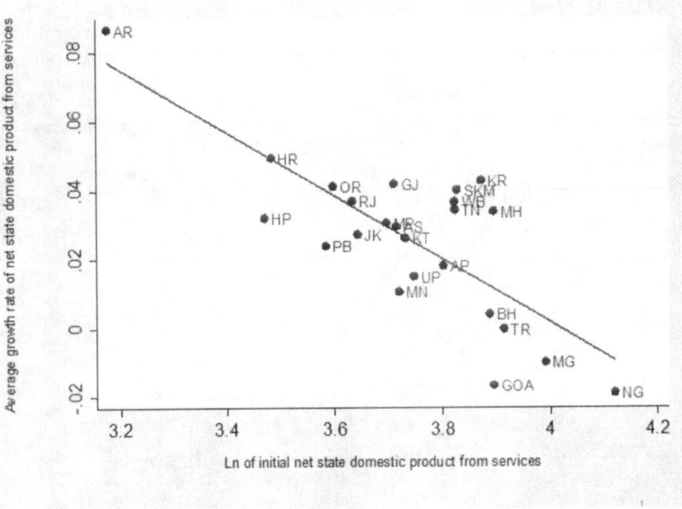

Fig. 4.30 Average growth rate of NSDP originating from services sector (1995-2000) against the ln of initial NSDP originating from services sector (1995).

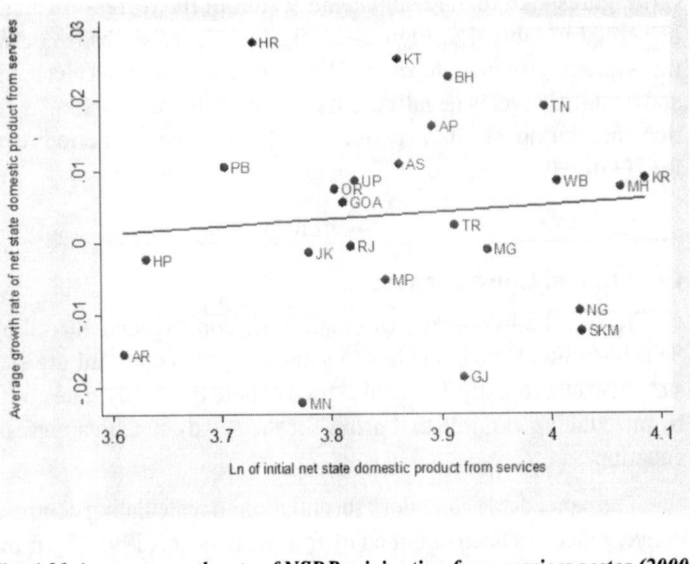

Fig. 4.31 Average growth rate of NSDP originating from services sector (2000-2005) against the ln of initial NSDP originating from services sector (2000).

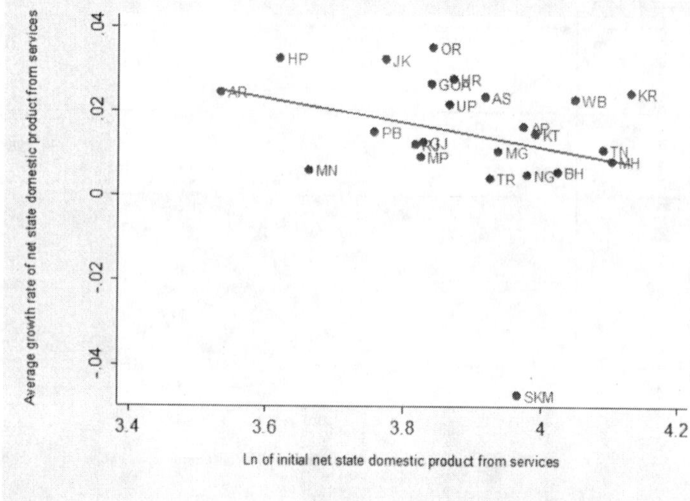

Fig. 4.32 Average growth rate of NSDP originating from services sector (2005-2011) against the ln of initial NSDP originating from services sector (2005).

Figures 4.26 to 4.32 shows the scatter of the regression analysis presented in table 4.8. Figures shows that the relationship between the average growth rate of NSDP originating from services sector and its initial level is negative and the poor states are catching up with rich ones during the whole period as well for all the sub-periods except for 2000-2005.

Section-II

Conditional Convergence:

To test the hypothesis of conditional convergence according to Sala-i-Martin (1996), one has to somehow, hold constant the steady state of each economy. I have also tried to hold the steady state constant by introducing variable that proxy for the steady state in a regression equation.

The panel data framework formulation for calculating conditional convergence has been obtained by following Islam (1995), by moving a single cross-section spanning period (1980-2011) to cross sections for the several periods. The total time period 1980-2011 has been divided into five-year shorter time periods to apply panel data framework. The constructed five-year periods are 1980-1985, 1985-1990, 1990-1995, 1995-2000, 2000-2005 and 2005-2011. Average annual growth rate of per capita income of each five-year span has been regressed on the natural log of per capita income at the beginning of each period and other explanatory variables.

Table 4.9: Conditional Convergence for Per Capita NSDP

Constant	0.6876 (0.00)
Coefficient	-0.0254** (0.01)
X1 (annual per capita electricity consumption)	0.0151** (0.02)
X2 (annual per capita industrial consumption of electricity)	0.0159*** (0.06)
X3 (net irrigated area as a % of net area sown)	0.0103 (0.20)
X4 (% share of agriculture in NSDP)	-0.0725* (0.00)
X5 (% share of industry in NSDP)	-0.0031 (0.82)
X6 (% share of services in NSDP)	-0.0438 (0.11)
X7 (bank deposits as a % of NSDP)	0.0108 (0.45)
X8 (bank advances as a % of NSDP)	-0.0061 (0.53)
X9 (population growth rate)	-0.0263* (0.00)
X10 (population per bank office (thousand)	-0.0094 (0.47)
X11 (% of villages electrified)	-0.0022 (0.88)
R^2	0.458
F-statistics	2.48* (P=0.000)
β-convergence	0.0499
Half-life Convergence	13.83
Hausman Specification Test	58.68* (P=0.000)
N	144

Note: Figures in parentheses are P-values; *, ** & *** denotes significance at 1 per cent, 5 per cent and 10 and level respectively.

The results of conditional convergence for per capita NSDP have been presented in table 4.9. Study found evidence of conditional convergence, as the co-efficient on per capita income is negative and statistically significant at 5 per cent level of significance. In other words, poor states grew faster than rich states once controls, that proxy for differences in steady states, are held constant. It has been found that Indian states have been converging conditionally at the speed of 5 per cent per year and will take only 14 years for half-life convergence.

Further, table shows that strong and clear effect comes only from the percentage share of agriculture in NSDP and population growth rate, as they exerts a highly significant and negative effect on per capita NSDP. Table reveals that the states with a greater initial dependence on agriculture grew more slowly. These results are in line with the Cherodian and Thirlwall (2013) which also found the negative impact of agricultural share and population growth on economic development in India. Whereas the percentage share of services and industry in NSDP exerts no significant impact on state per capita income which may be due to the location of industries in few states and concentration of services sector is also in few states. The other variables such as bank advances as a per cent of NSDP, population per bank office and percentage of villages electrified also have no significant impact on state per capita income. On the other hand per capita electricity consumption and industrial consumption of electricity exerts a positive and significant impact on per capita income. Furthermore, the table reveals that the net irrigated area as a percentage of net area sown and bank deposits as a percentage of NSDP affects per capita income positively but at an insignificant rate.

The results of the study are in line with Aiyar (2001), Adabar (2004) and Nagaraj et al. (1998). However, the estimate of my conditional convergence at the speed of 5 per cent per annum is relatively very small than the high speeds of convergence (34 per cent, 20 per cent and 12 per cent) found by Nagaraj et al. (1998), Aiyar (2001) and Adabar (2004) respectively in their studies. This may be due to differences in the time period and data set used.

Section-III

Time Series Unit Root Test for Stochastic Convergence

Most time series tests of convergence are related to the notion of 'stochastic convergence'. "Stochastic convergence implies that shocks to the income of a given country relative to the average income across a group of countries will be temporary. Thus, a common test for stochastic convergence involves testing for a unit root in the log of the ratio of per capita income relative to the group average. Failure to reject the unit root null hypothesis is an evidence of divergence, whereas rejection of the unit root null supports stochastic convergence" (Dawson and Strazicich, 2010). In the present study time series approach has been used to examine stochastic convergence. Stochastic convergence involves testing of a unit root, which requires that, for each state i, the natural logarithm of the ratio of per capita net state domestic Product (PCNSDP) relative to the average of all the states should be stationary.

$Y_{it} = \ln (PCNDP_{it} / \text{average } PCNDP_{t})$

There are various methods and tests to check for stationarity of any time series but in the present study an Augmented Dickey Fuller (ADF) unit root test has been applied to the natural log of relative income for each state. For each state, the null hypothesis of no convergence (non-stationarity) has been examined against alternative of convergence (stationarity). A rejection of null hypothesis implies stationarity and stochastic convergence. In other words, a unit root test for a state's relative income should be stationary.

Table 4.10, 4.11, 4.12 and 4.13 presents the results of Augmented Dickey Fuller test statistics for the per capita NSDP, NSDP originating from agriculture, industrial and services sector respectively for each state. Column II of each table gives the value of Augmented Dickey Fuller test statistics against which the null hypothesis has been tested whereas column III, IV and V of each table shows the Mackinnon critical values (1996) at 1 per cent, 5 per cent and 10 per cent level of significance respectively. If the value of test statistics exceeds the critical values at any level of significance then the null hypothesis is not to be rejected.

The estimated test statistics from the ADF unit root test presented in table 4.10 shows that the null hypothesis of a unit root has been rejected in favour of stationarity for Andhra Pradesh, Assam, Kerala, Meghalaya and Uttar Pradesh. This suggests that only these five states are stochastically converging with the average level of all the states, whereas the remaining 19 states have been diverging over the period of time. Majority of the states in India indicated no evidence of income convergence during the study period, as only five states out of twenty four states were in the convergence club, whereas the remaining 19 states were categorised under non-convergent club, following different steady-state paths. As most of the poor states except Assam, Meghalaya and Uttar Pradesh did not catch up with the rich ones due to wide disparities in geographic, demographic and economic features across the states. Thus the results are not enough to prove income convergence

Table 4.10: Stochastic Convergence for Per Capita NSDP

I	II	III	IV	V	VI
States	**Test Statistic**	**τ-critical value at 1%**	**τ-critical value at 5%**	**τ-critical value at 10%**	**Acceptance/Rejection of Null Hypothesis**
Andhra Pradesh	-3.658** (0)	-4.284	-3.563	-3.215	Reject H_0
Arunachal Pradesh	-2.189 (0)	-4.284	-3.563	-3.215	Cannot Reject H_0
Assam	-5.292* (4)	-4.339	-3.587	-3.230	Reject H_0
Bihar	-1.512 (4)	-4.339	-3.587	-3.230	Cannot Reject H_0
Goa	-2.007 (0)	-4.284	-3.563	-3.215	Cannot Reject H_0
Gujarat	-3.230 (4)	-4.339	-3.587	-3.230	Cannot Reject H_0
Haryana	-2.635 (6)	-4.374	-3.603	-3.238	Cannot Reject H_0
Himachal Pradesh	-2.392 (0)	-4.284	-3.563	-3.215	Cannot Reject H_0
Jammu and Kashmir	-2.544 (2)	-4.309	-3.574	-3.222	Cannot Reject H_0
Karnataka	-2.719 (0)	-4.284	-3.563	-3.215	Cannot Reject H_0
Kerala	-4.527* (5)	-4.356	-3.595	-3.233	Reject H_0
Madhya Pradesh	-1.967 (3)	-4.324	-3.581	-3.225	Cannot Reject H_0
Maharashtra	-2.332 (0)	-4.284	-3.563	-3.215	Cannot Reject H_0
Manipur	-2.229 (0)	-4.284	-3.563	-3.215	Cannot Reject H_0
Meghalaya	-3.233***(0)	-4.284	-3.563	-3.215	Reject H_0
Orissa	-3.047 (6)	-4.374	-3.603	-3.238	Cannot Reject H_0
Punjab	-0.747 (6)	-4.374	-3.603	-3.238	Cannot Reject H_0
Rajasthan	-1.175 (6)	-4.374	-3.603	-3.238	Cannot Reject H_0
Sikkim	-1.358 (0)	-4.284	-3.563	-3.215	Cannot Reject H_0
Nagaland	-2.861 (5)	-4.356	-3.595	-3.233	Cannot Reject H_0
Tamil Nadu	-2.855 (7)	-4.394	-3.613	-3.243	Cannot Reject H_0
Tripura	-2.610 (0)	-4.284	-3.563	-3.215	Cannot Reject H_0
Uttar Pradesh	-3.267*** (1)	-4.297	-3.568	-3.218	Reject H_0
West Bengal	-3.128 (7)	-4.394	-3.613	-3.243	Cannot Reject H_0

Note: *, ** and *** denote significance at 1, 5 and 10 per cent levels. Critical values are from Mackinnon (1996).

in India. The existence of different clubs (convergent and non-convergent) may be due to the reasons that the high income states like that of Goa, Maharashtra, Haryana, Punjab, Tamil Nadu, and Gujarat have been pulling away from the national average and are best performing states in one way or another. Goa is India's richest state with per capita income of ₹ 112602 at current prices during

2011-12 and was ranked as the best state by the Eleventh Finance Commission for its infrastructure. Maharashtra is India's leading Industrial state contributing 13 per cent of national industrial output and almost 46 per cent of the GSDP is contributed by industry.

Table 4.11: Stochastic Convergence for NSDP originating from Agricultural sector

I	II	III	IV	V	VI
States	**Test Statistic**	**τ-critical value at 1%**	**τ-critical value at 5%**	**τ-critical value at 10%**	**Acceptance/Rejection of Null Hypothesis**
Andhra Pradesh	-2.974 (0)	-4.284	-3.563	-3.215	Cannot Reject H_0
Arunachal Pradesh	-2.902 (4)	-4.339	-3.587	-3.230	Cannot Reject H_0
Assam	-3.609** (3)	-4.324	-3.581	-3.225	Reject H_0
Bihar	-3.533***(2)	-4.309	-3.574	-3.222	Reject H_0
Goa	-1.918 (6)	-4.374	-3.603	-3.238	Cannot Reject H_0
Gujarat	-4.778*(0)	-4.284	-3.563	-3.215	Reject H_0
Haryana	-1.077 (1)	-4.297	-3.568	-3.218	Cannot Reject H_0
Himachal Pradesh	-3.301*** (0)	-4.284	-3.563	-3.215	Reject H_0
Jammu and Kashmir	-2.225 (1)	-4.297	-3.568	-3.218	Cannot Reject H_0
Karnataka	-2.850 (0)	-4.284	-3.563	-3.215	Cannot Reject H_0
Kerala	-0.066 (2)	-4.309	-3.574	-3.222	Cannot Reject H_0
Madhya Pradesh	-2.273 (6)	-4.374	-3.603	-3.238	Cannot Reject H_0
Maharashtra	-3.866** (5)	-4.324	-3.581	-3.225	Reject H_0
Manipur	-0.899 (0)	-4.284	-3.563	-3.215	Cannot Reject H_0
Meghalaya	-2.514 (0)	-4.284	-3.563	-3.215	Cannot Reject H_0
Orissa	-3.098 (6)	-4.374	-3.603	-3.238	Cannot Reject H_0
Punjab	-0.034 (1)	-4.297	-3.568	-3.218	Cannot Reject H_0
Rajasthan	-4.548* (0)	-4.284	-3.563	-3.215	Reject H_0
Sikkim	-2.600 (0)	-4.284	-3.563	-3.215	Cannot Reject H_0
Nagaland	-1.538 (0)	-4.284	-3.563	-3.215	Cannot Reject H_0
Tamil Nadu	-3.239*** (0)	-4.284	-3.563	-3.215	Reject H_0
Tripura	-1.955 (0)	-4.284	-3.563	-3.215	Cannot Reject H_0
Uttar Pradesh	-1.594 (0)	-4.284	-3.563	-3.215	Cannot Reject H_0
West Bengal	-1.406 (1)	-4.297	-3.568	-3.218	Cannot Reject H_0

Note: *, ** and *** denote significance at 1, 5 and 10 and levels. Critical values are from Mackinnon (1996).

Table 4.11 shows that out of 24 states in the sample, only 7 states displayed tendency towards convergence as the null hypothesis of non-convergence has been rejected for Gujarat and Rajasthan at 1 per cent level of significance, for Assam and Maharashtra at 5 per cent level of significance, whereas at 10 per cent level for Bihar, Himachal Pradesh and Tamil Nadu. Bihar's success in catching up in terms of NSDP originating from agricultural sector is that Bihar's economy is basically agrarian in nature and is the eighth largest food grain producer in the country.

Table 4.12 shows that the null hypothesis of a unit root (non-stationarity) has been rejected for the six states only (Arunachal Pradesh, Gujarat, Himachal Pradesh, Karnataka, Rajasthan and Tamil Nadu) but it cannot be rejected for the remaining 18 states. Further, it has been found that Gujarat, Himachal Pradesh, Tamil Nadu and Rajasthan (Table 4.11 and 4.12) were the only states converging in terms of NSDP originating from agricultural and industrial sector. The Rajasthan Mega Highways Project, -which was being implemented by the Road Infrastructure Development Company of Rajasthan Ltd. (RIDCOR), aimed at improving and maintaining 1053 Km of roads and involving an investment of US $ 326mn- has been completed. This has not only driven industrialisation in the state but also generated employment. The tremendous boost in tourism augments growth in the state. Rajasthan Financial Corporation (RFC) is also providing financial support for setting up of new industries and expansion and renovation of existing industries. Investments in irrigation facilities, technology breakthrough and infrastructure development etc. are the factors affecting agricultural production in the Rajasthan.

The results displayed in table 4.13 shows that the unit root null hypothesis has been rejected for Arunachal Pradesh, Gujarat, Odisha at 10 per cent level, Madhya Pradesh and Tamil Nadu at 5 per cent level and Kerala at 1 per cent level of significance. It may be noted that Gujarat and Tamil Nadu were the only states converging in terms of NSDP originating from agricultural, industrial and services sector. Gujarat has been in first few states of India which initiated private sector investment. The strength of Gujarat's agricultural success has been contributed to diversified crops and cropping patterns, the existence of four agricultural universities in the state, which promotes

Table 4.12: Stochastic Convergence for NSDP originating from Industrial sector

I	II	III	IV	V	VI
States	**Test Statistic**	**τ-critical value at 1%**	**τ-critical value at 5%**	**τ-critical value at 10%**	**Acceptance/Rejection of Null Hypothesis**
Andhra Pradesh	-1.651 (0)	-4.284	-3.563	-3.215	Cannot Reject H_0
Arunachal Pradesh	-4.379* (0)	-4.284	-3.563	-3.215	Reject H_0
Assam	-3.117 (1)	-4.297	-3.568	-3.218	Cannot Reject H_0
Bihar	-0.964 (1)	-4.297	-3.568	-3.218	Cannot Reject H_0
Goa	-2.605 (0)	-4.284	-3.563	-3.215	Cannot Reject H_0
Gujarat	-3.557*** (0)	-4.284	-3.563	-3.215	Reject H_0
Haryana	0.4889 (7)	-4.394	-3.612	-3.243	Cannot Reject H_0
Himachal Pradesh	-3.829** (0)	-4.284	-3.563	-3.215	Reject H_0
Jammu and Kashmir	-2.651 (0)	-4.284	-3.563	-3.215	Cannot Reject H_0
Karnataka	-3.596** (1)	-4.297	-3.568	-3.218	Reject H_0
Kerala	-2.792 (0)	-4.284	-3.563	-3.215	Cannot Reject H_0
Madhya Pradesh	-2.742 (0)	-4.284	-3.563	-3.215	Cannot Reject H_0
Maharashtra	-2.283 (0)	-4.284	-3.563	-3.215	Cannot Reject H_0
Manipur	-2.510 (7)	-4.394	-3.612	-3.243	Cannot Reject H_0
Meghalaya	-2.951 (2)	-4.309	-3.574	-3.222	Cannot Reject H_0
Odisha	-2.231 (0)	-4.284	-3.563	-3.215	Cannot Reject H_0
Punjab	-3.014 (7)	-4.394	-3.612	-3.243	Cannot Reject H_0
Rajasthan	-4.598* (0)	-4.284	-3.563	-3.215	Reject H_0
Sikkim	-1.080 (0)	-4.284	-3.563	-3.215	Cannot Reject H_0
Nagaland	-1.898 (0)	-4.284	-3.563	-3.215	Cannot Reject H_0
Tamil Nadu	-4.481* (0)	-4.284	-3.563	-3.215	Reject H_0
Tripura	-2.076 (5)	-4.356	-3.595	-3.233	Cannot Reject H_0
Uttar Pradesh	-2.497 (0)	-4.284	-3.563	-3.215	Cannot Reject H_0
West Bengal	-2.372 (0)	-4.284	-3.563	-3.215	Cannot Reject H_0

Note: *, ** and *** denote significance at 1, 5 and 10 per cent levels. Critical values are from Mackinnon (1996).

research in agricultural sustainability and efficiency. Tamil Nadu is among the most industrialised states in the country and attracted several industrial projects and is amongst the highest FDI attracting states which helped in achieving greater technological advancement and more exportable products. Tamil Nadu is also a leading producer of agricultural products in India.

Table 4.13: Stochastic Convergence for NSDP originating from Services sector

I	II	III	IV	V	VI
States	**Test Statistic**	**τ-critical value at 1%**	**τ-critical value at 5%**	**τ-critical value at 10%**	**Acceptance/Rejection of Null Hypothesis**
Andhra Pradesh	-2.193 (0)	-4.284	-3.563	-3.215	Cannot Reject H_0
Arunachal Pradesh	-3.225*** (0)	-4.284	-3.563	-3.215	Reject H_0
Assam	-3.179 (0)	-4.284	-3.563	-3.215	Cannot Reject H_0
Bihar	-2.069 (1)	-4.297	-3.568	-3.218	Cannot Reject H_0
Goa	-1.995 (1)	-4.297	-3.568	-3.218	Cannot Reject H_0
Gujarat	-3.391*** (4)	-4.339	-3.587	-3.230	Reject H_0
Haryana	-1.772 (1)	-4.297	-3.568	-3.218	Cannot Reject H_0
Himachal Pradesh	-2.528 (0)	-4.284	-3.563	-3.215	Cannot Reject H_0
Jammu and Kashmir	-2.114 (0)	-4.284	-3.563	-3.215	Cannot Reject H_0
Karnataka	-2.048 (5)	-4.356	-3.595	-3.233	Cannot Reject H_0
Kerala	-4.568* (7)	-4.394	-3.612	-3.243	Reject H_0
Madhya Pradesh	-4.033** (0)	-4.284	-3.563	-3.215	Reject H_0
Maharashtra	-2.925 (0)	-4.284	-3.563	-3.215	Cannot Reject H_0
Manipur	-3.161 (7)	-4.394	-3.612	-3.243	Cannot Reject H_0
Meghalaya	-2.188 (0)	-4.284	-3.563	-3.215	Cannot Reject H_0
Orissa	-3.247*** (6)	-4.374	-3.603	-3.238	Reject H_0
Punjab	-2.365 (3)	-4.324	-3.581	-3.225	Cannot Reject H_0
Rajasthan	-2.592 (1)	-4.297	-3.568	-3.218	Cannot Reject H_0
Sikkim	-0.569 (0)	-4.284	-3.563	-3.215	Cannot Reject H_0
Nagaland	-1.644 (5)	-4.356	-3.595	-3.233	Cannot Reject H_0
Tamil Nadu	-3.619** (7)	-4.394	-3.612	-3.243	Reject H_0
Tripura	-1.779 (0)	-4.284	-3.563	-3.215	Cannot Reject H_0
Uttar Pradesh	-2.226 (6)	-4.374	-3.603	-3.238	Cannot Reject H_0
West Bengal	-1.618 (1)	-4.297	-3.568	-3.218	Cannot Reject H_0

Note: *, ** and *** denote significance at 1, 5 and 10 per cent levels. Critical values are from Mackinnon (1996).

Section-IV

Panel Data Unit Root Tests for Stochastic Convergence:

In this section, the convergence hypothesis has been examined in terms of per capita NSDP for the whole period (1980-81 to 2011-12) as well as for the two sub-periods i.e. pre-reform period (1980-81 to 1990-91) and post-reform period (1991-92 to 2011-12). For applying stochastic convergence framework, the natural logarithm of the ratio of per capita NSDP of each state relative to the average of all the states has been computed and then LLC, IPS, ADF Fisher, Fisher-PP and Hadri tests were applied to investigate unit roots in the relative per capita income. The null hypothesis of all panel unit root tests, with the exception of Hadri, is that states do not converge and series have a unit root (non-stationarity). On the other hand, for Hadri test the null hypothesis is of no unit root (stationarity), against the alternative of a unit root (non-stationarity) for time series data. In case of panel unit root tests, stationarity of the panel reveals convergence in state per capita income, whereas non-stationarity reveals divergence of state per capita income.

Table 4.14: Unit Root Tests for the Full Panel for 24 States

Types of test statistics	Test statistics	P-value
LLC	1.03630	0.8500
IPS	5.11018	0.9000
Fisher-ADF	4.75175	0.9000
Fisher-PP	63.8631	0.0624
Hadri	15.8103	0.0000

Source: Author's Calculation.

Table 4.14 reports the results of all the five panel unit root tests of 24 states for the entire period 1980-81 to 2011-12. The table reveals that null hypothesis of unit root is not rejected for all the tests except Fisher-PP test. The Hadri statistics also rejected the null of stationarity. So, the results of all the tests (except Fisher-PP test) highlights that the mean deviation of per capita income of Indian states poses a unit root. This indicates no sign of convergence of per capita income across

Indian states, suggesting that the poor states are not catching up with rich ones over the period 1980-81 to 2011-12.

Table 4.15: Unit Root Tests for the Pre-Reform Period for 24 States

Types of test statistics	Test statistics	P-value
LLC	2.06958	0.0192
IPS	3.03791	0.0012
Fisher-ADF	69.8210	0.0215
Fisher-PP	75.2151	0.0073
Hadri	-1.23387	0.8914

Source: Author's Calculation.

The results of panel unit root tests for 24 states for the pre-reform period (1980-81 to 1990-91) has been presented in table 4.15. Table reveals that the unit root null hypothesis has been rejected in all the four tests (LLC, IPS, Fisher-ADF and Fisher-PP) and the Hadri statistics also accepted the null of stationarity, which indicates convergence across Indian states during the pre-reform period. So, the gap between the states has declined in terms of per capita income over the period 1980-81 to 1990-91.

Table 4.16: Unit Root Tests for the Post-Reform Period for 24 States

Types of test statistics	Test statistics	P-value
LLC	2.12901	0.0166
IPS	0.23430	0.5926
Fisher-ADF	31.0419	0.9726
Fisher-PP	0.29205	0.6149
Hadri	12.3461	0.0000

Source: Author's Calculation.

The results of panel unit root tests for 24 states for the period 1991-92 to 2011-12 has been presented in table 4.16. Table reveals the evidence of divergence during the post-reform period as in case of all the tests, the null hypothesis is not rejected (except for LLC result, which indicates convergence across states during the post reform period). The Hadri statistics also indicates evidence of divergence by rejecting the null of stationarity.

Overall, the results of this section reveals that for the period 1980-81 to 2011-12, the states did not show any evidence of convergence, rather states have diverged. But the stationarity in the pre-reform period indicates stochastic convergence across states during the period 1980-81 to 1990-91. Whereas the non-stationarity achieved during the post-reform period (1991-92 to 2011-12), indicates that the rich states are becoming richer and poor are becoming poorer in case of per capita income and the gap is widening further during this period. The results of this section are in line with K. G. and Kumar (2011), who also by applying four different panel unit root tests (LLC, IPS, MW and PP Fisher Chi-square) found that Indian states in terms of per capita income did not show any indication of convergence for the period 1980-81 to 2008-09, rather were diverging during this period. According to their study, the Indian states are converging during the pre-reform period (1980-81 to 1990-91), however, non-stationary in the post-reform period indicated that the state per capita income has been diverging during the post-reform period (1991-92 to 2008-09).

The possible reason of divergence across Indian states could be that with the launching of economic reforms in 1991, few states such as Gujarat, Maharashtra, Tamil Nadu, Andhra Pradesh, and Karnataka have attracted larger FDI and were the big gainers from the process of economic liberalisation. Whereas states, such as Odisha, Bihar, Uttar Pradesh, Madhya Pradesh and Rajasthan lagged behind as being less attractive destinations of FDI. After opening up of economy, only few states- which were already industrialised- have gained in terms of industrial investment both domestic and foreign, thus widening the gap which was earlier bridging. Liberalisation and opening up of economy has helped some sectors to grow rapidly, but it also negatively affected the other sectors which could not compete internationally. This has increased inter-state inequality in the country. State level policy reform could be another reason for divergence. There are major differences across states in the area of policy reform. Few of the Indian states such as Gujarat, Tamil Nadu, Maharashtra, Karnataka and Andhra Pradesh have been more reform-oriented, but states such as Madhya Pradesh, Haryana, Kerala, Odisha, Punjab, Rajasthan and West Bengal have lagged behind in implementing economic reforms.

Section-V

Conclusion

The convergence hypothesis has been enamined across 24 Indian states in terms of per capita NSDP, NSDP originating from agricultural sector, industrial sector and services sector to know whether the regional inequality has been persisting across Indian states or not. The standard deviation of the natural log of the per capita NSDP and NSDP originating from agricultural sector have consistently increased over time, resulting in an increasing trend toward interstate disparities. The evidence of σ-convergence has been supported by fig. 4.3 and fig. 4.4 in terms of NSDP originating from industrial and services sector respectively. Thus it can be concluded that the states have been diverging in the sense of σ in terms of per capita NSDP and NSDP originating from agricultural sector, however, converging in terms of NSDP originating from industrial and services sector.

The result of the estimated cross-sectional unconditional β-convergence reveals that the Indian states have been diverging in terms of per capita NSDP and NSDP originating from agricultural sector over the period of time. Rich states grew faster than poor states, resulting in to increasing inequality among the states in terms of per capita NSDP and NSDP originating from agricultural sector. However, unconditional β-convergence has been observed in terms of NSDP originating from industrial and services sector. Further, study found an evidence of conditional convergence among Indian states in terms of per capita NSDP. It has been found that the states have been converging at the speed of 5 per cent per year and will take only 14 years for half-life convergence.

Estimating stochastic convergence by applying ADF unit root test statistics across Indian states, study found that while the null hypothesis of a unit root (non-stationarity) can be rejected for five states only (Andhra Pradesh, Assam, Kerala, Meghalaya and Uttar Pradesh) in case of per capita NSDP. The existence of different clubs (convergent and non-convergent) may be due to the reasons that the high income states like that of Goa, Maharashtra, Haryana, Punjab, Tamil Nadu, and Gujarat have been pulling away from the national average and are best performing states in one way or another. Study found that the null hypothesis of non-convergence has been rejected for Himachal Pradesh, Gujarat, Assam, Bihar, Maharashtra, Tamil Nadu and Rajasthan in terms of NSDP originating from agricultural sector. While the null hypothesis of no convergence can be rejected for six states each for NSDP originating from industrial sector (Himachal Pradesh, Arunachal Pradesh, Gujarat, Rajasthan, Karnataka and Tamil Nadu) and for the NSDP originating from services sector (Gujarat, Arunachal Pradesh, Odisha, Kerala, Madhya Pradesh and Tamil Nadu). Further, it has been found that Gujarat, Himachal Pradesh, Tamil Nadu and Rajasthan were the states converging in terms of NSDP originating from agricultural and industrial sector. Gujarat and Tamil Nadu were the only two states (out of 24 states) converging in terms of NSDP originating from agricultural, industrial and services sector.

Furthermore, the panel data unit root tests for stochastic convergence reveals that the states have been diverging in terms of per capita NSDP over the period 1980-81 to 2011-12. However, the states have been converging during 1980-81 to 1990-91 (pre-reform period). The non-stationarity found during 1991-92 to 2011-12 (post-reform period), indicated that the poor states are not catching up with the rich ones and the gap is widening further in terms of per capita NSDP. After opening up of economy, only few states- which were already industrialised- have gained in terms of industrial investment both domestic and foreign, thus widening the gap which was earlier bridging. Liberalisation and opening up of economy has helped some sectors to grow rapidly, but it also negatively affected the other sectors which could not compete internationally. This has increased inter-state inequality in the country.

The results of the study indicated that infrastructure development is the primary cause of diversity among the Indian states. The results suggests that improvement should be made in physical as well as social infrastructure in the lagging states, as it can help in promoting long run growth as well as in achieving convergence across Indian states in terms of per capita NSDP. More investment should be made especially in electricity and road infrastructure, since these factors have shown to exert a significant impact on growth in the study. Also quality electricity is now a pre-condition of almost all productive activities and its availability leads to economic development and hence can increase per capita income. Road density provides market access opportunities to people and helps the people get linked to economic and productive activities.

Regional convergence achieved in terms of NSDP originating from industrial and services sector could also help poorly performing states to achieve a higher growth rate and catch up with the better performing states in terms of per capita income.

Chapter 5

An Examination of Convergence Hypothesis in case of Human Development Index across Indian States

Human development enlarges people's choices, which are infinite and change over time. The essential choices before people are to lead a long and healthy life, to acquire knowledge and to have access to resources needed for a decent standard of living. If these essential choices are not available, many other opportunities remain inaccessible. However, there are many additional choices, highly valued by many people, ranging from social, political and economic freedom to opportunities for being creative and productive, and enjoying personal self respect are also important constituents of human development. No doubt, people always would like to have more and high income, but 'it is not the sum total of their lives'. "Development must, therefore, be more than just the expansion of income and wealth. Its focus must be people" (UNDP, 1990).

Human development is measured in terms of Human Development Index involving three dimensions of the quality of life- Longevity, Knowledge and Income. No doubt, there has been an improvement in the standard of living of the people of the world, but wide variations are found in the levels across countries and within the countries. It is really important to see whether this gap in the human development levels are bridging across countries and within the countries. The convergence hypothesis is one which can throw a light on this phenomenon. The present study examines the concept of convergence hypothesis to human resource development measured through human development index as well as its three components across 15 major Indian states namely Andhra Pradesh (AP), Assam (AS), Bihar (BH), Gujarat (GJ), Haryana (HR), Karnataka (KT), Kerala (KR), Madhya Pradesh (MP), Maharashtra (MH), Odisha (OR), Punjab (PB), Rajasthan (RJ), Tamil Nadu (TN), Uttar Pradesh (UP) and West Bengal (WB).

Knowledge, the first component of HDI has been represented by adult literacy rate, second- the longevity- by life expectancy at birth and the third-income-by per capita NSDP at constant prices (2004-05 prices).

For the purpose of analysis, the chapter has been divided into 6 sections. In Section-I, an examination of σ-convergence has been undertaken. Section-II deals with the analysis of cross-section unconditional β-convergence in terms of life expectancy. Section-III deals with the analysis of cross-section unconditional β-convergence in terms of adult literacy rate. In Section-IV analysis of cross-section unconditional β-convergence in terms of per capita NSDP has been undertaken. Section-V deals with the analysis of cross-section unconditional β-convergence in terms of human development index. The whole discussion has been concluded in Section-VI.

Section-I

σ-convergence

In the present section, σ-convergence has been examined for the health status, education status, per capita NSDP and the human development index by measuring the standard deviation across states of the natural log (ln) of life expectancy, adult literacy rate, per capita NSDP and the human development index is shown in table 5.1. On the basis of standard deviation summarised in table 5.1, the results for σ-convergence have been presented graphically in figures 5.1 to 5.4.

It is clear from table 5.1 that standard deviation of the natural log of life expectancy fell from 0.0870 in 1981-85 to 0.0498 in 2006-10. Fig. 5.1 plots the standard deviation across states of the natural log of life expectancy and reveals σ-convergence for life expectancy.

Table 5.1: Standard Deviation (σ-convergence)

Variables	Period	Standard Deviation	Variables	Period	Standard Deviation
Life Expectancy	1981-85	0.0870	Adult Literacy Rate	1981	0.2586
	1991-95	0.0762		1991	0.2316
	2001-05	0.0669		2001	0.1477
	2006-10	0.0498		2011	0.0961
Per Capita NSDP	1981	0.3007	Human Development Index	1981	0.2139
	1991	0.3414		1991	0.1827
	2001	0.4317		2001	0.1581
	2011	0.4742		2011	0.1004

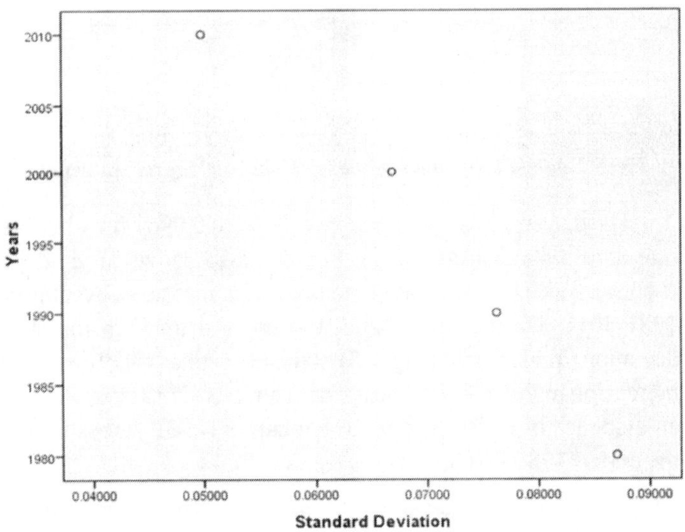

Fig. 5.1 Standard Deviation of the ln of life expectancy values of states

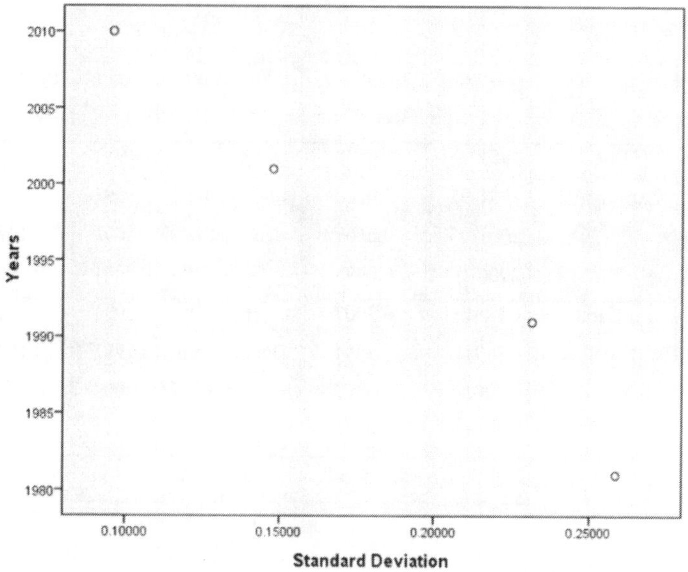

Fig. 5.2 Standard Deviation of the ln of adult literacy rate values of states

The dispersion decreases from 0.2586 to 0.0961 for adult literacy rate across states (Table 5.1). Fig. 5.2 also shows an evidence of σ-convergence in case of adult literacy rate across states over the period 1981-2011. On the other hand, the upward trend in the standard deviation (Table 5.1 and Fig. 5.3) of the per capita NSDP demonstrates increasing regional disparities in per capita NSDP across states. Thus an evidence of σ-divergence for per capita NSDP across states over the period 1981-2011.

In case of human development index, standard deviation of natural log (ln) of HDI, dropped from its highest value of 0.2139 in 1981 to 0.1004 in 2011 (Table 5.1) and the same has been supported by figure 5.4. Hence the σ-convergence has been found for HDI across states over the period 1981-2011. This convergence in HDI is broadly because of the presence of non-income indicators in HDI.

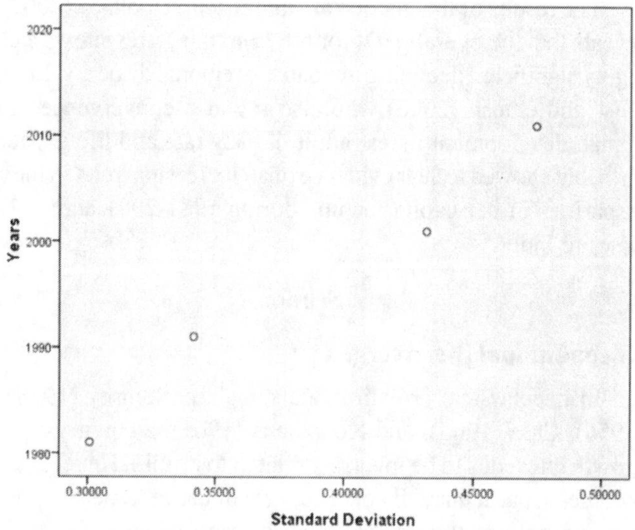

Fig. 5.3 Standard Deviation of the ln of per capita NSDP of states.

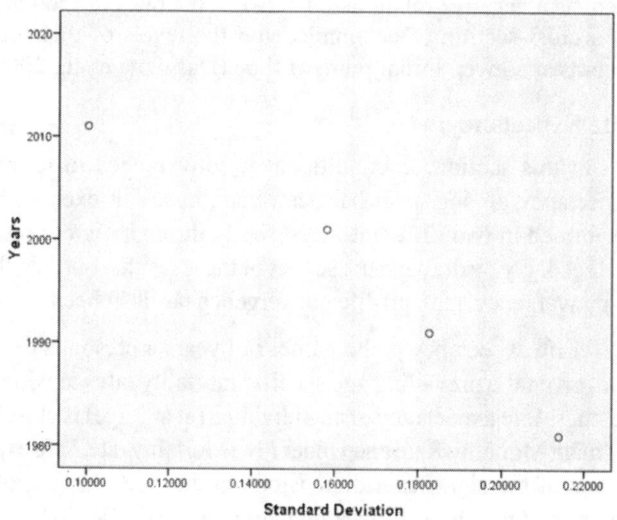

Fig. 5.4 Standard Deviation of the ln of HDI values of states.

The results of this section are in line with Dholakia (2003), which reveals that the overall HDI for the 15 major states shows a clear and highly significant declining trend in the regional disparity during 1981-2001 and Ghosh (2006) who also found σ-convergence in case of human development index, adult literacy rate and life expectancy at birth, but showed a clear evidence of an increasing trend in the regional disparities in per capita income during 1981-2001 across 15 major states in India.

Section-II

Unconditional β-convergence:

In neoclassical growth models such as Ramsey (1928), Solow (1956), Cass (1965), and Koopmans (1965), a country's per capita growth rate tends to be inversely related to its initial level of per capita income. In particular, "if countries are similar in respect to preferences and technology, then poor countries tend to grow faster than rich countries. Thus there is a force that promotes convergence in levels of per capita income across countries" (Barro, 1991). This leads to the hypothesis of absolute or unconditional β-convergence, which predicts a negative relationship between the rates of growth enjoyed by a cross-section of economies and the levels of their per capita outputs at a given initial point of time (Dasgupta et al., 2000).

Life Expectancy:

In this section, unconditional β-convergence in terms of life expectancy, among states has been examined. This exercise has been performed in two different ways, firstly through regression analysis and secondly by drawing the scatter of these results. Further, the speed of convergence and half-life convergence has also been worked.

"Life expectancy is the number of years a person is expected to live, given the prevailing age specific mortality rates to which he/she belongs. Life expectancy of an individual (at any age) is closely linked to Infant Mortality Rate and Under Five Mortality rate. Life expectancy is one of the significant dimensions in the development of human beings and thus human development index" (IHDR, 2011).

Table 5.2: Cross-Sectional Regression for Life Expectancy

Year	Constant	Coefficient	β-convergence	Half Life Convergence	R^2	Adjusted R^2	N	F-statistics
1981-85 to 1991-95	0.0735 (2.518)	-0.0164** (-2.267)	0.0179	38.55	0.283	0.228	15	5.137** (p=0.041)
1991-95 to 2001-05	0.0551 (9.216)	-0.0124* (-8.549)	0.0132	52.27	0.849	0.837	15	73.080* (p=0.000)
2001-05 to 2006-10	0.2489 (4.875)	-0.0578* (-4.703)	0.0682	10.11	0.630	0.601	15	22.120* (p=0.00)
1981-85 to 2001-05	0.0592 (4.717)	-0.0132* (-4.265)	0.0153	45.09	0.583	0.551	15	18.191* (p=0.000)
1991-95 to 2006-10	0.1084 (7.520)	-0.0250* (-7.132)	0.0313	22.04	0.796	0.781	15	50.867* (p=0.000)
1981-85 to 2006-10	0.0858 (7.268)	-0.0197* (-6.735)	0.0271	25.46	0.777	0.760	15	45.360* (p=0.000)

Note: * and ** denote significant at 1 and 5 per cent level respectively. Figures in parenthesis are t-values.

Table 5.2 reports the results of unconditional β-convergence for life expectancy for the whole period (1981-85 to 2006-10) and for the five sub-periods (1981-85 to 1991-95, 1991-95 to 2001-05, 2001-05 to 2006-10, 1981-85 to 2001-05 and 1991-95 to 2006-10). There has been tendency of convergence in life expectancy across states for the whole period as well as for the various sub-periods at 1 per cent level of significance. However, when the average growth rate of life expectancy for the period 1981-85 to 1991-95 has been regressed on the initial level (1981-85) of life expectancy, evidence of β-convergence has been found at 5 per cent level of significance during this period. This finding is also in tune with Ghosh (2006), who found that the co-efficients on initial level of life expectancy at birth are negative and statistically significant, implying that the regional disparities have been reduced across 15 major Indian states over the period 1981-2001 in terms of life expectancy at birth.

Further, it was found that the speed of convergence has varied over the period. The varying speed of convergence over the sub periods was the result of improvement in health expenditure and health facilities by the states. The speed of convergence increased from 1.79 per cent during the period 1981-85 to 1991-95 to 3.13 per cent during 1991-95 to 2006-10 and the highest speed of convergence (6.82 per cent) has been achieved during 2001-05 to 2006-10. This reveals the fact that states with initially lower life expectancy tended to grow at the fast speed due to the provision of better health and medical facilities over the period and these laggard states needs only 10 years to eliminate 50 per cent of the initial gap across states in terms of life expectancy.

Figures 5.5 to 5.10 corroborates the results found in table 5.2, as the relation between average growth rate and the natural log of initial life expectancy turns out to be negative. These scatter plots strengthen our conclusion that states with initially lower life expectancy are growing fast and reveals β-convergence in terms of life expectancy across Indian states.

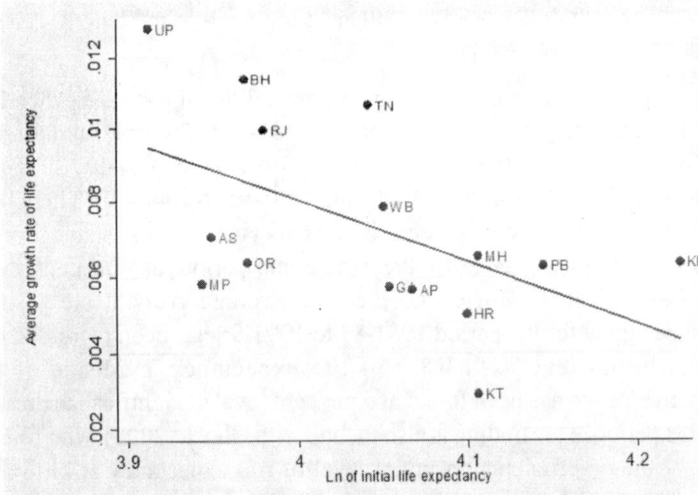

Fig. 5.5 Average growth rate of life expectancy (1981-85 to 1991-95) against the ln of initial life expectancy (1981-85).

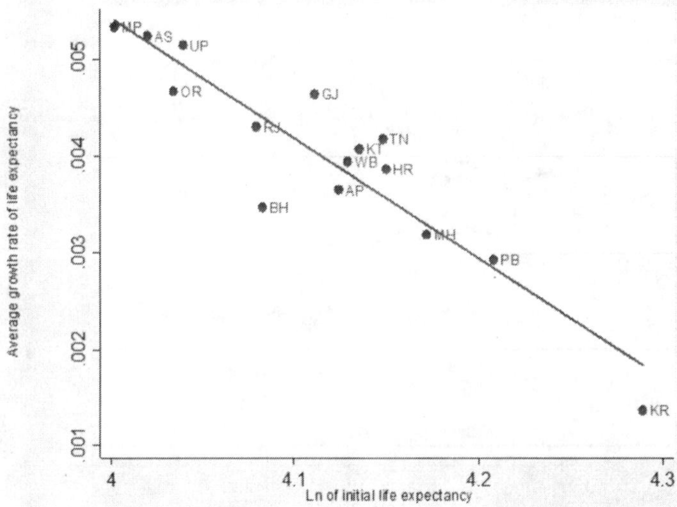

Fig. 5.6 Average growth rate of life expectancy (1991-95 to 2001-05) against the ln of initial life expectancy (1991-95).

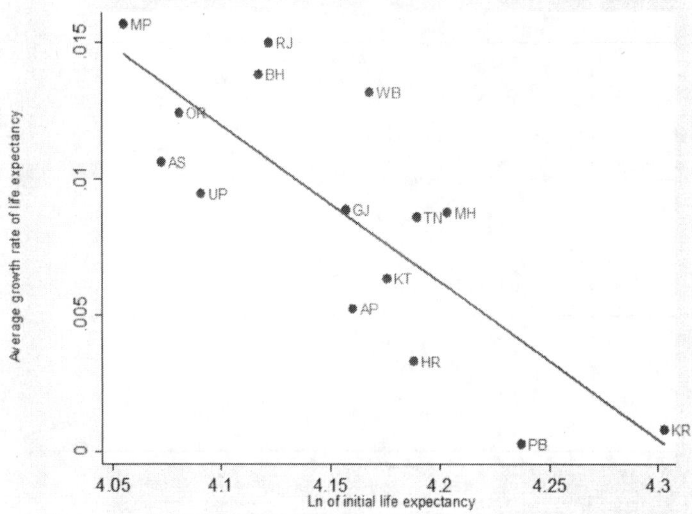

Fig. 5.7 Average growth rate of life expectancy (2001-05 to 2006-10) against the ln of initial life expectancy (2001-05).

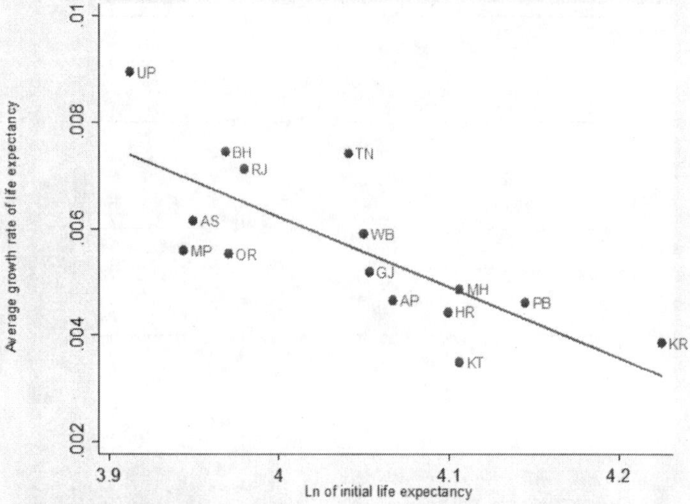

Fig. 5.8 Average growth rate of life expectancy (1981-85 to 2001-05) against the ln of initial life expectancy (1981-85).

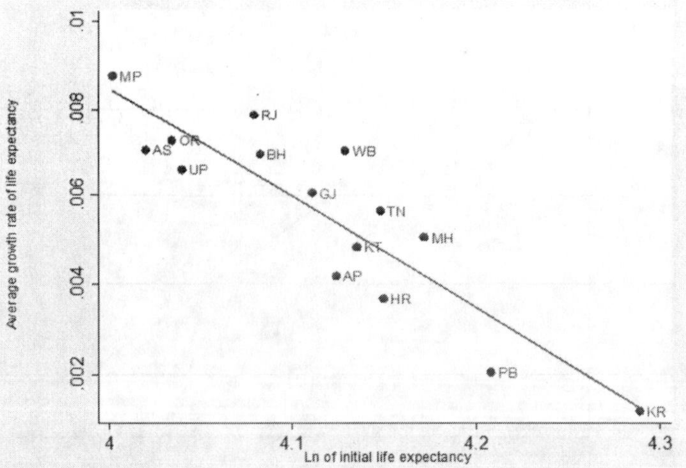

Fig. 5.9 Average growth rate of life expectancy (1991-95 to 2006-10) against the ln of initial life expectancy (1991-95).

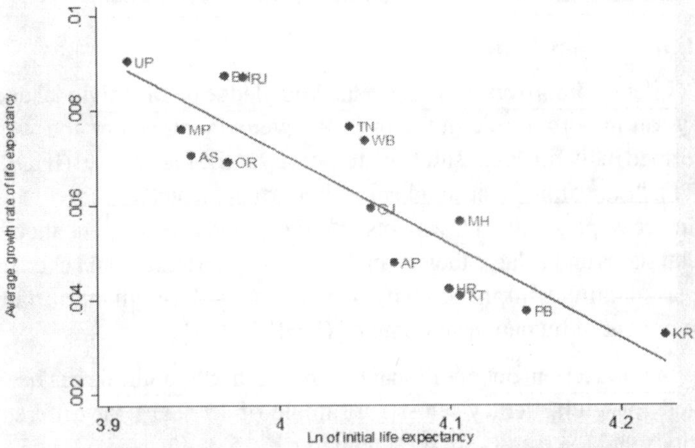

Fig. 5.10 Average growth rate of life expectancy (1981-85 to 2006-10) against the ln of initial life expectancy (1981-85).

Convergence observed in life expectancy over the period of time is broadly because of the fact that India has made improvement in various health outcomes over the last decade which is the result of better health and medical facilities being provided by the centre and state governments. Death rate, infant mortality rates (IMR) and under five mortality rates (U5MR), as well as the fertility rates have declined over the period. These along with other medical advances have improved life expectancy in the country. Another reason is the family planning, which helps in the spacing of children and improves the health status of mother and the child, thereby reducing infant and maternal mortality and thus improved life expectancy. Education has also contributed in improving the health of mother and children. The government's flagship programme- National Rural Health Mission (NRHM)-has played a critical role in reducing disparity in life expectancy, as it addressed the need of health infrastructure (physical, financial as well as man power). Improved tap water facilities, sanitation and hygienic conditions generated positive externalities in terms of better health, which also contributed to improved life expectancy across Indian states.

Section-III

Adult Literacy Rate:

Literacy improves awareness and knowledge of an individual and plays an important role in the overall development. Better and well informed individuals constitute better society at the macro level (IHDR, 2011). "Education is the single most important means for individuals to improve personal endowments, build capability levels, enhancing social status and enlarge their available set of opportunities and choices for a sustained improvement in well-being. It is an important component of human development" (NHDR, 2001).

In this section, unconditional β-convergence hypothesis has been tested for adult literacy rate for a sample of 15 states for different periods and the results are presented in table 5.3.

Table 5.3: Cross-Sectional Regression for Adult Literacy Rate

Year	Constant	Coefficient	β-convergence	Half Life Convergence	R^2	Adjusted R^2	N	F-statistics
1981-1991	0.0820 (2.556)	-0.0160** (-1.862)	0.0174	39.65	0.210	0.150	15	3.467** (p=0.085)
1991-2001	0.1818 (7.323)	-0.0403* (-6.453)	0.0516	13.37	0.762	0.744	15	41.644* (p=0.000)
2001-2011	0.1720 (7.509)	-0.0380* (-6.951)	0.0478	14.4	0.788	0.772	15	48.315* (p=0.000)
1981-2001	0.1153 (8.144)	-0.0249* (-6.596)	0.0345	20	0.770	0.752	15	43.507* (p=0.000)
1991-2011	0.1349 (31.679)	-0.0296* (-27.644)	0.0448	15.40	0.983	0.982	15	764.217* (p=0.000)
1981-2011	0.1009 (20.499)	-0.0219* (-16.670)	0.0357	19.33	0.955	0.952	15	277.893* (p=0.000)

Note: * and ** denote significant at 1 and 10 per cent level respectively. Figures in parenthesis are t-values.

The relationship between the initial level of adult literacy rate and its average growth rate across the states has turned out to be negative and significant for all the periods. Thus, the average growth rates of adult literacy of poor states have grown faster than that of the rich states during these periods. This confirms the evidence of convergence in adult literacy rate across states. This finding is also supported by Chikte (2011), who found an evidence of convergence across states for the period 1970 to 2005 and concluded that "the states have become more and more similar as far as the literacy rates are concerned".

Further β-convergence has been estimated at the speed of 3.57 per cent per year for the whole period and at the rate of 1.74 per cent, 4.78 per cent, 3.45 per cent and 4.48 per cent for 1981-1991, 2001-2011, 1981-2001and 1991-2011 periods respectively. This indicates that the gap between the states in terms of adult literacy rate has declined at the varying speeds. But, it has also been observed that once the process of convergence has started, the speed of convergence increased with the passage of time and the highest speed of 5.16 per cent per year was achieved during 1991-2001. Thus education differences have narrowed down across states over time and will take only 14 years for half- life convergence.

Figures 5.11 to 5.16 highlight the differential behaviour of states for different periods. For these states, the relation between average growth rate and the natural log of initial adult literacy rate turns out to be negative, confirming β-convergence. Thus, supporting the results of regression analysis presented in table 5.3.

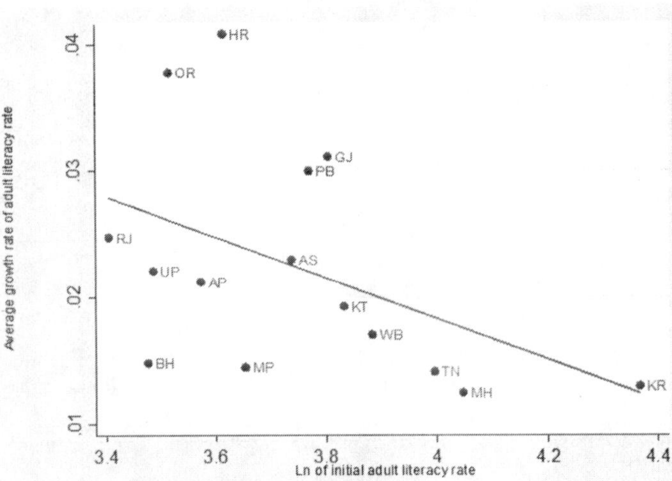

Fig. 5.11 Average growth rate of adult literacy rate (1981-1991) against the ln of initial adult literacy rate (1981).

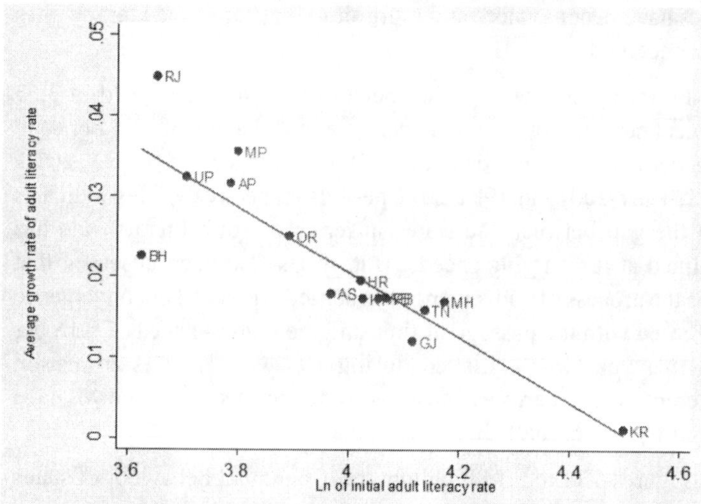

Fig. 5.12 Average growth rate of adult literacy rate (1991-2001) against the ln of initial adult literacy rate (1991).

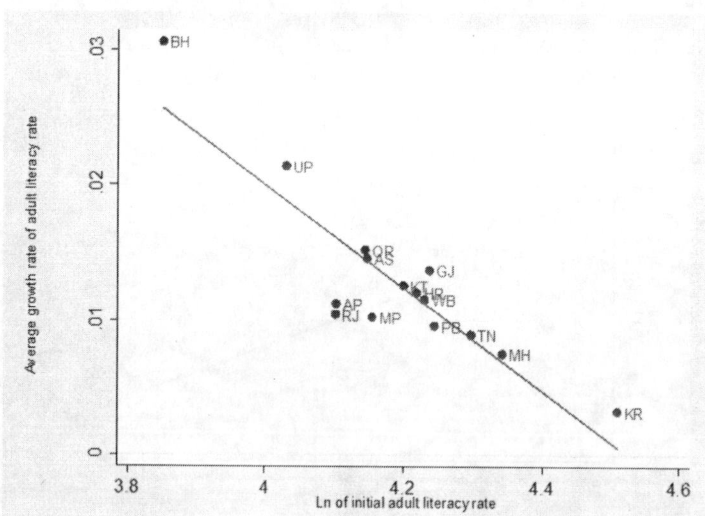

Fig. 5.13 Average growth rate of adult literacy rate (2001-2011) against the ln of initial adult literacy rate (2001).

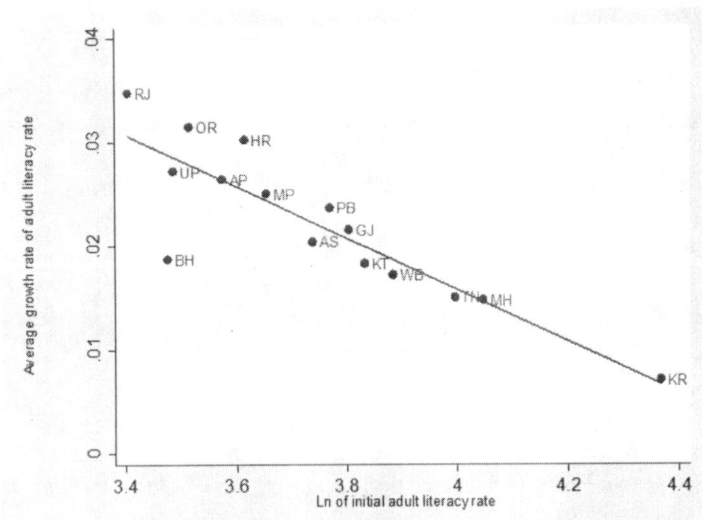

Fig. 5.14 Average growth rate of adult literacy rate (1981-2001) against the ln of initial adult literacy rate (1981).

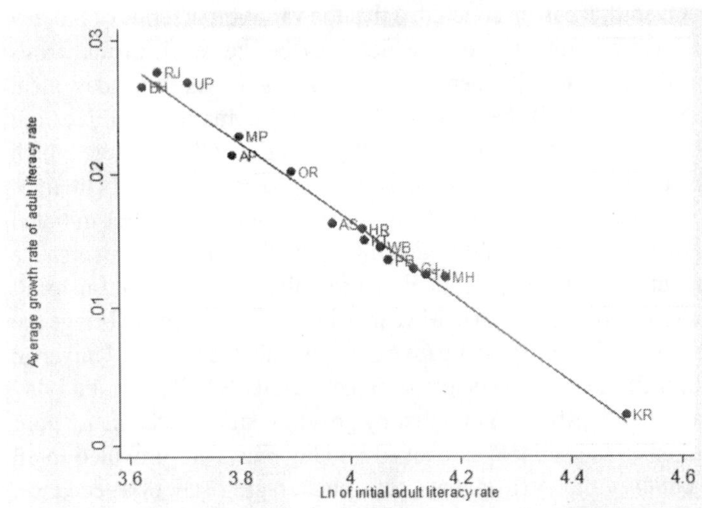

Fig. 5.15 Average growth rate of adult literacy rate (1991-2011) against the ln of initial adult literacy rate (1991).

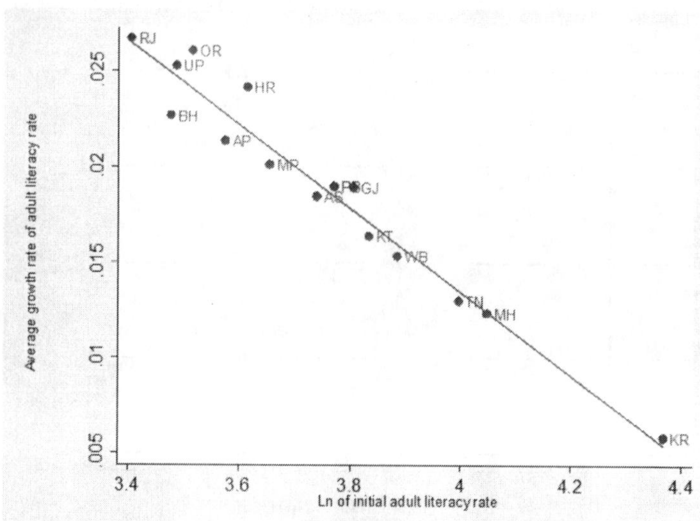

Fig. 5.16 Average growth rate of adult literacy rate (1981-2011) against the ln of initial adult literacy rate (1981).

Overall, it can be concluded that the variation in terms of literacy rates across states declined, which may be the result of numerous centrally sponsored schemes and programmes like mid-day meal scheme, Sarva Shiksha Abhiyan, National Programme for Education of Girls at Elementary Level and Right to Education Act etc which were initiated in all the states at par leading to convergence in literacy. Sarva Shiksha Abhiyan (SSA) is one of the major schemes initiated by government of India during the year 2002 in order to universalise elementary education. It aims at providing basic education to all children in the age group 6-14 years while endeavouring to bridge the regional, social and gender gaps existing within the country. Universal enrollment is one of the specific objectives of SSA. Further, mid-day meal scheme (MDMS) initiated by government attracted many poor children to the schools as cooked midday meals are provided to all the children of I-VIII classes, thus encouraging school attendance, which provided a boost to literacy rate in all the states. National Programme for Education of Girls at Elementary Level (NPEGEL) has been implemented in educationally backwards blocks where rural female literacy is low and it provided additional support for enhancing girl's education and hence giving push to female literacy rates (Economic Survey, 2011-12). Although these programmes might not have achieved the full success, but seems to be the probable reason for highest speed of convergence during the last decade.

Furthermore, a scheme of setting up 6000 model schools as benchmarks of excellence at block level with one school per block was launched in November 2008, helped in providing quality education to talented rural children. Free education for all children between the age of 6 and 14 has been made a fundamental right under the Right to Education Act 2009. Though these programmes have been implemented recently, the positivity of these will be seen in near future and it is expected that the speed of convergence in terms of adult literacy rate will increase further. Private sector participation in education at the school level is increasing in the country and these private institutions are being helped by the state in one form or another. As these schools are covered under Right to Education Act enacted by the government, it is expected that these private schools will start contributing positively in giving education to students from lower strata of the population. Although it is expected that this will enhance the literacy rate/education level in the country and improve quality education in the country, but it is only possible if the private sector take up its responsibility of giving admission to the students from poor strata as envisaged in the act, otherwise things may not change for poor people. Although, several programmes have been launched by the government for improving the health and education status of the population, still in order for the speed of convergence to rise further and eliminate the differences in the level of education and health among the states and different regions within the states, there is more need of public sector expenditure in both the education and health sector.

Section-IV

In the previous chapter unconditional β-convergence (or divergence) has been examined in terms of per capita NSDP for the whole period (1980-2011) as well as for the various sub-periods for 24 Indian states. The results show that the Indian states have been diverging but not statistically significant in terms of per capita NSDP over the period 1980-2011, 1985-1990, 1990-1995 and 2005-2011, however, diverging significantly at 10 per cent level of significance over the period 2000-2005, implying that poor states are not catching up with the rich ones during these periods. But when the annual average growth rate of per capita NSDP for the year 1980-1985 and 1995-2000 are regressed on the natural logarithm of initial level (1980 and 1995 respectively) of per capita NSDP, the co-efficient turns out to be negative but not significant, indicating the tendency of weak convergence. In this section, an attempt has been made to examine convergence hypothesis in terms of per capita NSDP for the overall period 1981 to 2011 as well as for the various sub-periods for 15 major Indian states and the results are presented in table 5.4.

Table 5.4: Cross-Sectional Regression for Per Capita NSDP

Year	Constant	Coefficient	β-convergence	R^2	Adjusted R^2	N	F-statistics
1981-1991	-0.0675 (-0.919)	0.0099 (1.260)	-0.0094	0.109	0.040	15	1.589 (p=0.229)
1991-2001	-0.1529 (-1.367)	0.019 (1.645)	-0.0174	0.172	0.108	15	2.705 (p=0.124)
2001-2011	0.0051 (0.052)	0.0057 (0.579)	-0.0055	0.025	-0.050	15	0.335 (p=0.572)
1981-2001	-0.1023 (-1.216)	0.0139 (1.549)	-0.0123	0.156	0.091	15	2.401 (p=0.145)
1991-2011	-0.0590 (-0.615)	0.0109 (1.087)	-0.0099	0.083	0.013	15	1.183 (p=0.296)
1981-2011	-0.0553 (-0.685)	0.0100 (1.160)	-0.0088	0.094	0.024	15	1.347 (p=0.267)

Note: Figures in parenthesis are t-values.

Average growth rates of per capita NSDP for 15 major states for different time periods have been computed and regressed on the natural log of their respective initial values of per capita NSDP. Positive but insignificant co-efficients of initial level of per capita NSDP has been found during the whole period as well as for the various sub-periods, inferring weak divergence across states. It indicates that the average growth rate of per capita NSDP of poor states has not been faster than that of the rich states and the states are becoming more dissimilar in respect of per capita NSDP over the period of time. It may be noted that the value of R^2 are relatively low in all regressions. This suggests that there may be some other explanatory variables which explain the behaviour of growth rates of per capita NSDP. The results in table 5.4 concurs with the finding of the latest study conducted by Cherodian and Thirlwall (2013), which also shows an evidence of β-divergence, but at an insignificant rate across Indian states over the period 1999-2000 to 2010-11. Although, insignificant divergence at varying speed has been found across states and maximum speed of 1.74 per cent per year has been recorded during the period 1991-2001, but later on it decreased with the passage of time and the lowest speed of 0.55 per cent per year has been observed during the last decade.

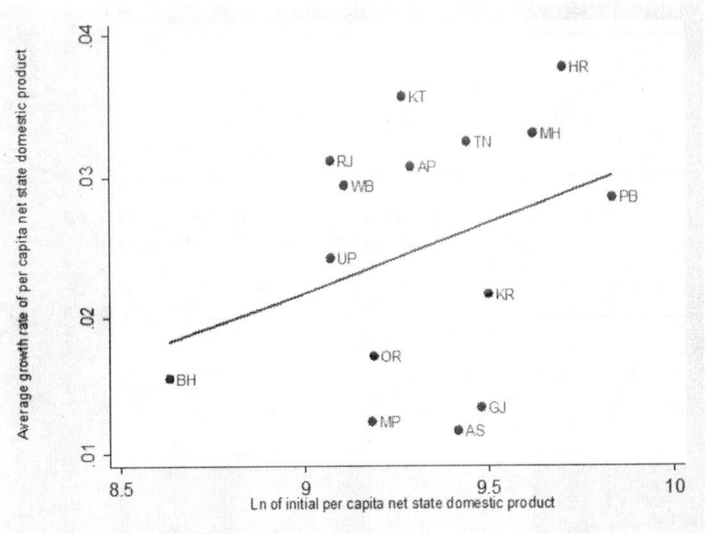

Fig. 5.17 Average growth rate of per capita NSDP (1981-1991) against the ln of initial per capita NSDP (1981).

Figures 5.17 to 5.22 also brings out the behaviour of 15 major states in terms of per capita NSDP, by plotting the average growth rate of the states for the respective period against the natural log of initial per capita income of that period. If there is convergence across states in the income level, the relationship should be downward sloping, but the positive lines obtained for these states, corroborates the existence of β-divergence over a shorter and longer period of

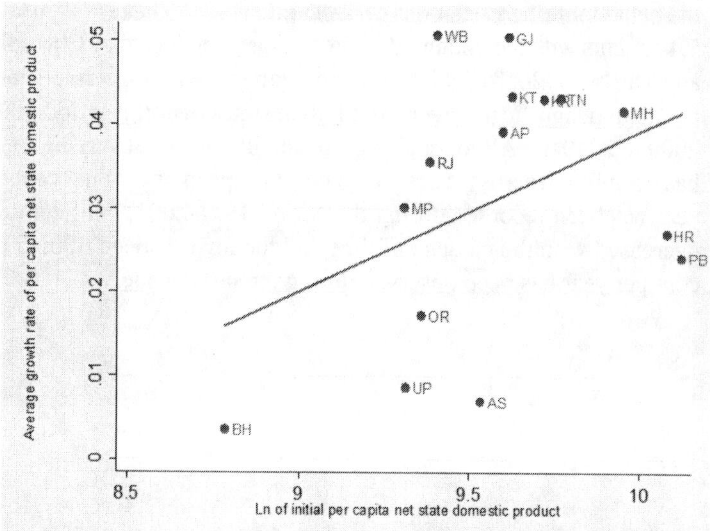

Fig. 5.18 Average growth rate of per capita NSDP (1991-2001) against the ln of initial per capita NSDP (1991).

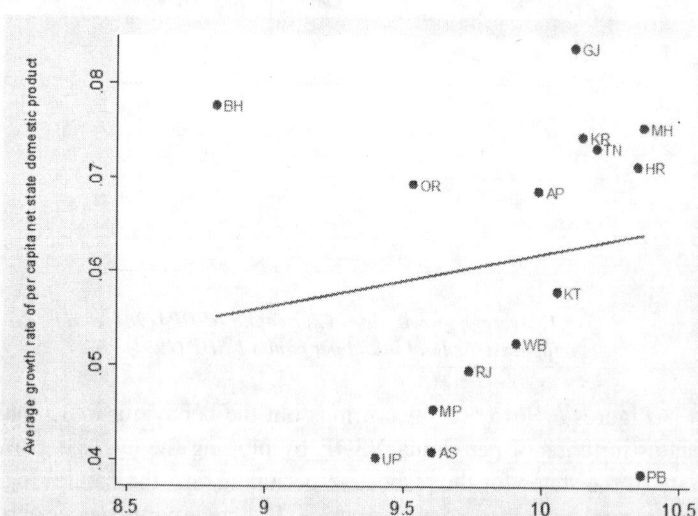

Fig. 5.19 Average growth rate of per capita NSDP (2001-2011) against the ln of initial per capita NSDP (2001).

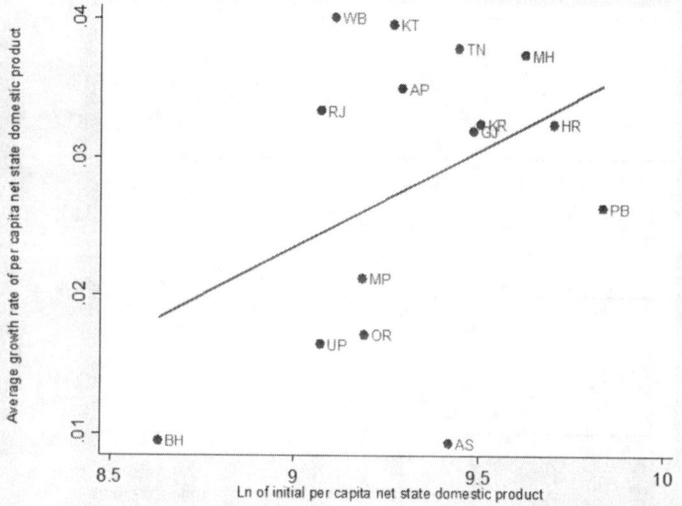

Fig. 5.20 Average growth rate of per capita NSDP (1981-2001) against the ln of initial per capita NSDP (1981).

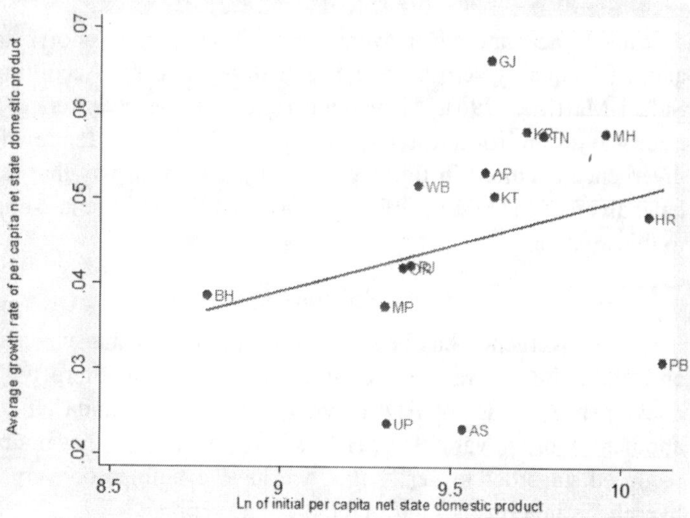

Fig. 5.21 Average growth rate of per capita NSDP (1991-2011) against the ln of initial per capita NSDP (1991).

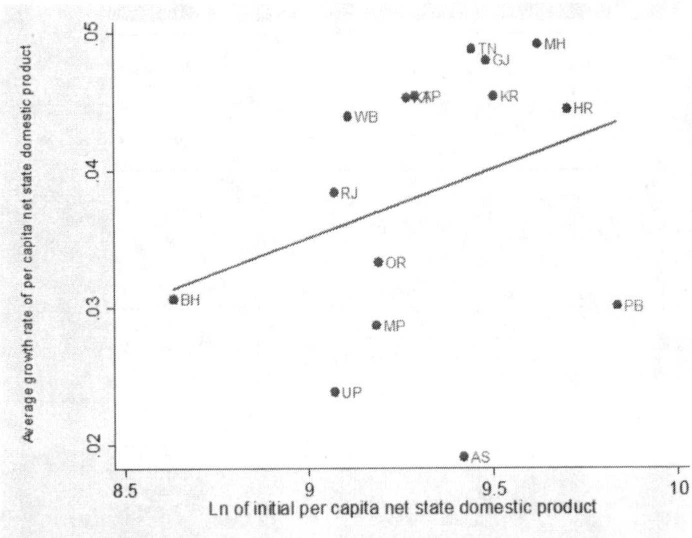

Fig. 5.22 Average growth rate of per capita NSDP (1981-2011) against the ln of initial per capita NSDP (1981).

time and richer states on an average grew faster than the poorer states and the inequality across states is actually increasing. According to Sala-i-Martin (1996), "The occurrence of β-convergence is a necessary condition for σ-convergence". The evidence of σ-divergence occurred in fig. 5.3 (pg. 106), which display that states have diverged in the sense of σ over the last 30 years, extends support to this argument.

Section-V

As convergence has been observed in case of life expectancy and adult literacy rate, so what we expect is that there will be convergence in case of HDI as well, although per capita NSDP is another important variable of HDI, where convergence has not been recorded. In order to verify this, we have examined convergence hypothesis in terms of HDI in the present section.

Table 5.5 reports the unconditional convergence for human development index. Table shows that co-efficient (-0.0182) turns out to be negative and statistical significant at 1 per cent level for the whole period (1981-2011) signalling unconditional β-convergence across states over the period 1981-2011 at the rate of 2.63 per cent per year. Further, the whole period has been divided into sub-periods i.e., 1981-1991, 1991-2001, 2001-2011, 1981-2001 and 1991-2011. Convergence in human development index has been observed in all the sub-periods also at 1 per cent level of significance, however, the speed of convergence has varied from period to period. As it can be seen from the table that the speed of convergence which was 1.74 per cent per year across states for pre-reform period (1981-1991), increased to 3.16 per cent per year during the post-reform period i.e. 1991-2011. The speed of convergence during the latest period (2001-2011) was the highest (4.88 per cent per year). Thus, it emerges that in case of Indian states, once the convergence started, speed of convergence has increased over period. Further, it was found that the half-life convergence - the time it takes for 50 per cent of the initial gap to be eliminated has reduced to 14 years for the latest period from more than 39 years in the initial period of study (1981-1991). Overall, it can be concluded that the speed of convergence has reached the maximum and half-life convergence to minimum in the last decade.

Table 5.5: Cross-Sectional Regression for Human Development Index

Year	Constant	Coefficient	β-convergence	Half Life Convergence	R^2	Adjusted R^2	N	F-statistics
1981-1991	0.004 (0.717)	-0.016* (-3.347)	0.0174	39.65	0.463	0.421	15	11.203* (p=0.005)
1991-2001	0.0007 (0.170)	-0.0148* (-3.508)	0.0160	43.12	0.486	0.447	15	12.303* (p=0.004)
2001-2011	-0.0205 (-5.801)	-0.0386* (-8.708)	0.0488	14.14	0.854	0.842	15	75.831* (p=0.000)
1981-2001	0.0018 (0.525)	-0.0146* (-4.912)	0.0173	39.89	0.650	0.622	15	24.124* (p=0.000)
1991-2011	-0.0096 (-5.471)	-0.0234* (-12.550)	0.0316	21.83	0.924	0.918	15	157.514* (p=0.000)
1981-2011	-0.0054 (-3.961)	-0.0182* (-15.814)	0.0263	26.23	0.950	0.947	15	250.079* (p=0.000)

Note: *denote significant at 1 per cent level. Figures in parenthesis are t-values.

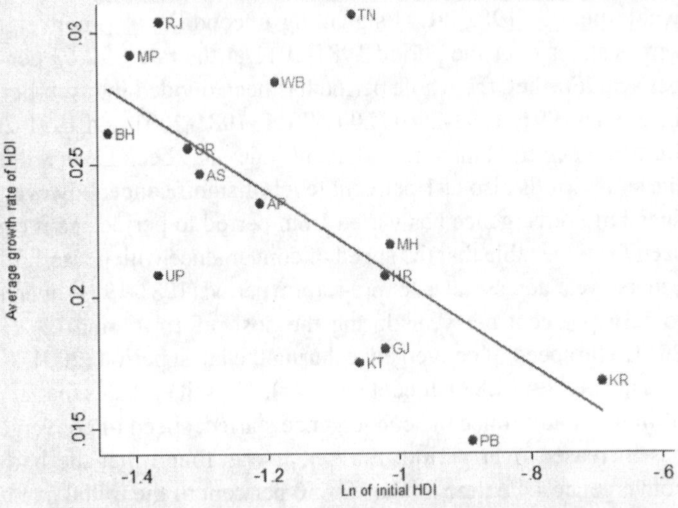

Fig. 5.23 Average growth rate of HDI (1981-1991) against the ln of initial HDI (1981).

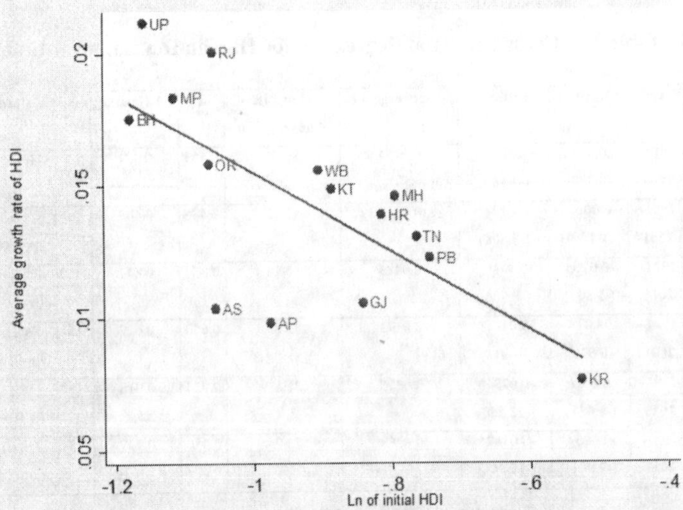

Fig. 5.24 Average growth rate of HDI (1991-2001) against the ln of initial HDI (1991).

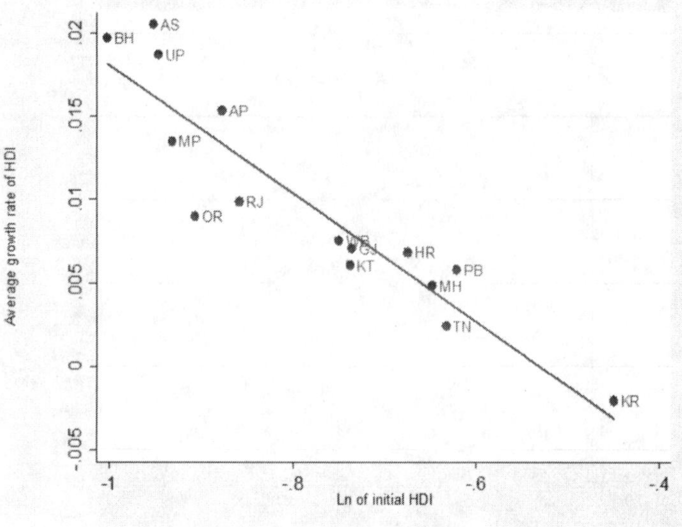

Fig. 5.25 Average growth rate of HDI (2001-2011) against the ln of initial HDI (2001).

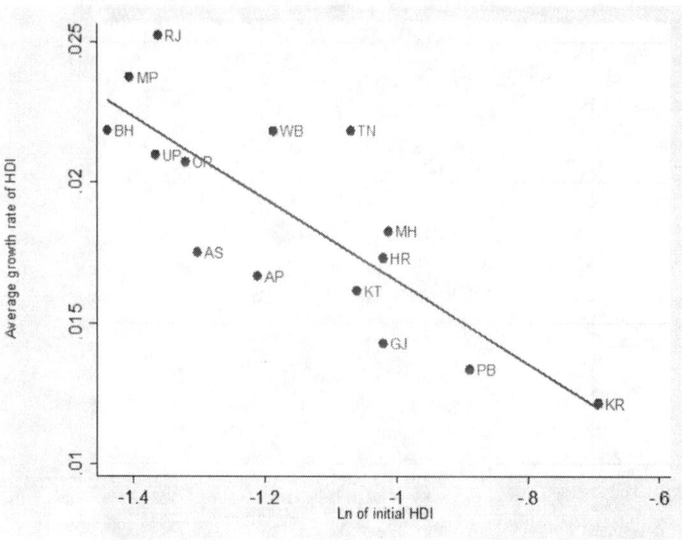

Fig. 5.26 Average growth rate of HDI (1981-2001) against the ln of initial HDI (1981).

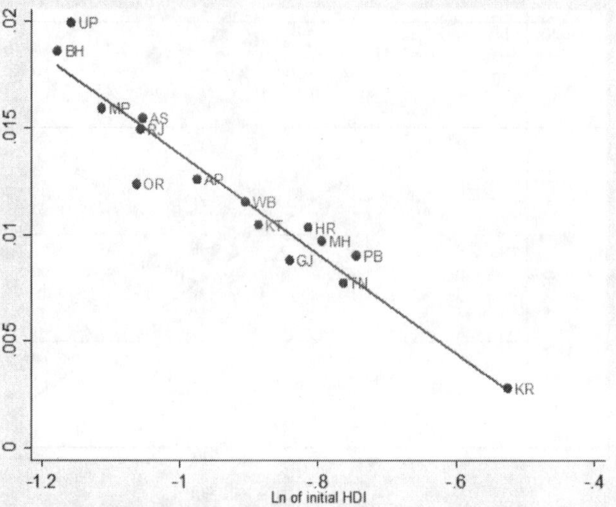

Fig. 5.27 Average growth rate of HDI (1991-2011) against the ln of initial HDI (1991).

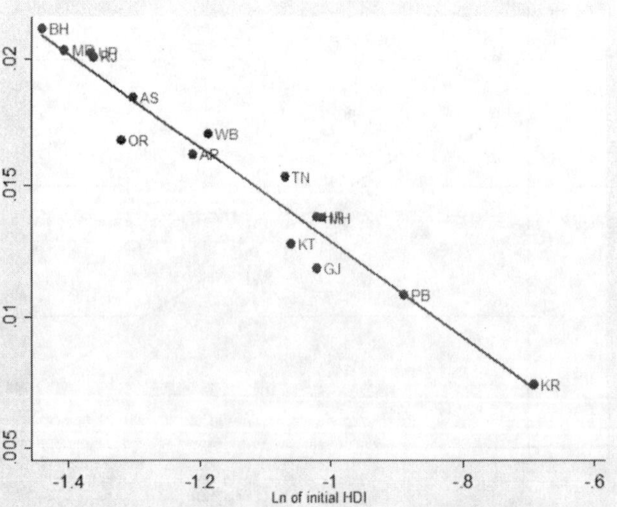

Fig. 5.28 Average growth rate of HDI (1981-2011) against the ln of initial HDI (1981).

Despite divergence in per capita income, the high rate of convergence in life expectancy and adult literacy rate made it possible to achieve sustained reductions in the regional disparities in human development index.

Figures 5.23 to 5.28 show the scatter across the set of 15 states in case of human development index for the sub-periods as well as for the whole period of the study. Figures show that the relation between average growth rate and the initial level of HDI is negative, which confirms the process of cross-state convergence in terms of HDI.

Section-VI

Conclusion

This chapter evaluates relative performance of 15 major states on human development index and its three components. The results show that the standard deviation across states tends to decline over time in terms of health status (measured by life expectancy), education status (measured by adult literacy rate) and human development index, supporting the existence of "sigma" convergence for life expectancy, adult literacy rate and human development index. However, the dispersion increased in case of per capita NSDP reflecting sigma divergence for per capita NSDP. Figures used for detecting sigma convergence or divergence on the basis of calculated standard deviations across states also reveals the existence of σ-convergence for health status (Fig. 5.1), education status (Fig. 5.2) and human development index (Fig. 5.4), but figure 5.3 reveals that the states are diverging in the sense of σ in terms of per capita NSDP over the past 30 years.

Regarding cross-sectional regression for unconditional β-convergence, the study found negative and statistically significant co-efficient for the whole period as well as for the various sub-periods, signalling unconditional β-convergence in terms of life expectancy, adult literacy rate and human development index. The estimated downward sloping lines (Fig. 5.5 to Fig. 5.10), (Fig. 5.11 to Fig. 5.16) and (Fig. 5.23 to Fig. 5.28), showing a negative relationship between the annual average growth rate and initial level of life expectancy, adult literacy rate and human development index respectively lends support to unconditional β-convergence in these three variables. Further, the analysis shows that the rate of unconditional β-convergence has varied across the different time periods for different variables. The study also found that once the process of convergence has started, the speed of convergence increased with the passage of time. The gap between the states has declined at the rate of 6.82, 4.78 and 4.88 per cent per year in terms of life expectancy, adult literacy rate and human development index respectively during the last decade. It has been found that the laggard states needs only 10 years in terms of life expectancy and will take 14 years each in case of adult literacy and human development index to eliminate 50 per cent of the initial gap across states.

Furthermore, positive but insignificant co-efficients of initial level of per capita NSDP has been found during the whole period as well for the various sub-periods, indicating that the average growth rate of poor states are becoming more dissimilar in respect of per capita NSDP over the period of time. However, the lowest speed of 0.55 per cent per year observed during the last decade reveals that the speed of divergence decreased with the passage of time.

Overall, the results of the study exhibited σ and significant unconditional β-convergence for health status (measured by life expectancy), education status (measured by adult literacy rate) and human development index across the states. However, in case of per capita NSDP neither σ nor unconditional β- convergence has been found, signalling that the poor states are getting relatively poorer and rich getting richer in terms of per capita income and the gap between the rich and the poor is widening further. So, the poor states that have failed to catch up with rich ones in terms of per capita income have managed to catch up in terms of human development index. The convergence observed in case of life expectancy and adult literacy rate helps in bringing convergence in terms of human development index also, despite considerable divergence in per capita NSDP. The presence of convergence in terms of indicators of education and health give some hope of convergence in income also, may be at the later stage because educated and healthy people means more efficient and productive labour which contributes positively to the economic activities leading to higher production and hence increasing income per capita.

From the above analysis it can be concluded that improvement in education and health facilities have a positive impact on the human development and because of the positive externalities of human development it leads to improvement in standard of living of the people through better incomes. There is a need for the governments particularly of the poor states to invest in both social as well as economic infrastructure, frame policies which improves investment in the states, which will ultimately lead to more production and employment and will help in reducing inequalities in the per capita income of different states.

Chapter 6

An Inter-State Analysis of Economic Development in India

Economic Development is a multidimensional process involving development of human capital, raising living standards, improving education, infrastructure, improvement of health, level of nutrition, quality of housing, distribution of goods and services and other areas that leads to increase in general welfare of the society. According to the World Bank Report (1992), "Development is about improving the well being of people. Raising living standards and improving education, health and equality of opportunity are all essential components of development." Economic development leads to improvement in all sectors of the economy. The indicators such as poverty ratio, literacy rates, infant mortality, per capita income and industrial and agriculture share can be used to measure the level of economic development in a country.

Economic development has become a matter of primary concern for almost every nation of the world including India. Since independence, policy-makers and planners in India have been concentrating on achieving balanced regional development in the country, but still the progress of states is not uniform in terms of economic development, as some states like Gujarat, Kerala and Maharashtra are experiencing fast progress, whereas others like that of Bihar, Uttar Pradesh and Madhya Pradesh are lagging behind. In this chapter an effort has been made to analyse and compare the position of Indian states by identifying the education, health, nutrition, sanitation and economic indicators responsible for the diversity in development, for which the Composite development index has been constructed .'Factor Analysis' has been employed to determine the relative weight of the selected indicators. The relative weights to various indicators have been assigned on the basis of all the principal components. Following eighteen indicators have been used for developing composite development index.

1. Per Capita Net State Domestic Product at 2004-05 Prices.
2. Adult Literacy Rate.
3. Female Literacy Rate.
4. Primary Pupil Teacher Ratio.
5. Upper Primary Pupil Teacher Ratio.
6. Secondary Pupil Teacher Ratio.
7. Primary Gross Enrollment Ratio.
8. Upper Primary Gross Enrollment Ratio.
9. Primary Drop-out Rate.
10. Percentage of Population below Poverty Line.
11. Percentage of Households with Access to Safe Drinking Water.
12. Percentage of Households with Access to Electricity.
13. Infant Mortality Rate per Thousand Live Births.
14. Crude Death Rate per Thousand Population.
15. Urban Population as percentage of Total Population.
16. Per Capita Consumption of Electricity.
17. Percentage Share of Industry in NSDP at 2004-05 Prices.
18. Percentage Share of Services in NSDP at 2004-05 Prices.

For this purpose the whole chapter has been divided into 3 sections. In Section-I analysis of 22 states has been undertaken and composite development index has been developed. Convergence and divergence in terms of indicators and composite development index has been presented in Section-II. The whole discussion has been concluded in Section-III.

Section-I

In this section composite development index has been developed by using the weights obtained from all principal components for the states. The analysis has been undertaken for 22 states namely Andhra Pradesh, Arunachal Pradesh, Assam, Bihar, Goa, Gujarat, Himachal Pradesh, Haryana, Karnataka, Kerala, Manipur, Madhya Pradesh, Meghalaya, Maharashtra, Odisha, Punjab, Sikkim, Rajasthan, Tripura, Tamil Nadu, Uttar Pradesh and West Bengal for the year 1981, 1991, 2001 and 2011.

Table 6.1: Results of Factor Analysis for the Year 1981

	Variables	Factor Loadings			Commu-nalities	weights	Wt in %
		Factor-1 F1	Factor-2 F2	Factor-3 F3			
		1	2	3			
1.	PCNSDP	**.798**	-.135	.480	.885	0.3320	7.41
2.	Adult Literacy Rate	**.850**	.107	-.470	.957	0.3536	7.89
3.	Female Literacy Rate	**.883**	.208	-.273	.914	0.3674	8.20
4.	Primary Gross Enrolment Ratio	**.925**	.110	-.060	.909	0.3848	8.59
5.	Upper Primary Gross Enrolment Ratio	**.861**	.395	-.003	.922	0.3582	8.00
6.	Primary Drop-out Rate	**.613**	-.293	-.003	.890	0.2550	5.69
7.	Households with Access to Electricity	**.783**	-.240	.542	.965	0.3258	7.27
8.	Infant Mortality Rate	**.652**	.561	-.064	.762	0.2713	6.06
9.	Crude Death Rate	**.726**	.458	-.153	.794	0.3021	6.74
10.	Urban Population	**.584**	-.426	-.195	.870	0.2430	5.42
11.	Per Capita Consumption of Electricity	**.621**	-.620	.199	.862	0.2584	5.77
12.	Share of Industry	**.662**	-.082	-.048	.461	0.2754	6.15
13.	Share of Services	**.484**	-.220	-.515	.637	0.2014	4.50
14.	Primary Pupil Teacher Ratio	.167	**.834**	.024	.788	0.1549	3.46
15.	Upper Primary Pupil Teacher Ratio	-.100	**.698**	.498	.747	0.1297	2.89
16.	Secondary Pupil Teacher Ratio	-.244	**.654**	.285	.664	0.1215	2.71
17.	Population Below Poverty Line	.541	.018	**.667**	.748	0.0826	1.84
18.	Households with Access to Safe Drinking Water	.142	-.450	**.507**	.631	0.0628	1.40
	Eigen Values	7.489	3.344	2.229		4.4798	
	% age Variance Explained	41.605	18.579	12.381			
	Cum % age Variance Explained	41.605	60.184	72.565			

Source: Author's calculations.

The results of factor analysis for the year 1981 are presented in the table 6.1. Table 6.1 shows the factor loadings with three factors derived from the selected indicators. The three factors (F_1, F_2 and F_3) explain 72.56 per cent inter-state variations in development indicators. Communalities for all the indicators varied between 46.1 to 96.5 per cent, indicating that these three factors account for most of the variations in the selected indicators. The first factor (F_1) explains 41.6 per cent variations in the variable set. The most important indicators in the first factor are primary gross enrollment ratio, female literacy rate, followed by upper primary gross enrollment ratio, adult literacy rate, per capita net state domestic product and households with access to electricity. The other indicators included in this set are crude death rate, percentage share of industry in NSDP, infant mortality rate, per capita consumption of electricity, primary drop-out rate, urban population as percentage of total population and percentage share of services in NSDP. Most of these indicators are related to education and health.

The second factor (F_2), which explains 18.57 per cent of variations, includes indicators like primary pupil teacher ratio, upper primary pupil teacher ratio and secondary pupil teacher ratio.

Population below poverty line and households with access to safe drinking water constitutes the third factor (F_3), explaining 12.38 per cent variations in the variable set.

Composite Development Index

The weights calculated for the selected 18 indicators from 'Principal Component' for 22 Indian states have been used to develop the Composite Development Index and is presented in the table 6.2 along with ranking of the different states.

Table 6.2 shows that the value of index varies within the range of 0.1439 to 0.8493. Goa was at the top with highest value (0.8493) of composite development index among 22 states during 1981 followed by Kerala (0.7488), Punjab (0.6319), Maharashtra (0.6022), Tamil Nadu (0.5608) and Himachal Pradesh (0.5210). These are developed states as per composite development index.

Table 6.2: Composite Development Index for the Year 1981

States	Composite Development Index	Ranks
Andhra Pradesh	0.3053	15
Arunachal Pradesh	0.1757	21
Assam	0.2496	18
Bihar	0.1439	22
Goa	0.8493	01
Gujarat	0.4897	08
Himachal Pradesh	0.5210	06
Haryana	0.4763	09
Karnataka	0.4210	10
Kerala	0.7488	02
Manipur	0.4974	07
Madhya Pradesh	0.2222	19
Meghalaya	0.3927	13
Maharashtra	0.6022	04
Orissa	0.2569	17
Punjab	0.6319	03
Sikkim	0.4158	11
Rajasthan	0.2583	16
Tripura	0.3744	14
Tamil Nadu	0.5608	05
Uttar Pradesh	0.2016	20
West Bengal	0.3993	12

Source: Author's calculations.

Table further shows that Bihar has the lowest composite development index (0.1439). Other states having low value of index, (but more than Bihar) were Arunachal Pradesh (0.1757), Uttar Pradesh (0.2016), Madhya Pradesh (0.2222), Assam (0.2496) and Odisha (0.2569). These states are less developed as per this composite index.

Table 6.3: Results of Factor Analysis for the Year 1991

S. No	Variables	Factor Loadings					Commu-nalities	Weights	Wt in %
		Factor-1 F1	Factor-2 F2	Factor-3 F3	Factor-4 F4	Factor-5 F5			
		1	2	3	4	5			
1.	PCNSDP	**.793**	-.159	.389	-.106	.147	.839	0.3443	7.61
2.	Adult Literacy Rate	**.903**	.200	-.226	-.114	-.094	.929	0.3920	8.66
3.	Female Literacy Rate	**.884**	.254	-.257	-.110	-.119	.938	0.3838	8.48
4.	Primary Gross Enrolment Ratio	**.888**	-.118	-.055	-.246	-.160	.891	0.3855	8.52
5.	Upper Primary Gross Enrolment Ratio	**.916**	.238	.066	-.201	-.124	.956	0.3977	8.79
6.	Primary Drop-out Rate	**.683**	-.245	-.253	-.512	.020	.853	0.2965	6.55
7.	Population Below Poverty Line	**.730**	-.306	.230	.243	.055	.742	0.3169	7.00
8.	Households with Access to Electricity	**.815**	-.217	.447	.001	-.027	.911	0.3538	7.82
9.	Infant Mortality Rate	**.768**	.219	-.172	.302	-.306	.852	0.3334	7.37
10.	Crude Death Rate	**.716**	.230	-.202	.407	-.236	.828	0.3108	6.87
11.	Urban Population	**.594**	-.503	-.257	.405	.203	.877	0.2579	5.70
12.	Per Capita Consumption of Electricity	**.563**	-.671	.208	.086	.155	.842	0.2444	5.40
13.	Primary Pupil Teacher Ratio	.464	**.763**	.250	-.056	.147	.885	0.1321	2.92
14.	Upper Primary Pupil Teacher Ratio	.208	**.768**	.309	-.028	.175	.760	0.1329	2.94
15.	Secondary Pupil Teacher Ratio	.059	**.660**	.266	.459	.089	.728	0.1143	2.52
16.	Households with Access to Safe Drinking Water	-.028	-.536	**.626**	.200	-.339	.835	0.0715	1.58
17.	Share of Services	.183	-.106	-.811	**.252**	.172	.796	0.0169	0.37
18.	Share of Industry	.477	-.060	.072	.020	**.716**	.749	0.0406	0.90
	Eigen Values	7.814	3.116	2.056	1.204	1.021		4.5253	
	% age Variance Explained	43.413	17.311	11.4211	6.691	5.672			
	Cum % age Variance Explained	43.413	60.723	72.144	78.835	84.508			

Source: Author's calculations.

The results of factor analysis of selected variables for 22 states for the year 1991 are presented in the table 6.3. Table shows that five factors derived from 18 indicators under consideration explain 84.50 per cent inter-state variations. The communalities for these factors vary between 72.8 per cent and 95.6 per cent. The first factor (F_1) explains 43.41 per cent of variations in the variable set. Upper primary gross enrolment ratio, adult literacy rate, primary gross enrollment ratio, female literacy rate, households with access to electricity, per capita net state domestic product, infant mortality rate, population below poverty line, crude death rate, primary drop-out rate, urban population as percentage of total population and per capita consumption of electricity are the important indicators of first factor.

The second factor (F_2) explains 17.31 per cent of variations in the variable set, having primary pupil teacher ratio, upper primary pupil teacher ratio and secondary pupil teacher ratio as important indicators.

Households with access to safe drinking water constitute the third factor (F_3), which explains 11.42 per cent of variation. The fourth factor (F_4) explains 6.69 per cent of the variations with percentage share of services in NSDP as an important factor. The fifth factor (F_5) explains 5.67 per cent of the variations in the variable set which is based on percentage share of industry in NSDP.

Composite Development Index:

Composite development index has been developed on the basis of the 18 selected indicators by using weights calculated from all the 'principal components' for 22 states for the year 1991 and resulting ranks of states are presented in the table 6.4.

Table 6.4 shows that the value of index varies within the range of 0.1326 to 0.8441. Goa was at the top with highest value (0.8441) of composite development index among 22 states for which analysis has been undertaken. Other states which followed Goa were Kerala (0.7599), Punjab (0.6536), Maharashtra (0.5943), Himachal Pradesh (0.5671) and Haryana (0.5452).

Table further shows that Bihar has the lowest index of (0.1326). The states for which value of index was very low but more than Bihar were Uttar Pradesh (0.1917), Odisha (0.2362), Madhya Pradesh (0.2487), Rajasthan (0.2491) and Arunachal Pradesh (0.2582).

The results of factor analysis for the year 2001 are presented in the table 6.5. The table shows that the five factors taken together explain 83.28 per cent of variations in the variable set. The communalities for all indicators varied between 53 per cent and 94.9 per cent. The first factor (F_1) based on variables per capita net state domestic product, adult literacy rate, female literacy rate, primary pupil teacher ratio, upper primary pupil teacher ratio, secondary pupil teacher ratio, upper primary gross enrollment ratio, primary drop-out rate, population below poverty line, households with access to electricity, infant mortality rate and percentage share of industry in NSDP explains 41.19 per cent variations.

Table 6.4: Composite Development Index for the Year 1991

States	*Composite Development Index*	*Ranks*
Andhra Pradesh	0.3503	13
Arunachal Pradesh	0.2582	17
Assam	0.2757	15
Bihar	0.1326	22
Goa	0.8441	01
Gujarat	0.5337	08
Himachal Pradesh	0.5671	05
Haryana	0.5452	06
Karnataka	0.4344	11
Kerala	0.7599	02
Manipur	0.4879	09
Madhya Pradesh	0.2487	19
Meghalaya	0.3485	14
Maharashtra	0.5943	04
Odisha	0.2362	20
Punjab	0.6536	03
Sikkim	0.4793	10
Rajasthan	0.2491	18
Tripura	0.3887	12
Tamil Nadu	0.5399	07
Uttar Pradesh	0.1917	21
West Bengal	0.2707	16

Source: Author's calculations.

Households with access to safe drinking water, urban population as percentage of total population and per capita consumption of electricity constitutes the second factor (F_2), which explains 17.19 per cent of variations in the variable set.

The third factor (F_3) based on percentage share of services in NSDP explains 11.96 per cent of variations in the variable set. The fourth factor (F_4) explains 6.87 per cent variations with primary gross enrollment ratio. The fifth factor (F_5) which explains 6 per cent variations in the variable set is based on crude death rate.

Table 6.5: Results of Factor Analysis for the Year 2001

S. No.	Variables	Factor Loadings					Commu-nalities	weights	Wt in %
		Factor-1 F1	Factor-2 F2	Factor-3 F3	Factor-4 F4	Factor-5 F5			
		1	2	3	4	5			
1.	PCNSDP	**.847**	.281	-.227	-.132	-.048	.868	0.3489	8.51
2.	Adult Literacy Rate	**.881**	-.008	.335	.108	-.158	.925	0.3629	8.86
3.	Female Literacy Rate	**.873**	-.105	.362	.051	-.181	.940	0.3596	8.78
4.	Primary Pupil Teacher Ratio	**.647**	-.557	-.109	-.037	-.104	.752	0.2665	6.50
5.	Upper Primary Pupil Teacher Ratio	**.613**	-.517	-.385	-.111	-.213	.848	0.2525	6.16
6.	Secondary Pupil Teacher Ratio	**.268**	-.679	-.441	.243	-.045	.788	0.1104	2.69
7.	Upper Primary Gross Enrolment Ratio	**.760**	-.148	.208	.352	.214	.812	0.3131	7.64
8.	Primary Drop-out Rate	**.765**	.370	.151	.109	-.210	.801	0.3152	7.69
9.	Population Below Poverty Line	**.691**	-.090	-.085	-.118	.149	.530	0.2847	6.95
10.	Households with Access to Electricity	**.824**	.250	-.255	.084	.253	.877	0.3395	8.28
11.	Infant Mortality Rate	**.708**	-.226	.399	-.399	.168	.899	0.2917	7.12
12.	Share of Industry	**.746**	.034	-.452	.160	-.008	.788	0.3073	7.50
13.	Households with Access to Safe Drinking Water	-.196	**.700**	-.395	-.192	.346	.841	0.1204	2.94
14.	Urban Population	.567	**.665**	.052	.135	.020	.785	0.1144	2.79
15.	Per Capita Consumption of Electricity	.530	**.708**	-.227	.162	.017	.861	0.1218	2.97
16.	Share of Services	.005	.243	**.846**	.076	-.109	.792	0.1012	2.47
17.	Primary Gross Enrolment Ratio	-.253	-.291	.157	**.726**	.483	.935	0.0499	1.22
18.	Crude Death Rate	.459	-.328	.228	-.420	**.634**	.949	0.0384	0.94
	Eigen Values	7.415	3.095	2.153	1.238	1.090		4.0984	
	% age Variance Explained	41.197	17.197	11.963	6.876	6.055			
	Cum % age Variance Explained	41.197	58.394	70.356	77.232	83.287			

Source: Author's calculations.

Composite Development Index:

Composite development index based on the weights derived from the factor analysis and the resulting ranks of 22 states for the year 2001 are presented in the table 6.6. The table shows that Goa (0.8476) was at the top position followed by Kerala (0.7422), Himachal Pradesh (0.6876), Maharashtra (0.6404), Punjab (0.6272) and Tamil Nadu (0.6233). The table further shows that Bihar (0.0944) was at the bottom, while Uttar Pradesh (0.2683), Odisha (0.3109), Rajasthan (0.3644), West Bengal (0.3812), Assam (0.3887) and Madhya Pradesh (0.4055) slightly better placed than Bihar.

Table 6.6: Composite Development Index for the Year 2001

States	Composite Development Index	Ranks
Andhra Pradesh	0.4292	15
Arunachal Pradesh	0.4398	14
Assam	0.3887	17
Bihar	0.0944	22
Goa	0.8476	01
Gujarat	0.5361	11
Himachal Pradesh	0.6876	03
Haryana	0.5676	07
Karnataka	0.5473	10
Kerala	0.7422	02
Manipur	0.5657	08
Madhya Pradesh	0.4055	16
Meghalaya	0.4767	13
Maharashtra	0.6404	04
Odisha	0.3109	20
Punjab	0.6272	05
Sikkim	0.5519	09
Rajasthan	0.3644	19
Tripura	0.4911	12
Tamil Nadu	0.6233	06
Uttar Pradesh	0.2683	21
West Bengal	0.3812	18

Source: Author's calculations.

Table 6.7: Results of Factor Analysis for the Year 2011

S. No.	Variables	Factor Loadings				Commu-nalities	weights	Wt in %
		Factor-1 F1	Factor-2 F2	Factor-3 F3	Factor-4 F4			
		1	2	3	4			
1.	PCNSDP	**.847**	-.206	.215	.150	.829	0.3530	8.06
2.	Adult Literacy Rate	**.804**	-.039	-.451	.063	.855	0.3350	7.65
3.	Female Literacy Rate	**.767**	-.139	-.340	-.195	.761	0.3196	7.30
4.	Primary Pupil Teacher Ratio	**.762**	.282	-.061	-.219	.712	0.3175	7.25
5.	Secondary Pupil Teacher Ratio	**.652**	.456	.056	-.463	.851	0.2717	6.21
6.	Upper Primary Gross Enrolment Ratio	**.589**	.203	-.197	.129	.444	0.2454	5.61
7.	Primary Drop-out Rate	**.740**	-.473	.018	.007	.772	0.3084	7.04
8.	Population Below Poverty Line	**.847**	-.103	.106	-.248	.800	0.3530	8.06
9.	Households with Access to Electricity	**.908**	-.059	.192	-.014	.864	0.3784	8.64
10.	Infant Mortality Rate	**.715**	.084	-.345	.523	.911	0.2980	6.81
11.	Urban Population	**.669**	-.421	-.071	.330	.738	0.2788	6.37
12.	Per Capita Consumption of Electricity	**.655**	-.369	.572	-.008	.892	0.2730	6.24
13.	Share of Industry	**.567**	.478	.503	.178	.835	0.2363	5.40
14.	Share of Services	**-.017**	-.772	-.536	-.156	.908	0.0071	0.16
15.	Upper Primary Pupil Teacher Ratio	.521	**.578**	.034	-.490	.847	0.1065	2.43
16.	Primary Gross Enrolment Ratio	-.163	**.857**	.000	.201	.801	0.1580	3.61
17.	Households with Access to Safe Drinking Water	-.076	-.470	**.736**	.196	.807	0.0825	1.88
18.	Crude Death Rate	.305	.505	-.151	**.634**	.772	0.0551	
	Eigen Values	7.501	3.318	2.017	1.565		4.3772	
	% age Variance Explained	41.672	18.432	11.203	8.694			
	Cum % age Variance Explained	41.672	60.104	71.307	80.001			

Source: Author's calculations.

Table 6.7 reveals the results of factor analysis for the year 2011 for 22 states. The table shows that the four factors under consideration explain 80 per cent variations in the variable set. The communalities for all factors varied between 44.4 and 91.1percent in the variable set.

The first factor (F_1) explains 41.67 per cent variations in the variable set. The most important indicators in this factor are households with access to electricity followed by per capita net state domestic product, population below poverty line, adult literacy rate, female literacy rate, primary pupil teacher ratio, primary drop-out rate, infant mortality rate, urban population as percentage of total population, per capita consumption of electricity and secondary pupil teacher ratio. The other important indicators are upper primary gross enrollment ratio, percentage share of industry in NSDP and percentage share of services in NSDP.

Table 6.8: Composite Development Index for the Year 2011

States	Composite Development Index	Ranks
Andhra Pradesh	0.4713	14
Arunachal Pradesh	0.4776	13
Assam	0.2882	20
Bihar	0.0913	22
Goa	0.8446	01
Gujarat	0.5255	11
Himachal Pradesh	0.6899	04
Haryana	0.5420	10
Karnataka	0.5586	09
Kerala	0.7153	02
Manipur	0.4791	12
Madhya Pradesh	0.3749	17
Meghalaya	0.4369	15
Maharashtra	0.6015	07
Odisha	0.3476	19
Punjab	0.6574	06
Sikkim	0.6929	03
Rajasthan	0.3528	18
Tripura	0.5777	08
Tamil Nadu	0.6619	05
Uttar Pradesh	0.1840	21
West Bengal	0.4027	16

Source: Author's calculations.

The second factor (F_2) which explains 18.43 per cent variations includes indicators like upper primary pupil teacher ratio and primary gross enrollment ratio.

Households with access to safe drinking water constitute the third factor (F_3) which explains 11.20 per cent variations in the variable set. The fourth factor (F_4) explains 8.69 per cent variations in the variable set. The only important indicator in this set is crude death rate.

Composite Development Index:

Composite development index has been developed on the basis of 18 indicators by using weights calculated on the basis of factor analysis for 22 states and the resulting rank of states for the year 2011 are presented in the table 6.8.

The table shows that the index varies between 0.0913 and 0.8446. Goa occupies the top position with highest value (0.8446), followed by Kerala (0.7153), Sikkim (0.6929), Himachal Pradesh (0.6899), Tamil Nadu (0.6619) and Punjab (0.6574). Bihar with index value (0.0913) lies at the bottom with Uttar Pradesh (0.1840), Assam (0.2882), Odisha (0.3476), Rajasthan (0.3528) and Madhya Pradesh (0.3749) slightly better placed.

Section-II

Convergence-Divergence:

This section examines the trend of inequality in various indicators across states over the period of time, for which co-efficient of variation as a measure of convergence has been applied.

Co-efficients of variation of indicators have been worked out across states at four points of time 1981, 1991, 2001 and 2011 and are presented in the table 6.9.

Table reveals that the co-efficients of variation of indicators like per capita net state domestic product, primary pupil teacher ratio, upper primary pupil teacher ratio, secondary pupil teacher ratio, primary drop-out rate, percentage of population below poverty line, infant mortality rate and urban population as percentage of total population is increasing over the period 1981 to 2011, which indicates that the gap between the states has been widening in respect of these indicators. Whereas, the co-efficients of variation in respect of adult literacy rate, female literacy rate, primary gross enrollment ratio, upper primary gross enrollment ratio, household with access to safe drinking water, household with access to electricity, crude death rate, per capita consumption of electricity, percentage share of industry in NSDP and percentage share of services in NSDP has declined over the period, revealing convergence across states from 1981 to 2011 in respect of these indicators.

Table 6.9: Convergence/Divergence in Various Indicators for 22 states

S. No.	Variables	1981			1991			2001			2011		
		Mean	S.D.	C.V. (%)	Mean	S.D.	C.V. (%)	Mean	S.D.	C.V. (%)	Mean	S.D.	C.V. (%)
1.	PCNSDP	11775.32	3623.77	30.77	16128.41	5972.18	37.03	23231.65	10734.84	46.21	43567.76	22090.81	50.70
2.	Adult Literacy Rate	43.76	12.76	29.16	55.52	12.42	22.37	67.51	9.53	14.12	76.88	7.65	9.95
3.	Female Literacy Rate	33.17	14.34	43.24	43.90	14.85	33.83	58.02	11.73	20.21	69.34	10.94	15.78
4.	Primary Pupil Teacher Ratio	37.00	8.12	21.96	38.45	11.92	30.99	38.50	14.30	37.13	34.62	18.49	53.41
5.	Upper Primary Pupil Teacher Ratio	29.32	8.77	29.91	32.43	12.26	37.80	29.41	11.25	38.25	30.59	15.92	52.06
6.	Secondary Pupil Teacher Ratio	26.38	4.41	16.72	29.14	9.73	33.40	29.77	9.88	33.17	29.14	14.97	51.37
7.	Primary Gross Enrolment Ratio	52.10	15.58	29.91	56.20	16.17	28.77	99.56	17.81	17.89	123.60	31.55	25.52
8.	Upper Primary Gross Enrolment Ratio	54.74	12.93	23.61	67.20	12.08	17.97	68.01	16.94	24.91	90.39	13.01	14.39
9.	Primary Drop-out Rate	52.85	18.51	35.02	40.16	21.08	52.49	35.35	18.84	53.29	20.58	20.77	100.93
10.	Percentage of Population Below Poverty Line	39.04	13.39	34.29	33.61	10.40	30.96	33.39	10.56	31.64	25.02	12.03	48.09
11.	Households with Access to Safe Drinking Water	36.46	18.03	49.45	58.85	18.09	30.74	71.78	19.32	26.91	79.66	17.80	22.35
12.	Households With Access to Electricity	30.00	15.92	53.06	48.55	21.70	44.70	61.29	24.49	39.96	72.89	23.62	32.40
13.	Infant Mortality Rate	89.68	31.43	35.05	70.45	24.40	34.64	54.68	21.44	39.20	36.68	15.18	41.39
14.	Crude Death Rate	11.09	3.07	27.73	9.23	2.21	23.94	7.67	1.52	19.85	6.78	1.05	15.50
15.	Urban Population	20.79	8.59	41.34	23.13	9.57	41.40	25.56	11.20	43.83	30.61	13.28	43.38
16.	Per Capita Consumption of Electricity	127.08	88.88	69.94	254.41	160.53	63.10	369.91	245.35	66.33	838.16	516.40	61.61
17.	Share of Industry	21.03	6.75	32.10	23.09	7.23	31.32	24.97	6.85	27.45	28.01	8.23	29.40
18.	Share of Services	34.49	5.63	16.33	40.63	5.61	13.80	48.36	6.90	14.27	53.97	8.59	15.92

Source: Author's calculations.

Table 6.10: Convergence/Divergence in Composite Development Index

Variables	1981			1991			2001			2011		
	Mean	S.D.	C.V. (%)	Mean	S.D.	C.V. (%)	Mean	S.D.	C.V. (%)	Mean	S.D.	C.V. (%)
22 States	0.4179	0.1871	44.7749	0.4268	0.1902	44.5613	0.4994	0.1687	33.7846	0.4988	0.1824	36.5766

Source: Author's calculations.

The extent of convergence or divergence in respect of composite development index has been worked out and results are presented in the table 6.10. Table shows that the coefficient of variation remains more or less same from 1981 to 1991, but decreased to 33.78 per cent in 2001 from 44.56 per cent in 1991 indicating that the poor states are catching up with rich ones in terms of composite development index during this time period. However, study shows diverging tendencies across Indian states in terms of composite development index from 2001 to 2011.

Section-III

Conclusion

This chapter analyses and compares the position of 22 Indian states for the year 1981, 1991, 2001 and 2011 by constructing composite development index on the basis of education, health, nutrition, sanitation and economic indicators. The results of the study shows that the value of the index varies within the range of 0.1439 to 0.8493 and Goa was at the top with highest value (0.8493) of composite development index during the year 1981 among 22 states followed by Kerala, Punjab, Maharashtra, Tamil Nadu and Himachal Pradesh. Bihar remained at the last position with lowest (0.1439) value of index. In the year 1991, Goa again occupied the top position with highest value (0.8441) of composite development index followed by Kerala, Punjab, Maharashtra, Himachal Pradesh and Haryana. Bihar again remained at its lowest position with (0.1326) value of index. It is noted that the four states namely Goa, Kerala, Punjab and Maharashtra remained stick to its position by occupying 1st, 2nd, 3rd and 4th positions respectively during the year 1981 and 1991.

For the year 2001, Goa (0.8476) again was at the top most position followed by Kerala, Himachal Pradesh, Maharashtra, Punjab and Tamil Nadu. However, Punjab drifted from third position in 1991 to fifth in

2001. Bihar (0.0944) remained at the last position, while Uttar Pradesh, Odisha, Rajasthan, West Bengal, Assam and Madhya Pradesh slightly better placed than Bihar. The analysis for the year 2011 also found Goa at the first position with highest (0.8446) value of index, followed by Kerala, Sikkim, Himachal Pradesh, Tamil Nadu and Punjab. Bihar has the lowest (0.0913) index during 2011 also. It is also notable that Goa and Kerala were the only states which remained at 1st and 2nd positions respectively at four points of time. Punjab further drifted to 6th position in 2011 from 5th in 2001.

Further, the extent of convergence or divergence in respect of various indicators and composite development index has been worked out by using co-efficient of variation as a measure of convergence/ divergence. The analysis of convergence or divergence of various indicators reveals that the co-efficients of variation in respect of adult literacy rate, female literacy rate, primary gross enrollment ratio, upper primary gross enrollment ratio, household with access to safe drinking water, household with access to electricity, crude death rate, per capita consumption of electricity, percentage share of industry in NSDP and percentage share of services in NSDP has declined over the period, revealing convergence across states from 1981 to 2011 in respect of these indicators. However, divergence in terms of remaining 8 indicators.

Regarding the composite development index, study shows that the co-efficient of variation of the composite development index remains more or less constant (44 per cent) from 1981 to 1991, but declined to 33.78 per cent in 2001 from 44.56 per cent in 1991 indicating that poor states catched up with rich ones in terms of composite development index during this period. However, the co-efficient of variation increased to 36.57 per cent in 2011 from 33.78 per cent in 2001 revealing that the states have diverged in terms of composite development index during 2001 to 2011. It is also notable that the states have been converging in terms of composite development index for the overall period (1981 to 2011), as the co-efficient of variation decreased from 44 per cent to 36 per cent respectively.

Overall, the study concludes that not much change has occured in the ranks of the states, as the best performing states (like Goa,

Kerala Maharashtra, Himachal Pradesh and Tamil Nadu) remains the best and the worst performing states (like Bihar, Madhya Pradesh, Odisha, Rajasthan and Uttar Pradesh) remains the worst. Furthermore, study reveals a clear evidence of an increasing trend in the regional disparity in per capita net state domestic product as the co-efficient of variation increased to 50.70 per cent in 2011 from 30.77 per cent in 1981. This suggests that poor states have failed to catch up with rich ones in terms of per capita income. Thus, there is a need for policy measures on the part of the poor states to improve their per capita income as other issues will be addressed automatically in order to catch up with rich ones.

Chapter 7

Measuring Human Poverty in India: An Inter-State Analysis

Poverty is a complex phenomenon and is difficult to define in a simple way. In terms of human survival, poverty means shortage of food, but in economic terms, poverty may be defined as the inability of a person to get the minimum needs fulfilled for leading a simple and healthy life. These minimum needs include food, clothing, housing, education and basic health requirements. Thus, poverty is the state, where a person is in want of basic necessities of human existence (Ganguli, 1971). Poverty inflicts suffering on individuals. The capacity of a person to acquire the necessities of life divides the individuals into the category of economically well off and the poor. At the individual level, it leads to a life full of hardship and suffering. At the national level it manifests as shortage of resources and non-availability of essential goods and services to meet the requirement of a growing population (Ramaswamy, 1980).

The problem of poverty in India has received considerable attention among researchers and policy makers. Alleviation of poverty has been one of the primary objectives of Indian planning. The concerns for achieving high growth, improving the standard of living of the population and alleviation of poverty, have been expressed in government's policies and programmes (Ghosh, 2013). The inter-State differences in human poverty are quite striking. It was in the range of 55-60 per cent in the early eighties for the worse off States, namely Odisha, Bihar, Arunachal Pradesh, Assam and Uttar Pradesh and between 32-35 per cent in the better off States like Kerala, Punjab and Himachal Pradesh. The magnitude of human poverty in early nineties had declined in all the States. However, the relative positions of different States remained quite similar to the earlier period. The decline in human poverty was significant in case of Himachal Pradesh, Tamil Nadu, Maharashtra, Jammu and Kashmir, Karnataka and Kerala. In case of Bihar, Uttar Pradesh and Rajasthan, the decline was only marginal (NHDR, 2001).

The concept of Human Poverty Index (HPI) introduced in the Human Development Report 1997, concentrates on deprivation in three basic elements of human life-health, knowledge and a decent living standard. The present study examines the deprivations in these three basic elements of human life and work out the level of human poverty in the light of the experience of 25 Indian states namely Andhra Pradesh, Arunachal Pradesh, Assam, Bihar, Goa, Gujarat, Himachal Pradesh, Haryana, Jammu and Kashmir, Karnataka, Kerala, Manipur, Madhya Pradesh, Meghalaya, Maharashtra, Mizoram, Odisha, Nagaland, Punjab, Sikkim, Rajasthan, Tripura, Tamil Nadu, Uttar Pradesh and West Bengal for the year 2001 and 2011. Effort has also been made to compare the positions of 15 major states of India with respect to human development index, human poverty index and per capita NSDP. This comparison has been done to see the relative performances of these states with respect to these two indices and to find out whether there has occurred any change in the relative position of these states in the year 2011 as compared to the year 2001.

For this purpose the chapter has been divided into 4 Sections. Section I represents the computations of HPI for 25 Indian states for the years 2001 and 2011. In Section II HPI in 2011 which is based on human deprivation has been compared with poverty head count ratio for the year 2009-10. Section III represents the relative comparison of 15 major Indian states with respect to HDI, HPI and Per Capita NSDP. The whole discussion has been concluded in Section IV.

Section–I

Following the UNDP's methodology, human poverty index (HPI) based on three deprivations viz., health, knowledge and economic for 25 Indian states for the year 2001and 2011has been computed in this section.

Table 7.1: Health Deprivation (P_1) Captured by the Infant Mortality Rate and Undernourished Children: 2001 and 2011.

States	Health Deprivation (P_1)		Difference in 2011 over 2001
	2001	2011	(Per cent)
Andhra Pradesh	50.1	36.4	13.7
Arunachal Pradesh	30.25	30.8	-0.55
Assam	54.65	45.4	9.25
Bihar	57.1	49.5	7.6
Goa	20.15	16.2	3.95
Gujarat	50.8	41.15	9.65
Himachal Pradesh	45.25	34.55	10.7
Haryana	47.95	41.1	6.85
Jammu and Kashmir	38.6	32.5	6.1
Karnataka	48.3	34.1	14.2
Kerala	16.35	16.6	2.8
Manipur	20.05	15.25	4.8
Madhya Pradesh	68.4	58.45	9.95
Meghalaya	42.3	47.45	-5.15
Maharashtra	44.9	28.75	16.15
Mizoram	19.4	24.15	-4.75
Odisha	70.65	48.2	22.45
Nagaland	15.9	22.3	-6.4
Punjab	38.35	26.8	11.55
Sikkim	28.75	21.65	7.1
Rajasthan	63.35	44.45	18.9
Tripura	25.55	32.1	-6.55
Tamil Nadu	40.25	23.95	16.3
Uttar Pradesh	65.55	49.25	16.3
West Bengal	48.15	34.8	13.35
India	54.35	42.2	12.15

Note: A positive difference indicates that the health deprivation (P_1) has improved over time and a negative value indicates deterioration.

Source: Author's calculations.

Health Deprivation:

Health deprivation (P_1) was derived on the basis of infant mortality rate and child undernourishment. Health deprivation (P_1) for the year 2001 and 2011, along with differences in 2011 over 2001 is presented in table 7.1.

Table shows that the value of P_1 had declined over time, except in case of North-Eastern states- Arunachal Pradesh, Meghalaya, Mizoram, Nagaland and Tripura- where it has increased by 0.55, 5.15, 4.75, 6.4 and 6.55 per cent respectively. Table shows that for the year 2001, Odisha (70.65), Madhya Pradesh (68.4), Uttar Pradesh (65.55), Rajasthan (63.35), Bihar (57.1), Assam (54.65), Gujarat (50.8), Andhra Pradesh (50.1), Karnataka (48.3), West Bengal (48.15) and Haryana (47.95) were the other states having high health deprivation, however, health deprivation decline has been observed for these states in 2011. The improvement made by these states lies between 7 to 22 per cent points and of these states, only six states namely Odisha, Madhya Pradesh, Uttar Pradesh, Rajasthan, Bihar and Assam were the states having health deprivation higher than the All India Average. It is also notable that Odisha (70.65) was the worst performing state in 2001, however, it has shown the maximum improvement of 22.45 per cent points over time. Manipur with a decline of just 4.8 per cent is the state after Kerala which has least health deprivation for the year 2011.

Table also shows that although the health deprivation for almost all the states has gone down overtime but the worst performing state in 2001 (like Madhya Pradesh, Uttar Pradesh, Odisha and Bihar) remains the worst performing in 2011 as well and the best performing states in 2001 (like Kerala, Goa and Manipur) still continues to be best in 2011.

Knowledge Deprivation:

Knowledge deprivation (P_2), based on illiteracy rate and non-enrollment ratio for the year 2001 and 2011 is presented in table 7.2. Table shows that the knowledge deprivation has declined overtime in all the states. Among the states, education deprivation was highest in Bihar in both the years under consideration (64 in 2001 and 35.67 in 2011). Although, Bihar was the worst performing state in both the years, however, it has shown an improvement of (28.33 per cent) overtime. For the year 2001, Uttar Pradesh (56.96), Andhra Pradesh

(44.85), Odisha (41.59) and West Bengal (40.95) were the other states having high educational deprivation but the deprivation for these four states also declined in 2011. Of these Uttar Pradesh had shown better performance on this front whereas, Andhra Pradesh and Odisha had shown the same improvement with 20.60 per cent.

Table 7.2: Knowledge Deprivation Captured by the Illiteracy Rate and Non-enrolment Ratio: 2001 and 2011

States	Knowledge Deprivation (P2)		Difference in 2011 over 2001 (Per cent)
	2001	2011	
Andhra Pradesh	44.85	24.25	20.60
Arunachal Pradesh	35.47	7.99	27.48
Assam	31.95	30.25	1.70
Bihar	64.00	35.67	28.33
Goa	25.45	7.14	18.31
Gujarat	29.87	16.54	13.33
Himachal Pradesh	12.86	-3.29	16.15
Haryana	33.44	18.90	14.53
Jammu and Kashmir	32.21	14.39	17.83
Karnataka	28.62	14.59	14.04
Kerala	4.65	-0.40	5.05
Manipur	24.71	4.06	20.64
Madhya Pradesh	39.17	9.37	29.80
Meghalaya	38.56	14.43	24.13
Maharashtra	14.50	10.92	3.58
Mizoram	16.95	-0.17	17.13
Odisha	41.59	20.99	20.60
Nagaland	37.52	32.96	4.56
Punjab	33.45	12.06	21.39
Sikkim	32.66	20.01	12.65
Rajasthan	29.33	22.97	6.36
Tripura	30.45	9.55	20.90
Tamil Nadu	14.12	-1.11	15.23
Uttar Pradesh	56.96	23.66	33.30
West Bengal	40.95	16.93	24.03
India	31.06	18.51	12.55

Note: A positive difference indicates that the knowledge deprivation (P_2) has improved over time and a negative value indicates deterioration.

Source: Author's calculations.

Further, table shows that the worst performing states like Uttar Pradesh, Madhya Pradesh and Bihar were the states which have shown maximum improvement of 33.30, 29.80 and 28.33 per cent during the period and the gap between the worst performing states (Bihar, Uttar Pradesh and Odisha) and best performing states (Kerala, Tamil Nadu and Maharashtra) has narrowed down overtime.

Economic Deprivation:

Economic deprivation (P_3) for the year 2001 and 2011 is presented in table 7.3. Table shows that by 2011, the proportion of population with economic deprivation had declined in all the states. Among all the states, economic deprivation was highest in Bihar in 2001(65.46) as well as in 2011(57.44). The other states for which deprivation was high in both the years were Assam, Madhya Pradesh, Meghalaya, Odisha, Rajasthan and Uttar Pradesh. However, Goa, Himachal Pradesh, Haryana, Punjab and Tamil Nadu were the states with least economic deprivation in both the years. By 2011, economic deprivation for Bihar, Assam, Madhya Pradesh, Meghalaya, Odisha, Rajasthan and Uttar Pradesh declined between 4 to 13 per cent. Table highlights that even in Kerala, a high proportion (32.48 per cent in 2001 and 22.72 per cent in 2011) was deprived in terms of economic provisioning, but overtime the deprivation has declined by 9.76 per cent. Further, Punjab (20.5 per cent) in 2001 and Goa (13.56 per cent) in 2011 were the states with best performance on economic deprivation. Himachal Pradesh, Sikkim, Punjab, Haryana and Tamil Nadu were the other five states besides Goa with better performance during 2011 on this front.

Furthermore, the table shows that the worst performing states like that of Bihar, Odisha, Madhya Pradesh, Uttar Pradesh and Assam of 2001 remains the worst performing in 2011 as well and the best performing states like Goa, Punjab and Tamil Nadu remains the best over the period of time. At the all India level, economic deprivation has fallen by just 7.7 per cent and still very high proportion of population (37.32) is economically deprived.

Indices on three aspects of deprivation viz. health (P_1), knowledge (P_2) and economic (P_3) have been used to construct the composite index of deprivation, called human poverty index. The values of the human poverty index (HPI) for the year 2001 and 2011 are presented in table 7.4 and 7.5 respectively. Further, the ranking of different states for the human poverty index has been presented in Table 7.6.

Table 7.3: Economic Deprivation (P_3) captured by the proportion of population below poverty line, proportion of population not fully vaccinated, proportion of population without safe Drinking water, proportion of population without electricity and without toilet facility: 2001 and 2011

States	Economic Deprivation (P_3) 2001	Economic Deprivation (P_3) 2011	Difference in 2011 over 2001 (Per cent)
Andhra Pradesh	38.12	28.56	9.56
Arunachal Pradesh	44.48	38.24	6.24
Assam	53.82	46.92	6.9
Bihar	65.46	57.44	8.02
Goa	24	13.56	10.44
Gujarat	33.9	27.96	5.94
Himachal Pradesh	24.54	15.14	9.4
Haryana	29.58	20.38	9.2
Jammu and Kashmir	31.5	25.92	5.58
Karnataka	34.56	27.86	6.7
Kerala	32.48	22.72	9.76
Manipur	43.32	39.44	3.88
Madhya Pradesh	52.76	44.5	8.26
Meghalaya	53.78	43.14	10.64
Maharashtra	33.46	29.06	4.4
Mizoram	32.24	27.62	4.62
Odisha	61.5	48.98	12.52
Nagaland	42.8	37.6	5.2
Punjab	20.5	16.46	4.04
Sikkim	34.32	15.7	18.62
Rajasthan	53.04	43.64	9.4
Tripura	32.86	29.16	3.7
Tamil Nadu	28.22	20.4	7.82
Uttar Pradesh	53.72	49.44	4.28
West Bengal	44.16	31.38	12.78
India	45.02	37.32	7.7

Note: A positive difference indicates that the economic deprivation (P_3) has improved over time and a negative value indicates deterioration.

Source: Author's Calculations.

Table 7.4: Human Poverty Index Based on P_1, P_2, P_3, for the year 2001

States	P_1	P_2	P_3	P_1^3	P_2^3	P_3^3	$\sum_{i=1}^{3} P_i^3$	$\frac{\sum_{i=1}^{3} P_i^3}{3}$	$\sqrt[3]{\frac{\sum_{i=1}^{3} P_i^3}{3}}$
Andhra Pradesh	50.10	44.85	38.12	125751.50	90237.91	55393.48	271382.89	90460.96	44.89
Arunachal Pradesh	30.25	35.47	44.48	27680.64	44618.00	88002.36	160301.00	53433.67	37.67
Assam	54.65	31.95	53.82	163218.92	32623.83	155894.60	351737.35	117245.78	48.94
Bihar	57.10	64.00	65.46	186169.41	262199.30	280496.86	728865.57	242955.19	62.40
Goa	20.15	25.45	24.00	8181.35	16475.29	13824.00	38480.64	12826.88	23.41
Gujarat	50.80	29.87	33.90	131096.51	26638.48	38958.22	196693.21	65564.40	40.32
Himachal Pradesh	45.25	12.86	24.54	92652.20	2126.78	14778.27	109557.26	36519.09	33.18
Haryana	47.95	33.44	29.58	110246.76	37378.64	25881.80	173507.20	57835.73	38.67
Jammu and Kashmir	38.60	32.21	31.50	57512.46	33431.37	31255.88	122199.70	40733.23	34.41
Karnataka	48.30	28.62	34.56	112678.59	23446.45	41278.24	177403.28	59134.43	38.96
Kerala	16.35	4.65	32.48	4370.72	100.45	34264.79	38735.96	12911.99	23.46
Manipur	20.05	24.71	43.32	8060.15	15079.29	81295.28	104434.72	34811.57	32.65
Madhya Pradesh	68.40	39.17	52.76	320013.50	60077.39	146863.66	526954.55	175651.52	56.00
Meghalaya	42.30	38.56	53.78	75686.97	57353.92	155547.27	288588.16	96196.05	45.82
Maharashtra	44.90	14.50	33.46	90518.85	3049.26	37460.87	131028.97	43676.32	35.22
Mizoram	19.40	16.95	32.24	7301.38	4871.93	33510.82	45684.14	15228.05	24.79
Orissa	70.65	41.59	61.50	352644.00	71957.56	232608.38	657209.93	219069.98	60.28
Nagaland	15.90	37.52	42.80	4019.68	52837.80	78402.75	135260.23	45086.74	35.59
Punjab	38.35	33.45	20.50	56402.21	37428.97	8615.13	102446.30	34148.77	32.44
Sikkim	28.75	32.66	34.32	23763.67	34834.43	40424.24	99022.33	33007.44	32.08
Rajasthan	63.35	29.33	53.04	254237.65	25238.84	149214.33	428690.82	142896.94	52.28
Tripura	25.55	30.45	32.86	16679.10	28233.32	35481.56	80393.98	26797.99	29.92
Tamil Nadu	40.25	14.12	28.22	65207.52	2816.36	22473.52	90497.39	30165.80	31.13
Uttar Pradesh	65.55	56.96	53.72	281655.40	184842.33	155027.24	621524.97	207174.99	59.17
West Bengal	48.15	40.95	44.16	111632.04	68689.28	86116.66	266437.99	88812.66	44.62
India	54.35	31.06	45.02	160545.69	29959.97	91246.55	281752.22	93917.41	45.46

Source: Author's Calculations.

Table 7.5: Human Poverty Index Based on P_1, P_2, P_3, for the year 2011

States	P_1	P_2	P_3	P_1^3	P_2^3	P_3^3	$\sum_{i=1}^{3} P_i^3$	$\frac{\sum_{i=1}^{3} P_i^3}{3}$	$\sqrt[3]{\frac{\sum_{i=1}^{3} P_i^3}{3}}$
Andhra Pradesh	36.40	24.25	28.56	48228.54	14267.57	23295.64	85791.76	28597.25	30.58
Arunachal Pradesh	30.80	7.99	38.24	29218.11	510.56	55918.26	85646.93	28548.98	30.56
Assam	45.40	30.25	46.92	93576.66	27686.13	103293.74	224556.54	74852.18	42.14
Bihar	49.50	35.67	57.44	121287.38	45396.14	189514.87	356198.38	118732.79	49.15
Goa	16.20	7.14	13.56	4251.53	363.99	2493.33	7108.85	2369.62	13.33
Gujarat	41.15	16.54	27.96	69680.22	4522.00	21858.05	96060.28	32020.09	31.75
Himachal Pradesh	34.55	-3.29	15.14	41242.42	-35.71	3470.38	44677.10	14892.37	24.60
Haryana	41.10	18.90	20.38	69426.53	6752.34	8464.72	84643.59	28214.53	30.44
Jammu and Kashmir	32.50	14.39	25.92	34328.13	2977.28	17414.26	54719.67	18239.89	26.32
Karnataka	34.10	14.59	27.86	39651.82	3102.55	21624.36	64378.74	21459.58	27.79
Kerala	13.55	-0.40	22.72	2487.81	-0.07	11728.03	14215.78	4738.59	16.80
Manipur	15.25	4.06	39.44	3546.58	67.05	61349.46	64963.08	21654.36	27.87
Madhya Pradesh	58.45	9.37	44.50	199688.73	822.53	88121.13	288632.38	96210.79	45.82
Meghalaya	47.45	14.43	43.14	106833.79	3005.93	80286.11	190125.84	63375.28	39.87
Maharashtra	28.75	10.92	29.06	23763.67	1302.71	24540.69	49607.07	16535.69	25.48
Mizoram	24.15	-0.17	27.62	14084.82	-0.01	21070.31	35155.13	11718.38	22.71
Orissa	48.20	20.99	48.98	111980.17	9251.08	117505.00	238736.25	79578.75	43.01
Nagaland	22.30	32.96	37.60	11089.57	35811.37	53157.38	100058.31	33352.77	32.19
Punjab	26.80	12.06	16.46	19248.83	1754.92	4459.53	25463.29	8487.76	20.40
Sikkim	21.65	20.01	15.70	10147.84	8012.01	3869.89	22029.74	7343.25	19.44
Rajasthan	44.45	22.97	43.64	87824.42	12117.87	83110.18	183052.47	61017.49	39.37
Tripura	32.10	9.55	29.16	33076.16	871.67	24794.91	58742.74	19580.91	26.95
Tamil Nadu	23.95	-1.11	20.40	13737.78	-1.37	8489.66	22226.07	7408.69	19.49
Uttar Pradesh	49.25	23.66	49.44	119458.95	13249.80	120846.86	253555.62	84518.54	43.89
West Bengal	34.80	16.93	31.38	42144.19	4849.98	30900.02	77894.20	25964.73	29.61
India	42.20	18.51	37.32	75151.45	6342.93	51978.64	133473.01	44491.00	35.43

Source: Author's Calculations.

Table 7.6: Human Poverty Index for the Year 2001 and 2011

States	Human Poverty Index			
	2001		2011	
	Value	Rank	Value	Rank
Andhra Pradesh	44.89	18	30.58	16
Arunachal Pradesh	37.67	13	30.56	15
Assam	48.94	20	42.14	21
Bihar	62.40	25	49.15	25
Goa	23.41	1	13.33	1
Gujarat	40.32	16	31.75	17
Himachal Pradesh	33.18	9	24.60	7
Haryana	38.67	14	30.44	14
Jammu and Kashmir	34.41	10	26.32	9
Karnataka	38.96	15	27.79	11
Kerala	23.46	2	16.80	2
Manipur	32.65	8	27.87	12
Madhya Pradesh	56.00	22	45.82	24
Meghalaya	45.82	19	39.87	20
Maharashtra	35.22	11	25.48	8
Mizoram	24.79	3	22.71	6
Odisha	60.28	24	43.01	22
Nagaland	35.59	12	32.19	18
Punjab	32.44	7	20.40	5
Sikkim	32.08	6	19.44	3
Rajasthan	52.28	21	39.37	19
Tripura	29.92	4	26.95	10
Tamil Nadu	31.13	5	19.49	4
Uttar Pradesh	59.17	23	43.89	23
West Bengal	44.62	17	29.61	13
India	45.46		35.43	

Source: Author's Calculations.

Table 7.6 shows that Bihar is the worst performing state in terms of HPI for both the years 2001 and 2011. For the year 2001, Odisha (60.28), Uttar Pradesh (59.17), Madhya Pradesh (56.00) Rajasthan

(52.28) and Assam (48.94) were the other worst performing states besides Bihar which occupied 24th, 23rd, 22nd, 21st and 20th ranks respectively. On the other hand Goa, Kerala, Mizoram, Tripura and Tamil Nadu were the states with low HPI during 2001. Further during the year 2011, Madhya Pradesh (45.82), Uttar Pradesh (43.89), Odisha (43.01) and Assam (42.14) were the other worst performing states besides Bihar whereas Goa, Kerala, Sikkim, Tamil Nadu and Punjab were the states with best performance on this front. Overtime, the rank of Rajasthan (19 from 21) and Odisha improved to (22 from 24), whereas that of Madhya Pradesh worsened (24 from 22) and the rank of Bihar and Uttar Pradesh remained same. The states of Goa and Kerala occupied same positions and remained best performing states during both the years. Furthermore, Karnataka, Maharashtra, Haryana, Andhra Pradesh, Gujarat and West Bengal were the six states which occupied middle order ranks for HPI for both the years i.e. 2001 and 2011.

It is clear from the table that although the values of HPI had declined for most of the states by the year 2011 still the gap between the worst performing states (Bihar, Odisha and Uttar Pradesh) and best performing states (Kerala, Tamil Nadu and Punjab) has remained almost the same.

Section–II

In this section effort has been made to analyse the relative performance of different states in terms of HPI in 2011 based on human deprivation and poverty head count ratio for the year 2009-10.

Human Poverty Index and Poverty Head Count Ratio for the year 2009-10 is presented in table 7.7.

Table shows that Kerala was the best performing state with least human poverty index as well as poverty head count ratio. Bihar remained the worst performing by occupying 15th rank in both the concepts. Overall, it shows that all worst performing states (in terms of HPI) like Bihar, Uttar Pradesh, Madhya Pradesh and Odisha remained worst in terms of poverty head count ratio and the best were the best on both the counts.

Table 7.7: Relative Performance of 15 Indian States on HPI and Poverty Head Count Ratio

States	Human Poverty Index		Poverty Head Count Ratio* (%)	
	2011		2009-10	
	Value	Rank	Value	Rank
Andhra Pradesh	30.58	8	21.1	5
Assam	42.14	11	37.9	14
Bihar	49.15	15	53.5	15
Gujarat	31.75	9	23.0	6
Haryana	30.44	7	20.1	4
Karnataka	27.79	5	23.6	7
Kerala	16.8	1	12.0	1
Madhya Pradesh	45.82	14	36.7	11
Maharashtra	25.48	4	24.5	8
Orissa	43.01	12	37.0	12
Punjab	20.4	3	15.9	2
Rajasthan	39.37	10	24.8	9
Tamil Nadu	19.49	2	17.1	3
Uttar Pradesh	43.89	13	37.7	13
West Bengal	29.61	6	26.7	10
India	35.43		29.8	

Note: *Figures of poverty are estimated by Tendulkar Methodology.

Source: Government of India, Planning Commission, November, 2009

Section–III

In this section, fifteen major states have been ranked according to HDI, HPI and PCNSDP. The relative performance of each state in the context of these indices has been analysed for the years 2001 and 2011. For a better understanding, the states are classified on the basis of their ranks. Hence, states with ranks 1 to 5 could be considered to be better performers than others and those with ranks 11 to 15 as worst performers. HDI, HPI and PCNSDP for major states with ranks in 2001 are presented in table 7.8.

Table 7.8: Relative Performance of 15 Major States on HDI, HPI and PCNSDP for the year 2001

States	2001					
	HDI		HPI		Per capita NSDP* (Rs.)	
	Value	Rank	Value	Rank	Value	Rank
Andhra Pradesh	0.416	10	44.89	9	21776	8
Assam	0.386	14	48.94	10	14813	12
Bihar	0.367	15	62.40	15	6777	15
Gujarat	0.479	6	40.32	7	24787	6
Haryana	0.509	5	38.67	5	31191	3
Karnataka	0.478	7	38.96	6	23327	7
Kerala	0.638	1	23.46	1	25545	5
Madhya Pradesh	0.394	12	56.00	12	14874	11
Maharashtra	0.523	4	35.22	4	31821	1
Odisha	0.404	11	60.28	14	13780	13
Punjab	0.537	2	32.44	3	31631	2
Rajasthan	0.424	9	52.28	11	16928	10
Tamil Nadu	0.531	3	31.13	2	26876	4
Uttar Pradesh	0.388	13	59.17	13	12071	14
West Bengal	0.472	8	44.62	8	20103	9
All India	0.472		45.46		20906	

Note: * denotes PCNSDP for 2001-02 at 2004-05 prices.

Table 7.8 shows that HDI was 0.472 for the country as a whole whereas HPI and Per Capita NSDP were 45.46 and ₹20906 respectively. For the year 2001, Kerala {with HDI (0.638) and HPI

(23.46)} occupied first position amongst major states while in terms of Per Capita NSDP (₹ 25545), Kerala was at 5th rank. Maharashtra, which was at the top in terms of Per Capita NSDP (₹ 31821), occupied 4th position in terms of HDI (0.523) and HPI (35.22). Punjab, on the other hand ranked 2nd in terms of HDI (0.537) and Per Capita NSDP (₹ 31631) and 3rd in terms of HPI. Haryana, which occupied 5th position in terms of HDI and HPI, occupied 3rd rank in terms of Per Capita NSDP. Tamil Nadu occupied 3rd rank in terms of HDI (0.531), 2nd in terms of HPI (31.13), whereas 4th in terms of Per Capita NSDP. Gujarat, which remained at 6th position in terms of HDI and PCNSDP, ranked 7th for HPI. Table also shows that Bihar, Odisha, Assam, Uttar Pradesh and Madhya Pradesh were worst performing states in terms of all the three measures. Of these states, Bihar in terms of HDI (0.367), HPI (62.40) and PCNSDP (₹ 6777) was at the bottom (15th position), amongst all the 15 major states. On the other hand, Madhya Pradesh and Uttar Pradesh occupied 12th and 13th positions in terms of HDI and HPI and ranked 11th and 14th in terms of Per Capita NSDP respectively for the year 2001.

HDI, HPI and Per Capita NSDP for 15 major states for the year 2011 are presented in table 7.9. Table shows that Kerala showed the same performance by remaining at the top position with (0.625) HDI and HPI (16.80) but occupied 5th position in terms of Per Capita NSDP (₹ 53877) as was during 2001. Tamil Nadu was at the top in terms of Per Capita NSDP (₹ 84496), followed by Maharashtra (₹ 64951), Haryana (₹ 62927) and Gujarat (₹ 57508). On the other hand Tamil Nadu occupied 2nd rank in terms of HPI, followed by Punjab, Maharashtra and Karnataka. In terms of HDI, after Kerala, Punjab occupied 2nd rank (0.569), followed by Maharashtra (0.549), Haryana (0.545) and Tamil Nadu (0.544). Further, Odisha, Bihar, Madhya Pradesh, Assam and Uttar Pradesh were again the five worst performing states in terms of HDI, HPI and Per Capita NSDP for the year 2011. Overtime comparison shows that the gap between the worst performing state and best performing state has narrowed down in terms of human poverty index and human development index. However, in case of per capita NSDP the gap between the worst performing state and best performing state has widened over the period of time. As compared to the year 2001, these 15 states had experienced some changes in their positions in the year 2011. However, worst performing states like Bihar, Uttar Pradesh, Odisha and Madhya Pradesh in terms of HDI, HPI and Per Capita NSDP in 2001 remained the worst performer in 2011 also. Further, according to HDI, HPI and Per Capita NSDP the states like Kerala, Punjab, Haryana, Gujarat, Tamil Nadu and Maharashtra were the best performers in both the years.

Table 7.9: Relative Performance of 15 Major States on HDI, HPI and PCNSDP for the year 2011

States	2011					
	HDI		HPI		Per capita NSDP* (Rs.)	
	Value	Rank	Value	Rank	Value	Rank
Andhra Pradesh	0.485	9	30.58	8	42119	8
Assam	0.474	10	42.14	11	22910	13
Bihar	0.447	14	49.15	15	13178	15
Gujarat	0.514	6	31.75	9	57508	4
Haryana	0.545	4	30.44	7	62927	3
Karnataka	0.508	8	27.79	5	42218	7
Kerala	0.625	1	16.80	1	53877	5
Madhya Pradesh	0.451	13	45.82	14	24395	11
Maharashtra	0.549	3	25.48	4	64951	2
Odisha	0.442	15	43.01	12	24134	12
Punjab	0.569	2	20.4	3	46422	6
Rajasthan	0.468	11	39.37	10	28851	10
Tamil Nadu	0.544	5	19.49	2	84496	1
Uttar Pradesh	0.468	11	43.89	13	18249	14
West Bengal	0.509	7	29.61	6	34166	9
All India	0.504		35.43		35993	

Note: * denotes PCNSDP for 2011-12 at 2004-05 prices.

Section–IV

Conclusion:

Health deprivation (P_1), knowledge deprivation (P_2), and economic deprivation (P_3) has been worked to construct Human Poverty Index. Study found that in terms of health deprivation (P_1), Odisha was the worst performing state in 2001 and Madhya Pradesh in 2011, whereas the best performing states were Nagaland and Kerala during 2001 and 2011 respectively. In terms of knowledge deprivation (P_2), Bihar was the worst performing state in 2001 as well as in 2011. On the other hand, Kerala and Himachal Pradesh were the states with best performance during this period. Further, among the states, economic deprivation (P_3) was highest in Bihar in both the years. On the other hand, Punjab and Goa performed best in terms of economic deprivation during 2001 and 2011 respectively. The study also found that Sikkim was the state which showed maximum improvement (18.62 per cent) in economic deprivation over time. It is clear from the analysis that in respect of the position of 25 states based on deprivations in 2001 and 2011 that the gap between the worst performing state and best performing state had remained almost same in case of human poverty index.

When all the 25 Indian states were ranked according to index of human poverty calculated on the basis of three deprivations viz. health deprivation (P_1), knowledge deprivation (P_2), and economic deprivation (P_3) for 2001 and 2011, it was found that there was improvement in ranks for 44 per cent of states, deterioration of ranks for 36 per cent of states and ranks remained same for the remaining 20 per cent of states by the year 2011. Further, there was improvement in the ranks of some of the major states of India. The value of HPI is estimated to be 45.46 and 35.43 for 2001 and 2011 respectively. Seven states (Assam, Bihar, Madhya Pradesh, Meghalaya, Odisha, Rajasthan and Uttar Pradesh) out of 25 states had HPI more than the All India average during 2001 as well as 2011, implying greater deprivation as compared to the All India average. In the remaining 18 states, the rate of deprivation is lower than the All India average.

Relative comparison of human poverty index of 15 major states with poverty head count ratio reveals that the worst performing states in terms of HPI like Bihar, Madhya Pradesh, Odisha and Uttar Pradesh remains worst in terms of poverty head count ratio and the best performing states were best in terms of both the concepts.

The study found that the ranks of fifteen major states of India according to human development index, human poverty index and per capita NSDP did not remain same in 2011 as compared to 2001. Overtime comparison also shows that the gap between the worst and the best performing state in terms of human development index and human poverty index has narrowed down from 0.271 to 0.183 and from 38.94 to 32.35 respectively, whereas in case of per capita NSDP the gap between the richest state (Goa) and the poorest state (Bihar) has widened. Andhra Pradesh was the only state that had both HDI and HPI lower than the All India average during both the years. This means that it had both low attainment and low deprivation. However, the situation is different for other states, where low HDI is matched with high HPI. This is true for Assam, Bihar, Madhya Pradesh, Odisha, Rajasthan and Uttar Pradesh during both the years. It was only the state of Kerala for which ranks on three indices did not change overtime. But it is also notable that worst performing states performed worst and best performing state remained the best in 2011 as compared to the year 2001.

Chapter 8

Summary, Conclusions and Policy Implications

Economic development is the primary objective of every nation. It is associated with a rising level of income over a long period of time. Development implies change. It is a multidimensional process which involves changes in economic and social structures. Development means the eradication of poverty, acceleration of economic growth, an access to clean drinking water, sanitation, higher standards of health and nutrition, better education and more equality of opportunity. It aims at an elimination of unemployment, malnutrition, illiteracy and inequality. Development can be distinguished from growth, it is no longer considered identical with growth. Economic development implies growth plus change. An economy may grow but it may not develop because unemployment, illiteracy, poverty and inequalities may continue to persist due to absence of technological and structural changes.

Since independence, there are significant disparities in the levels of economic development across Indian states. All states have not grown at same rate as some states like Kerala, Maharashtra, Karnataka and Gujarat etc. are growing rapidly than others like Uttar Pradesh, Bihar, Madhya Pradesh, Assam and Odisha. There are also differences in the levels of education, literacy, per capita incomes and health standards, which causes disparities in the standard of living and regional inequalities are still persisting across states. This provides a strong motivation for studying the variability of inter-state development and to find out the various reasons responsible for existing variations among Indian states.

In the above mentioned context, the present study has been undertaken to examine the convergence hypothesis across Indian states over the period 1980-81 to 2011-12.

Objectives of the Study:

The specific objectives of the study are:

1. To examine the hypothesis of convergence in respect of per capita NSDP and NSDP originating from agricultural, industrial and services sector of Indian states for the period since 1980's.
2. To examine the issue of convergence hypothesis in case of Human Development Index as well as in term of its three components and to measure the speed of convergence and the half-life convergence - the time it takes for 50 per cent of the initial gap to be eliminated.
3. To construct Composite Development Index based on socio-economic and demographic indicators with an objective to examine the convergence hypothesis for it.
4. To examine the deprivations in three basic elements of human life (health, knowledge and a decent living standard) and work out the level of human poverty in the light of the experience of Indian states and to compare the positions of major states of India with respect to human development index, human poverty index and per capita NSDP.
5. Identify reasons for the convergence or lack of it among the Indian states.

Data Base and Methodology:

The present study entitled "Economic Growth and Regional Disparities in India" is based on secondary data. First of all, list of all possible indicators related to study was prepared. An attempt was made to collect the data regarding the maximum possible number of indicators for maximum possible number of states. The data used in the study were collected from Central Statistical Organisation, National

Human Development Report 2001, Census of India, Statistical Abstract of Punjab (various issues), Data book for the use of Deputy Chairman (Planning Commission 2011), UNDP India 2011, Centre for Monitoring Indian Economy (CMIE) Report (various issues), Economic Survey (various issues), Economic and Political Weekly Research Foundation 2011, National Family Health Survey (NFHS I and II), Manpower Profile, India Human Development Report 2011. The study has been undertaken for the period 1980 to 2011, the earliest and the latest years as per the availability of data. In order to obtain comparable data for per capita NSDP at 2004-05 prices for the period 1980-81 to 2011-12, shifting of base year from 1980-81 to 1993-94, from 1993-94 to 1999-2000 and then from 1999-2000 to 2004-05 constant prices is necessary. So, as per the requirement, state-wise per capita NSDP at 1980-81 constant prices has been converted into 1993-94 constant prices for each state and then from 1993-94 to 1999-2000 and furthermore, the per capita NSDP at 1999-2000 constant prices for each state has been converted into 2004-05 prices for the entire period 1980-81 to 2011-12. Analysis has been performed by applying various types of econometric techniques and models including σ-convergence, Unconditional β-convergence, Conditional β-Convergence, Panel Data Regression Models, Factor Analysis, Co-efficient of Variation, Time Series Unit Root Tests and Panel Data Unit Root Tests.

Plan of the Study:

To achieve the objectives, the study has been divided into eight chapters. The first chapter introduces the problem. The second chapter reviews the literature related to economic development, growth and convergence hypothesis while data base and methodology used in the study have been discussed in chapter third. Convergence hypothesis in respect of per capita NSDP and NSDP originating from agricultural, industrial and services sector has been examined in chapter fourth. The issue of convergence hypothesis in case of Human Development Index as well as in term of its three components has been examined in chapter fifth. Composite Development Index based on socio-economic and demographic indicators has been constructed in chapter sixth with an objective to examine the convergence hypothesis for it. Human Poverty Index calculated to compare the positions of major states of

India with respect to human development index, human poverty index and per capita NSDP forms the subject matter of chapter seventh. Chapter eighth contains summary, conclusions along with policy implications derived from the study.

Main Findings of the Study:

Since Independence in 1947, India has achieved success in many areas of economic and social development due to the continuous efforts made by the governments through various Five Year Plans, but still the economy suffers from large inequalities. With the launching of economic reforms in 1991, few states such as Gujarat, Maharashtra, Tamil Nadu, Andhra Pradesh, and Karnataka have attracted larger FDI and were the big gainers from the process of economic liberalisation. Whereas states, such as Odisha, Bihar, Uttar Pradesh, Madhya Pradesh and Rajasthan lagged behind as being less attractive destinations of FDI. This has increased inter-state inequality in the country. Various factors such as per capita income, literacy rate, health standards and different level of infrastructure development contribute to the present inequalities among Indian states. There is a substantial literature covering different time periods which examined the issue of convergence or divergence across states and results are, more or less sensitive to the sample, period and estimation techniques. Inspite of many efforts and much progress made in recent past, there is still a wide scope for testing the convergence hypothesis in respect of economic development by taking into consideration various socio-economic and human development indicators which have non-income components also.

In the fourth chapter, σ-convergence and unconditional β-convergence in terms of per capita NSDP and NSDP originating from agricultural, industrial and services sector has been examined across 24 Indian states and study found that the inter-state disparities in terms of per capita NSDP and NSDP originating from agricultural sector have consistently increased over time (1980-2011) for 24 Indian states.

Regional disparities measured in terms of standard deviation of the natural log of NSDP originating from industrial sector shows an evidence of σ-convergence across 24 states over the period 1980-2011. In case of NSDP originating from services sector the dispersion decreases from 0.2473 in 1980 to 0.1785 in 1990 to 0.1286 in 2000 and then further to 0.1560 during 2011, however, providing an evidence of σ-convergence across states from 1981 to 2011. Thus, the states have been diverging in the sense of σ in terms of per capita NSDP and NSDP originating from agricultural sector, however, converging in terms of NSDP originating from industrial and services sector. The result of the estimated cross-sectional unconditional β-convergence reveals that the Indian states have been diverging in terms of per capita NSDP and NSDP originating from agricultural sector over the period of time. The states with higher initial level of per capita income grew faster than those with lower initial level, resulting into increasing inequality among the states in terms of per capita NSDP and NSDP originating from agricultural sector. However, unconditional β-convergence has been observed in terms of NSDP originating from industrial and services sector.

Further, study found an evidence of conditional convergence among Indian states in terms of per capita NSDP. Poor states grew faster than rich states once controls, that proxy for differences in steady states, are held constant. It has been found that the states have been converging at the speed of 5 per cent per year and will take only 14 years for half-life convergence. The only strong and clear effect comes from the percentage share of agriculture in NSDP and population growth rate, as they exerts a highly significant and negative effect on per capita NSDP. Whereas the percentage share of services and industry in NSDP exerts no significant impact on state per capita income which may be due to the location of industries in few states and concentration of services sector is also in few states. The other variables such as bank advances as a percentage of NSDP, population per bank office and percentage of villages electrified also have no significant impact on state per capita income. On the other hand per capita electricity consumption and industrial consumption of electricity exerts a positive and significant impact on per capita income. Furthermore, the table reveals that the net irrigated area as a percentage of net area sown and bank deposits as a percentage of NSDP affects per capita income positively but at an insignificant rate. Estimating stochastic convergence by applying ADF unit root test statistics across Indian states, study found that while the null hypothesis of a unit root (non-stationarity) can be rejected for five states only (Andhra Pradesh, Assam, Kerala, Meghalaya and Uttar Pradesh) in case of per capita NSDP. This suggests that only these five states are stochastically converging with the average level of all the states, whereas the remaining 19 states have been diverging over the period of time. The null hypothesis of no convergence has been rejected for Assam, Bihar, Gujarat, Himachal Pradesh, Maharashtra, Rajasthan and Tamil Nadu in terms of NSDP originating from agricultural sector. While the null hypothesis of no convergence can be rejected for six states each for NSDP originating from industrial sector (Arunachal Pradesh, Gujarat, Himachal Pradesh, Karnataka, Rajasthan and Tamil Nadu) and for the NSDP originating from services sector (Arunachal Pradesh, Gujarat, Kerala, Madhya Pradesh, Odisha and Tamil Nadu). Further, it has been found that Gujarat, Himachal Pradesh, Tamil Nadu and Rajasthan were the states converging in terms of NSDP originating from agricultural and industrial sector. Gujarat and Tamil Nadu were the only two states (out of 24 states) converging in terms of NSDP originating from agricultural, industrial and services sector.

The panel data unit root tests for stochastic convergence reveals that the states have been diverging in terms of per capita NSDP over the period 1980-81 to 2011-12. However, the states have been converging during the pre-reform period (1980-81 to 1990-91). The non-stationarity found in the post-reform period (1991-92 to 2011-12), indicated that the poor states are not catching up with the rich ones and the gap is widening further in terms of per capita NSDP.

In the fifth chapter, an effort has been made to analyse the convergence hypothesis in case of human development index and its non-income indicators across 15 major Indian states. The standard deviation across states tends to decline over time in terms of health status (measured by life expectancy), education status (measured by adult literacy rate) and human development index, supporting the existence of "sigma" convergence for life expectancy, adult literacy rate and human development index. However, the dispersion increased in case of per capita NSDP reflecting sigma divergence for per capita

NSDP in terms of 15 major Indian states over the past 30 years (1981-2011).

Regarding cross-sectional regression for unconditional β-convergence, the study found negative and statistically significant co-efficient for the whole period as well as for the various sub-periods, signalling unconditional β-convergence in terms of life expectancy, adult literacy rate and human development index. Convergence observed in life expectancy over the period of time is broadly because of the fact that over the last decade India has made improvement in various health outcomes which is the result of better health and medical facilities being provided by the centre and state governments. The variation in terms of literacy rates across states declined, which may be the result of numerous centrally sponsored schemes and programmes like mid-day meal scheme, Sarva Shiksha Abhiyan, National Programme for Education of Girls at Elementary Level and Right to Education Act etc. which were initiated in all the states at par leading to convergence in literacy. The convergence in human development index is broadly because of the presence of non-income indicators in HDI.

Further, the analysis shows that the rate of unconditional β-convergence has varied across the different time periods for different variables. The study also found that once the process of convergence has started, the speed of convergence increased with the passage of time. The gap between the states has declined at the rate of 6.82, 4.78 and 4.88 per cent per year in terms of life expectancy, adult literacy rate and human development index respectively during the last decade. It has been found that the laggard states needs only 10 years in terms of life expectancy and will take 14 years each in case of adult literacy and human development index to eliminate 50 per cent of the initial gap across states. Positive but insignificant co-efficients of initial level of per capita NSDP has been found during the whole period as well for the various sub-periods, indicating that the average growth rate of poor states are becoming more dissimilar in respect of per capita NSDP over the period of time. However, the lowest speed of 0.55 per cent per year observed during the last decade reveals that the speed of divergence decreased with the passage of time.

The results of the study exhibited σ and significant unconditional β-convergence for health status (measured by life expectancy), education status (measured by adult literacy rate) and human development index across the states. However, in case of per capita NSDP neither σ nor unconditional β- convergence has been found, signalling that the poor states are getting relatively poorer and rich getting richer in terms of per capita income and the gap between the rich and the poor is widening further. So, the poor states that have failed to catch up with rich ones in terms of per capita income have managed to catch up in terms of human development index. The convergence observed in case of life expectancy and adult literacy rate helps in bringing convergence in terms of human development index also, despite considerable divergence in per capita NSDP. The presence of convergence in terms of indicators of education and health give some hope of convergence in income also, may be at the later stage because educated and healthy people means more efficient and productive labour which contributes positively to the economic activities leading to higher production and hence increasing income per capita.

Using the Composite development index, an effort has been made to analyse and compare the position of Indian states by identifying the education, health, nutrition, sanitation and economic indicators responsible for the diversity in development in chapter sixth. Goa was at the top with highest value of composite development index among 22 states during 1981 followed by Kerala, Punjab, Maharashtra, Tamil Nadu and Himachal Pradesh. These are developed states as per composite development index. Bihar has the lowest composite development index. Other states having low value of index, (but more than Bihar) were Arunachal Pradesh, Uttar Pradesh, Madhya Pradesh, Assam and Odisha. These states are less developed as per this composite index. For the year 1991, Goa was at the top with highest value of composite development index among 22 states for which analysis has been undertaken. Other states which followed Goa were Kerala, Punjab, Maharashtra, Himachal Pradesh and Haryana. Bihar has the lowest index. The states for which value of index was very low but more than Bihar were Uttar Pradesh, Odisha, Madhya Pradesh, Rajasthan and Arunachal Pradesh. It is noted that the four states namely

Goa, Kerala, Punjab and Maharashtra remained stick to its position by occupying 1st, 2nd, 3rd and 4th positions respectively during the year 1981 and 1991.

For the year 2001, again Goa was at the top position followed by Kerala, Himachal Pradesh, Maharashtra, Punjab and Tamil Nadu. However, Punjab drifted from third position in 1991 to fifth in 2001. Bihar was at the bottom, while Uttar Pradesh, Odisha, Rajasthan, West Bengal, Assam and Madhya Pradesh slightly better placed than Bihar. For the year 2011, Goa again occupies the top position with highest value, followed by Kerala, Sikkim, Himachal Pradesh, Tamil Nadu and Punjab. Bihar lies at the bottom with Uttar Pradesh, Assam, Odisha, Rajasthan and Madhya Pradesh slightly better placed. It is also notable that Goa and Kerala were the only states which remained at 1st and 2nd positions respectively at four points of time. Punjab further drifted to 6th position in 2011 from 5th in 2001.

Further, the extent of convergence or divergence in respect of various indicators and composite development index has been worked out by using co-efficient of variation as a measure of convergence/divergence. The analysis of convergence or divergence of various indicators reveals that the co-efficients of variation in respect of adult literacy rate, female literacy rate, primary gross enrollment ratio, upper primary gross enrollment ratio, household with access to safe drinking water, household with access to electricity, crude death rate, per capita consumption of electricity, percentage share of industry in NSDP and percentage share of services in NSDP has declined over the period, revealing convergence across states from 1981 to 2011 in respect of these indicators. However, divergence in terms of remaining 8 indicators.

Regarding the composite development index, study found that the co-efficient of variation of the composite development index remains more or less constant (44 per cent) from 1981 to 1991, but declined to 33.78 per cent in 2001 from 44.56 per cent in 1991 indicating that poor states catched up with rich ones in terms of composite development index during this period. However, the co-efficient of variation increased to 36.57 per cent in 2011 from 33.78 per cent in 2001 revealing that the states have diverged in terms of composite development index during 2001 to 2011.

Study found that not much change has occurred in the ranks of the states, as the best performing states (like Goa, Kerala, Maharashtra, Himachal Pradesh and Tamil Nadu) remains the best and the worst performing states (like Bihar, Madhya Pradesh, Odisha, Rajasthan and Uttar Pradesh) remains the worst, but the inter-state variations have declined in terms of composite development index for the overall period (1981 to 2011), as the co-efficient of variation decreased from 44 per cent to 36 per cent respectively. Furthermore, study reveals a clear evidence of an increasing trend in the regional disparity in per capita NSDP. This suggests that poor states have failed to catch up with rich ones in terms of per capita income. Thus there is a need for policy measures on the part of the poor states to improve their per capita income as other issues will be addressed automatically in order to catch up with rich ones.

Apart from the above, in chapter seventh, study examines the deprivations in three basic elements of human life (health, knowledge and a decent living standard) and work out the level of human poverty in the light of the experience of 25 Indian states for the year 2001 and 2011. Effort has also been made to compare the positions of 15 major states of India with respect to human development index, human poverty index and per capita NSDP. This comparison has been done to see the relative performances of these states with respect to these two indices and to find out whether there has occurred any change in the relative position of these states in the year 2011 as compared to the year 2001.

The human poverty index based on health deprivation (P_1), knowledge deprivation (P_2), and economic deprivation (P_3) has been constructed. Study found that in terms of longevity deprivation (P_1), Odisha was the worst performing state in 2001 and Madhya Pradesh in 2011, whereas the best performing states were Nagaland and Kerala during 2001 and 2011 respectively. In terms of knowledge deprivation (P_2), Bihar was the worst performing state in 2001 as well as in 2011. On the other hand, Kerala and Himachal Pradesh were the states with best performance during this period. Further, among the states, economic deprivation (P_3) was highest in Bihar in both the years. On the other hand, Punjab and Goa performed best in terms of economic deprivation during 2001 and 2011 respectively. The study also found that Sikkim was the state which showed maximum improvement (18.62 per cent) in economic deprivation over time. It has been found that in respect of position of 25 states based on deprivations in 2001 and 2011 that the gap between the worst performing state and best performing state had remained almost same in case of human poverty index.

When all the 25 Indian states were ranked according to index of human poverty calculated on the basis of three deprivations viz. health deprivation (P_1), knowledge deprivation (P_2), and economic deprivation (P_3) for 2001 and 2011, it was found that there was improvement in ranks for 44 per cent of state, deterioration of ranks for 36 per cent of states and ranks remained same for the remaining 20 per cent of states by the year 2011. Further, there was improvement in the ranks of some of the major states of India. Seven states (Assam, Bihar, Madhya Pradesh, Meghalaya, Odisha, Rajasthan and Uttar Pradesh) out of 25 states had HPI more than the All India average during 2001 as well as 2011, indicating greater deprivation as compared to the All India average. In the remaining 18 states, the rate of deprivation is lower than the All India average.

Relative comparison of human poverty index of 15 major states with poverty head count ratio reveals that the worst performing states in terms of HPI like Bihar, Madhya Pradesh, Odisha and Uttar Pradesh remains worst in terms of poverty head count ratio and the best performing states performed best in both the concepts. The ranks of fifteen major states of India according to human development index, human poverty index and per capita net state domestic product did not remain same in 2011 as compared to 2001. Overtime comparison also shows that the gap between the worst and the best performing state in terms of human development index and human poverty index has narrowed down, whereas in case of per capita NSDP the gap between the richest state (Goa) and the poorest state (Bihar) has widened. Andhra Pradesh was the only state that had both HDI and HPI less than the All India average during both the years. This means that it had both low attainment and low deprivation. However, the situation is different for other states, where low HDI is matched with high HPI. This is true for Assam, Bihar, Madhya Pradesh, Odisha, Rajasthan and Uttar Pradesh during both the years. It was only the state of Kerala for which ranks on three indices did not change overtime. But it is also notable that worst performing states performed worst and best performing state remained the best in 2011 as compared to the year 2001.

Policy Implications:

Many policy implications flow from the analysis and results of the study.

1. No doubt, relatively poor states received proportionately larger amount of funds from the central government without much effect on the development process because these were not being utilised efficiently. Thus funds distributed must flow into desired channels through good governance and effective implementation. Proper utilisation of these funds by the lagging states could help them in catching up with the better off states.
2. In the recent years states like Bihar, Madhya Pradesh, Uttar Pradesh and Odisha with per capita income below the national average seemed to have focused more on economic development. There also has been more emphasis by state governments on social sector development as reflected in the increase in social sector expenditure. However, given the relatively low level of development in these states, cohesive efforts of the state and central governments in this direction should be undertaken to support growth.
3. Special attention should be given to overpopulated states and special policy efforts to promote investment are required in these states to bridge the economic and social gap among the leading and laggard states.
4. The results of the study indicated that different level of infrastructure development is the primary cause of diversity among the Indian states. So, improvement should be made in physical as well as social infrastructure in the lagging states, as it can help in promoting long run growth as well as in achieving convergence across Indian states in terms of per capita NSDP. Physical infrastructure helps in bringing the

regions closer to the international market and creating new job opportunities.

5. Study found regional convergence in terms of NSDP originating from industrial and services sector. So, targeting public investment on infrastructure that enhances industrial productivity constitutes an important element of a strategy of growth in India. This will also help poorly performing states to achieve a higher growth rate and catch up with the better performing states in terms of per capita income.
6. Significant investment in the power sector and roads will drive growth as indicated by the study. Availability of quality power (electricity) is now a pre-condition of almost all productive activities and its availability leads to economic development and hence increased per capita income. Road density provides market access opportunities to people and helps the poor get connected to core economic activities and thus allowing them to access additional productive activities.
7. Poor performing states such as Bihar, Madhya Pradesh, Odisha, Assam and Uttar Pradesh can improve their growth performance by attracting FDI through well targeted initiatives that involve state as well as central government participation.
8. Government must give priority to investment in improving human capital through better facilities in education and health which will help them to participate in the growth process.
9. The states and central government should not withdraw from social sector–particularly education and health, as leaving this section to private players will make these services available to only few who afford to buy these in the market. Large mass of people will be deprived of these facilities if government withdraws.

Bibliography

Adabar, Kshamanidhi (2004), "*Economic Growth and Convergence in India"*, Working Paper: Institute for Social and Economic Change, Nagarbhavi, India. http://www.isid.ac.in/~planning/ka.pdf.

Aiyar, Shepherd (2001), "Growth Theory and Convergence across Indian States: A Panel Study", in Tim Cullen, Patricia Reynolds and Christopher Towel (eds.) *India at the Cross roads: Sustaining Growth and Reducing Poverty,* International Monetary Fund. Washington D.C.

Akkina, Krishna Rao (1999), "Convergence and the Role of Infrastructure and Power Shortages on Economic Growth across States in India", *The Indian Economic Journal,* 47 (2), pp. 42-53.

Asteriou D., S. Karagianni and C. Siriopoulos (2002), "Testing the Convergence Hypothesis Using Time Series Techniques: The Case of Greece 1971-1996", *The Journal of Applied Business Research,* 18 (2), pp. 125-130.

Bai, Jushan and Serena Ng (2004), "A Panic Attack on Unit Root and Cointegration", *Econometrica*, 72 (4), pp. 1127-1177.

Baltagi, Badi H. (2001), *Econometric Analysis of Panel Data,* John Wiley and Sons Ltd., The Atrium, Chichester, England.

__________ (2005), *Econometric Analysis of Panel Data,* 3rd ed. John Wiley and Sons Ltd., The Atrium, Chichester, England.

Barro, Robert J. (1991), "Economic Growth in a Cross Section of Countries", *The Quarterly Journal of Economics*, 106 (2), pp. 407-443.

Barro, Robert J. and Xavier Sala-i-Martin (1992), "Convergence", *Journal of Political Economy,* 100 (2), pp. 223-251.

__________ (1995), *Economic Growth,* New York: McGraw Hill.

Baumol, William J. (1986), "Productivity Growth, Convergence and Welfare: what the Long-Run Data Show", *American Economic Review,* 76 (5), pp. 1072-1116.

Bernard, Andrew B. and Steven N. Durlauf (1995), "Convergence in International Output", *Journal of Applied Econometrics,* 10 (2), pp. 97-108.

Bhattacharya, B. B. and S. Sakthivel (2004), "Regional Growth and Disparity in India: Comparison of Pre- and Post-Reform Decades", *Economic and Political Weekly,* 39 (10), pp. 1071-1077.

Bougheas S. D., Panicos O. and E. L. W. Morgenroth (1999), "Infrastructure, transport costs and trade", *Journal of International Economics,* 47 (1), pp. 169-189.

Breusch, T. S., and A. R. Pagan (1980), "The Lagrange Multiplier Test and its Applications to Model Specification in Econometrics", *Review of Economic Studies,* 47 (1), pp. 239-253.

Cahin, Paul and Ratna Sahay (1996), "*Internal Migration, Centre-State Grants and Economic Growth in the States of India",* IMF Working Paper, WP/95/58, Washington D.C.

Cass, David (1965), "Optimum Growth in an Aggregative Model of Capital Accumulation", *The Review of Economic Studies,* 32 (3), pp. 233-240.

Central Statistical Organisation, *National Accounts Statistics*, Ministry of Statistics and Programme Implementation, Government of India, Various Issues.

Centre for Monitoring Indian Economy , *Centre for Monitoring Indian Economy Pvt. Ltd. (CMIE)*, New Delhi, Various Issues.

Chenery, Hollis and Moises Syrquin (1975), *Patterns of Development 1950-1970,* Published for the World Bank by Oxford University Press, Oxford.

Cherodian, Rowan and A. P. Thirlwall (2013), *"Regional Disparities in Per Capita Income in India: Convergence or Divergence?",* KDPE 1313, School of Economics Discussion Papers, University of Kent. http://www.kent.ac.uk/economics/documents/research/papers/2013/1313.pdf.

Chikte, Rasika P. (2011), "Income Convergence and Regional Growth in India: Before and After the Economic Liberalisation", *South Asia Economic Journal,* 12 (2), pp. 239-269.

Choi, I. (2001), "Unit Root Tests for Panel Data", *Journal of International Money and Finance,* 20 (2), pp. 249-272.

_______ (2004), "Combination Unit Root Tests for Cross-Sectionally Correlated Panels", in P. C. B. Phillips, Dean Corbae, Steven N. Durlauf and Bruce E. Hansen (eds.), *Econometric Theory and Practice: Frontiers of Analysis and Applied Research,* Essays in Honor of Peter C. B. Phillips, Cambridge: Cambridge University Press.

Chowdhury, Khorshed (2004), "*Convergence of Per Capita GDP across SAARC Countries*", Working Paper No. 04-07, working paper series, School of Economics, University of Wollongong. www.uow.edu.au/commerce/econ/wpapers.html.

Costantini, Mauro and Claudio Lupi (2005), "Stochastic Convergence among European Economies", *Economics Bulletin,* 3 (38), pp. 1-17.

Cunado, J. and F. Perez de Gracia (2006), "Real Convergence in Africa in the Second-half of the 20th Century", *Journal of Economics and Business,* 58 (2), pp. 153-167.

Cunado, Juncal (2011), "Structural Breaks and Real Convergence in OPEC Countries", *Journal of Applied Economics,* 14 (1), pp. 101-117.

Cutanda, A and Joaquina Paricio (1994), "Infrastructure and Regional Economic Growth: The Spanish Case", *Regional Studies,* 28 (1), pp. 69–77.

Das, Abhiman (1999), "Socio-Economic Development in India: A Regional Analysis", *Development and Society,* 28 (2), pp. 313-345.

Dasgupta Dipankar, Pradip Maiti, Robin Mukherjee, Subrata Sarkar and Subhendu Chakrabarti (2000), "Growth and Interstate Disparities in India", *Economic and Political Weekly,* 35 (27), pp. 2413-2422.

Dasgupta, P. (1993), *An Inquiry into Well-being and Destitution,* Clarendon Press, Oxford.

Dawson, John W. and Mark C. Strazicich (2010), "Time-Series Tests of Income Convergence with Two Structural Breaks: Evidence from 29 Countries", *Applied Economics Letters,* 17 (9), pp. 909-912.

Dayanandan, Ajit and Lawrence Arbenser (2009), "Convergence in Human Development Levels across Regions, An Empirical Investigation: 1975-2005", *The Indian Economic Journal*, 57 (2), pp. 143-155.

Debasri, Mukherjee (2006), "New Economic Reform and Sector-Wise Convergence of Indian States", *Indian Journal of Economics and Business,* 5 (1), pp. 41-48.

Dholakia, Ravindra H. (2003), "Regional Disparity in Economic and Human Development in India", *Economic and Political Weekly,* 38 (39), pp. 4166-4172.

Dickey, D. A. and W. A. Fuller (1979), "Distribution of the Estimators for Autoregressive Time Series with a Unit Root", *Journal of the American Statistical Association,* 74 (366), pp. 427-431.

Dobsan, Stephen and Carlyn Ramlogan (2002), "Convergence and Divergence in Latin America, 1970-1998", *Applied Economics,* 34 (4), pp. 465-470.

EPW Research Foundation (2011), *Domestic Product of States of India: 1960-61 to 2006-07*, A Unit of Sameeksha Trust, Mumbai.

Erdal Fuat, Emre Can and Gaye Kocabas (2006), "*Convergence of Human Development Levels*", Proceedings of the International Conference on Human and Economics Resources, Izmir University of Economics, pp. 207-212. http://eco.ieu.edu.tr/wp- content/proceedings/2006/0618.pdf.

Esfahani, H. S. and M. T. Ramirez (2003), "Institutions, infrastructure, and economic growth", *Journal of Development Economics*, 70 (2), pp. 443–477.

Evans, Paul and Georgios Karras (1996), "Do Economies Converge? Evidence from a Panel of U.S. States", *The Review of Economics and Statistics*, 78 (3), pp. 384-388.

Friedman, Milton (1992), "Do Old Fallacies Ever Die", *Journal of Economic Literature*, 30 (4), pp. 2129-2132.

Ganguli, B. N. (1971), *Challenge of Poverty in India*, Vikas Publications, New Delhi.

Gaur, Achal Kumar (2010), *"Regional Disparities in Economic Growth: A Case Study of Indian States"*, Paper Presented at the 31st General Conference of The International Association for Research in Income and Wealth, St-Gallen, Switzerland, Aug 22-28, http://www.iariw.org/papers/2010/poster1 Gaur.pdf.

Ghosh Buddhadeb, Sugata Marjit and Chiranjib Neogi (1998), "Economic Growth and Regional Divergence in India, 1960 to 1995", *Economic and Political Weekly*, 33 (26), pp. 1623-1630.

Ghosh, Madhusudan (2006), "Economic Growth and Human Development in Indian States", *Economic and Political Weekly*, 41 (30), pp. 3321-3329.

__________ (2012), "Regional Economic Growth and Inequality in India during the Pre- and Post-reform periods", *Oxford Development Studies,* 40 (2), pp. 190-212.

__________ (2013), *Liberalisation, Growth and Regional Disparities in India,* India Studies in Business and Economics, Springer, New Delhi.

Goli Srinivas, Arokiasamy Perianayagam and Reddy Bhemeshawar (2013), *"Socioeconomic Progress across the Major Indian States: Converging or Diverging",* MPRA Paper No. 48978. http://mpra.ub.uni-muenchen.de/48978/4/MPRA_paper_48978.pdf

Gorsuch, R. L. (1974), *Factor Analysis*, W. B. Saunders Company, Philadelphia.

Goulet, D. (1971), *The Cruel Choice: A New Concept on the Theory of Development*, New York: Atheneum.

Government of India, *Census of India (2011),* Office of the Registrar General and Census Commissioner, India, New Delhi.

Government of India, *Economic Survey,* Ministry of Finance, Various Issues.

Government of Punjab, *Statistical Abstract of Punjab*, Department of Planning, Various Issues.

Greene, William H. (2008), *Econometrics Analysis*, 6th ed. Upper Saddle River, NJ: Prentice Hall.

Gunji, Hiroshi and Yuko Nikaido (2004), "Convergence across Indian States: A Re-evaluation", SSRN:http://ssrn.com/abstract=630281.

Hadri, Kaddour (2000), "Testing for Unit Roots in Heterogeneous Panel Data", *Econometrics Journal,* 3 (2), pp. 148-161.

Harman, H. H. (1967), *Modern Factor Analysis*, University Press, Chicago.

Hausman, Jerry A. (1978), "Specification Tests in Econometrics", *Econometrica*, 46 (6), pp. 1251-1271.

Hayami, Yujiro and Yoshihisa Godo (2005), *Development Economics: From the Poverty to the Wealth of Nations,* Oxford University Press, pp. 3-4. http://www.oecd.org/dev/1922509.pdf.

Im Kyung So, M. Hashem Pesaran and Yongcheol Shin (2003), “Testing for Unit Roots in Heterogeneous Panels”, *Journal of Econometrics,* 115 (1), pp. 53-74.

Indrayan A, M. J. Wysocki, A. Chawla, R. Kumar and N. Singh (1999), “3-Decade Trend in Human Development Index in India and Its Major States”, *Springer,* 46 (1), pp. 91-120.

Institute of Applied Manpower Research (IAMR) (2003), *India Year Book,* Manpower Profile, Report No. 7, New Delhi.

International Institute for Population Sciences, *National Family Health Survey (NFHS-1) India,* (1992-93), Mumbai, India.

International Institute for Population Sciences, *National Family Health Survey (NFHS-2) India,* (1998-99), Mumbai, India.

Islam, Nazrul (1995), “Growth Empirics: A Panel Data Approach”, *The Quarterly Journal of Economics,* 110 (4), pp. 1127-1170.

Ismail, Normazwana (2008), “Growth and Convergence in ASEAN: A Dynamic Panel Approach”, *International Journal of Economics and Management,* 2 (1), pp. 127-140.

Jan, Sajjad Ahmad and A. R. Chaudhary (2011), “Testing the Conditional Convergence Hypothesis for Pakistan”, *Pakistan Journal of Commerce and Social Sciences,* 5 (1), pp. 117-128.

Jayanthakumaran, Kankesu (2010), “Economic Reforms and Income Convergence/Divergence in Regional India”, *Indian Economic Review,* 45 (1), pp. 29-48.

Jones, Basil (2002), “Economic Integration and Convergence of Per Capita Income in west Africa”, *African Development Review*, 14 (1), pp. 18-47.

Jr, A. F. Galvao and F. A. Reis Gomes (2007), “Convergence or Divergence in Latin America? A Time Series Analysis”, *Applied Economics,* 39 (11), pp. 1353-1360.

K. G., Suresh and Mukund Kumar (2011), “Examining the Income Convergence among Indian States: A Panel Data Approach”, *Economic Research Guardian,* 1 (1), pp. 42-48.

Kalita, Mamoni and Aviral Kumar Tiwari (2012), “Testing Income Convergence: Evidence from Indian States Using Panel Linear and NonLinear Unit Root Tests”, *The Economic Research Guardian,* 2 (1), PP. 60-69.

Kalra, Sanjay and Piyaporn Sodsriwiboon (2010), *“Growth Convergence and Spillovers among Indian States: What Matters? What Does not?”,* International Monetary Fund, Working Paper No. 10/96. https://www.imf.org/external/pubs/ft/wp/2010/wp1096.pdf

Konya, Laszlo and Maria-Carmen Guisan (2008), “What Does Human Development Index Tell Us about Convergence?”, *Applied Econometrics and International Development,* 8 (1), pp. 19-40.

Koopmans, Tjalling C. (1965), "*On the Concept of Optimal Economic Growth*", Cowles Foundation Discussion Paper No. 163, Cowles Foundation for Research in Economics, Yale University, USA. http://cowles.econ.yale.edu/p/cd/do1b/do163.pdf.

Kumar, Utsav and Arvind Subramanian (2012), "Growth in India's States in the First Decade of the 21st Century: Four Facts", *Economic and Political Weekly,* 67 (3), pp. 48-57.

Lee, Junsoo and Mark C. Strazicich (2001), "Break Point Estimation and Spurious Rejections With Endogenous Unit Root Tests", *Oxford Bulletin of Economics and Statistics,* 63 (5), pp. 535-558.

Levin Andrew, Chien-Fu Lin and James Chu (2002), "Unit Root Tests in Panel Data: Asymptotic and Finite-Sample Properties", *Journal of Econometrics,* 108 (1), pp. 1-24.

Looney, Robert E. (1997), "Infrastructure and private sector investment in Pakistan", *Journal of Asian Economics*, 8 (3), pp. 393-420.

Mackinnon, J. G. (1996), "Numerical Distribution Functions for Unit Root and Cointegration Tests", *Journal of Applied Econometrics*, 11 (6), pp. 601-618.

Maddala, G. S. and S. Wu (1999), "A Comparative Study of Unit Root Tests with Panel Data and a New Simple Test", *Oxford Bulletin of Economics and Statistics,* 61 (S1), pp. 631-652.

Mankiw N. Gregory, David Romer and David N. Weil (1992), "A Contribution to the Empirics of Economic Growth", *The Quarterly Journal of Economics,* 107 (2), pp. 407-437.

Marques, Alfredo and Elias Soukiazis (1998), "*Per Capita Income Convergence across Countries and across Regions in the European Union: Some New Evidence*", Paper presented at the international meeting of European Economy. www4.fe.uc.pt/ceue/working_papers/iconver.pdf.

Mathur, Somesh K. (2005), "Economic Growth and Conditional Convergence: Its Speed for Selected Regions for 1961-2001", *Indian Economic Review*, 40 (2), pp. 185-208.

Meghalaya Human Development Report (2008), Government of Meghalaya, Shillong, http://megplanning.gov.in/MHDR/Human_De.pdf.

Mehta, Arun C. and A. Shamshed Siddiqui (2008), *Educational Development Index (EDI), A Suggestive Framework for Computation,* National University of Education Planning and Administration, New Delhi.

Meier, G. M. (1973), *Leading Issues in Economic Development Studies in International Poverty,* London: Oxford University Press.

Moon, Hyungsik Roger and Benoit Perron (2004), "Testing for a Unit Root in Panels with Dynamic Factors", *Journal of Econometrics*, 122 (1), pp. 81-126.

Nagaraj Rayoprolu, Aristomene Varoudakis and Marie-Ange Veganzones (1998), *"Long-Run Growth Trends and Convergence across Indian States"*, OECD Development Centre, Working Paper No. 131.

Nauriyal, D. K. and Bimal Kishore Sahoo (2010), "Economic Growth Across Indian States: Role of Education, Infrastructure and Health", in Anil Kumar Thakur and Shyam Sunder Singh (eds.) *Inter Regional Disparities in India,* Deep and Deep Publishers, New Delhi.

Nayyar, Gaurav (2008), "Economic Growth and Regional Inequality in India", *Economic and Political Weekly,* 43 (6), pp. 58-67.

Noorbakhsh, Farhad (2006), "*International Convergence and Inequality of Human Development: 1975-2001*", Working Papers 2006-03, Department of Economics, University of Glasgow. www.gla.ac.UK/media/media_ 22173 _en.pdf.

Park, Donghyun (1997), "An Examination of Global Income Convergence for 1960-1990", *Journal of Economic Development*, 22 (1), pp. 43-55.

Park, Hun Myoung (2011), *"Practical Guides To Panel Data Modeling: A Step-by-Step Analysis Using Stata"*, Tutorial Working Paper, Graduate School of International Relations, International University of Japan, Japan.

Pesaran, M Hashem (2005), *A Simple Panel Unit Root Test in the Presence of Cross Section Dependence*, Cambridge University and USC, mimeo.

Planning Commission (2002), *National Human Development Report (2001),* Government of India.

__________ (2009), *Report of the Expert Group to Review Methodology for Estimation of Poverty,* Government of India, New Delhi.

__________ (2011), *India Human Development Report 2011-Towards Social Inclusion IHDR (2011),* Institute of Manpower Research, Oxford University press, New Delhi.

__________ (2012), *Data for Use of Deputy Chairman,* Planning Commission, Government of India, New Delhi, Available at http:// Planning Commission.govt.in, Accessed on 5th December 2012.

Purfield, Catriona (2006), *"Mind the Gap- Is Economic Growth in India Leaving Some States Behind?"*, International Monetary Fund Working Paper No. 06/103. https://www.imf.org/external/pubs/ft/wp/2006/wp06103.pdf.

Quah, D. T (1995), *"International Patterns of Growth Persistence, Path Dependence and Sustained Take off in Growth Transition"*, Working Paper, Department of Economics, London School of Economics, London.

Raju, Swati (2012), "Growth across States in the 2000s- Evidence of Convergence", *Economic and Political Weekly,* 67 (23), pp. 76-79.

Ramaswamy, T. (1980), *The Cure for Poverty*, Anand Press, Cochin.

Ramsey, Frank P. (1928), "A Mathematical Theory of Saving", *The Economic Journal,* 38 (152), pp. 543-559.

Rao M. Govinda, R. T. Shand and K. P. Kalirajan (1999), "Convergence of Incomes across Indian States: A Divergent View", *Economic and Political Weekly,* 34 (13), pp. 769-778.

Rassekh, Farhad (1998), "The Convergence Hypothesis: History, Theory and Evidence", *Open Economies*, 9 (1), pp. 85-105.

Ray, Debraj (2001), *Development Economics,* Oxford University Press, New Delhi.

_________ (2004), *Development Economics,* Oxford University Press, New Delhi.

Romer, Paul M. (1986), "Increasing Returns and Long-Run Growth", *Journal of Political Economy,* 94 (5), pp. 1002-1036.

Roy, Hiranmoy and Kaushik Bhattacharjee (2009), "*Convergence of Human Development across Indian States",* IGIDR Proceedings/Project Reports Series, http://www.igidr.ac.in/pdf/publication pp-062-22.pdf.

Sachs Jeffrey D., Nirupam Bajpai and Ananthi Ramiah (2002), "*Understanding Regional Economic Growth in India",* (CID Working Paper No. 88), Cambridge, MA: Centre for International Development, Harvard University.

Sala-i-Martin, Xavier (1996), "The Classical Approach to Convergence Analysis", *The Economic Journal*, 106 (437), pp. 1019-1036.

_________ (1997), "I Just Ran Two Million Regressions", *American Economic Review,* 87 (2), pp. 178-183.

Sarkar, Prabirjit (1997), "Are Poor Countries Coming Closer to the Rich?", *Economic and Political Weekly*, 32 (31), pp. 1979-1984.

Sen, A. K. (1985), *Commodities and Capabilities,* North-Holland, Amsterdam.

_________ (1987), *Standard of Living,* Cambridge University Press, New York.

Shah, Ismail and Vinod Gosavi (2010), *Human Development Index and Human Poverty Index for Indian States, 2005: Multivariate Statistical Analysis of Basic Indicators,* Master Thesis (15 ECTS), Department of Statistics, School of Economics and Management, LUND University, Sweden.

Shiller, Ilona (2009), "Regional Convergence in Per Capita Personal Income in the US and Canada", *International Journal of Human and Social Sciences,* 4 (13), pp. 956-965.

Solow, Robert M. (1956), "A Contribution to the Theory of Economic Growth", *The Quarterly Journal of Economics*, 70 (1), pp. 65-94.

Stavros, Mavroudeas and Syriopoulos Costas (1998), "Convergence or Divergence: The Data from Greece", *Journal of Applied Business Research,* 14 (1), pp. 1-11.

Thirlwall, A. P. (2006), *Growth and Development with Special Reference to Developing Economics,* Palgrave Macmillan, p. 17.

Tilak, Jandhyala B. G. (2005), "*Post-Elementary Education, Poverty and Development in India",* Post-Basic Education and Training, Working Paper Series- No. 6, Centre of African Studies, University of Edinburgh.

Todaro, M. P. (1977), *Economic Development in the Third World: An Introduction to Problems and Policies in a Global Perspective*, London: Longman.

Todaro, M. P. and Stephen C. Smith (2007), *Economic Development,* Dorling Kindersley (India) Pvt. Ltd., New Delhi, pp. 51 & 57.

Trivedi, Kamakshya (2002), *"Regional Convergence and Catch-up in India between 1960 and 1992"*, Working Paper No. 2003-W01, Nuffield College, University of Oxford, http://www.nuff.ox.ac.uk/economics/papers/ 2003/W1/convergencewp1.pdf.

United Nations Development Programme (UNDP), *Human Development Report*, New York, Oxford University Press, Various Issues.

__________ (UNDP) (2011), *Inequality Adjusted Human Development Index for India's States,* New Delhi, India.

World Bank (1992), *World Development Report 1992: Development and the Environment,* New York, Oxford University Press.

__________ (1994), *World Development Report 1994: Infrastructure for Development*, New York, Oxford University Press.

__________ (2006), *India-Inclusive Growth and Service Delivery: Building of India's Success*, Development Policy Review, Report No. 34580-IN, Document of the World Bank.

__________ (2008), *The Growth Report- Strategies for Sustained Growth and Inclusive Development*, Commission on Growth and Development, Washington: The World Bank May 2008. (www.Growthcommission.org)

Websites Consulted:

www.cmie.com

www.epw.org

www.indiastat.com

www.mospi.nic.in

www.planningcommission.com

Index

V

W

Z